Third Edition

Spanish Is Fun

Lively Lessons for Advancing Students

Book 2

Heywood Wald, Ph.D.
Former Chairman
Foreign Language Department
Martin Van Buren HS
New York

AMSCO SCHOOL PUBLICATIONS, INC.,
a division of Perfection Learning®

Audio Program

An audio program with script to accompany Spanish Is Fun, Book 2, 3rd Edition is available separately from the publisher (ordering code 14861). It is designed to reinforce the skills presented in the textbook and in the accompanying ancillaries. The voices are those of native speakers of Spanish.

Text Illustrations by Ed Malsberg, Thinkstock
Cover and part opener photographs: Thinkstock

© 2015 by Amsco School Publications, Inc., a division of Perfection Learning®

Please visit our Web sites at:
www.amscopub.com and *www.perfectionlearning.com*

When ordering this book, please specify:

Hardcover: ISBN 978-1-62974-848-1 or **1486606**
Softcover: ISBN 978-1-62974-670-8 or **1486601**
eBook: ISBN 978-1-62974-961-7 or **14866D**

3   4   5   6   7   EBM   21   20   19   18   17

Printed in the United States of America

Preface

SPANISH IS FUN, BOOK 2 offers a program that makes language acquisition a natural, personalized, enjoyable, and rewarding experience. The book provides all the elements for a one-year course.

SPANISH IS FUN, BOOK 2 is designed to help students attain a desirable level of proficiency in the four basic skills—speaking, listening, reading, and writing—developed through simple materials in visually focused topical contexts that students can easily relate to their own experiences. Students are asked questions that require them to speak about their daily lives, express their opinions, and supply real information.

The **THIRD EDITION** has retained the proven organization and successful program of previous ones:

1. An introductory chapter serves as a diagnostic test, reviewing material usually covered during the first year of a Spanish-language course.
2. All lesson materials are built on a clearly focused content topic.
3. Each lesson follows a consistent program sequence.
4. Most exercises are presented in a communicative framework, with greater emphasis on personalized communication. Also found throughout this third edition is "Discusión," an exercise designed to encourage oral group discussion and critical thinking.
5. Situational conversations and dialogue exercises in cartoon-strip fashion are included in every lesson.
6. "Cápsula Cultural" (Cultural Note) sections follow each lesson, with comprehension questions. In this third edition, several notes also include "Para investigar," an open-ended research exercise that expands on the topic in question.
7. The Appendix containing introduces additional linguistic material that will discuss topics like noun formation, proverbs,onomatopeia, and other interesting topics.
8. A separate **CUADERNO DE EJERCICIOS** provides additional practice.
9. An audio program to supplement the **THIRD EDITION** is available separately.

SPANISH IS FUN, BOOK 2 consists of five parts. Each part ends with a Repaso (Review), in which each structure is recapitulated and practiced through various Actividades. These include games and puzzles, as well as more conventional exercises.

Each lesson includes a step-by-step sequence of elements designed to make the materials immediately accessible as well as give students the feeling that they can have fun learning and practicing their Spanish.

Vocabulary

Each lesson begins with topically related sets of drawings that convey the meanings of new words in Spanish without recourse to English. This device enables students to make a direct and vivid association between the Spanish terms and their meanings. The exercises also use pictures to practice Spanish words and expressions.

To facilitate comprehension, the book uses cognates of English words wherever suitable. Beginning a course in this way shows the students that Spanish is not so "foreign" after all and helps them overcome any fears they may have about the difficulty of learning a foreign language.

Structures

SPANISH IS FUN, BOOK 2 uses a simple, straightforward, guided presentation of new structural elements. These elements are introduced in small learning components at a time—and are directly followed by appropriate Actividades, many of them visually cued, personalized, and communicative. Students thus gain a feeling of accomplishment and success by making their own discoveries and formulating their own conclusions.

Dialogues

To encourage students to use Spanish for communication and self-expression, most lessons include a Diálogo—sometimes practical, sometimes humorous conversations which students complete by filling empty "balloons" with appropriate bits of information. These dialogues serve as springboards for additional personalized conversation.

Reading

Each lesson contains a short, entertaining narrative or playlet that features new structural elements and vocabulary and reinforces previously learned grammar and expressions. These passages deal with topics that are related to the everyday experiences of today's student generation. Cognates and near-cognates are used extensively.

Culture

Each lesson is followed by a Cápsula Cultural. These twenty-one cultural notes offer students picturesque views and insights into well-known and not so well-known aspects of Hispanic culture.

Cuaderno

SPANISH IS FUN, BOOK 2 has a companion workbook, **CUADERNO DE EJERCICIOS**, which features additional writing practice and stimulating puzzles to supplement the textbook exercises.

Teacher's Manual and Key

A separate Teacher's Manual and Key provides suggestions for teaching all elements in the book, additional oral practice materials, two achievement tests, and a complete Key to all exercises, puzzles, and quizzes.

Audio Program

An audio program on compact discs (CDs), available separately with corresponding script from the publisher, includes for each lesson oral exercises, the narrative or playlet, questions or completions, and the conversation, all with appropriate pauses for response or repetition.

The Author

Contents

Segunda Parte

Tercera Parte

Cuarta Parte

Quinta Parte

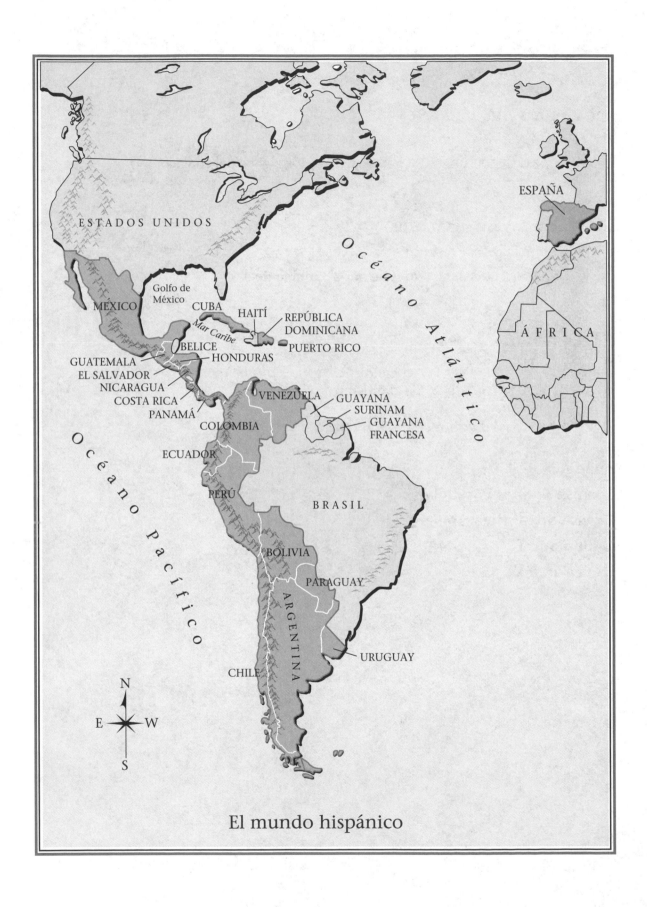

El mundo hispánico

Spanish America

What is Spanish America? Ask an American to give you an example of a country or place where there are Hispanic people, and the answer is likely to be Mexico, Cuba, or Puerto Rico. That would be a correct and logical answer, of course, because of the more than ten million United States citizens who originally came from those countries.

Spanish America is a lot more, however. In the vast area south of the United States there are eighteen independent Spanish-speaking countries. Together with Spain and Puerto Rico, these countries cover over sixteen percent of the surface of the Earth, with a growing population of over a quarter of a billion people. Spanish is, after English, the most widely used language in the world today.

Let's take a quick bird's-eye view of the Spanish-speaking world. First, there is Mexico, our immediate neighbor to the south, with a population of over eighty million people and an area approximately one-fourth that of the United States.

To the south of Mexico is Central America, with its six Spanish-speaking countries: Guatemala, Costa Rica, El Salvador, Honduras, Nicaragua, and Panama.

East of Mexico and Central America is the Caribbean Sea, with the Spanish-speaking countries of Cuba, the Dominican Republic, and Puerto Rico.

Finally, there is the vast continent of South America, with nine Spanish-speaking countries: Argentina, Bolivia, Colombia, Chile, Ecuador, Peru, Paraguay, Uruguay, and Venezuela. The largest of these countries, Argentina, is one-third the size of the United States.

These countries and their peoples cover a wide spectrum of cultures, climates, races, and human experiences. Together they make up *Hispanoamérica*.

Review Exercises of Level 1

A. Definite Articles (**el, la, los, las**); Indefinite Articles (**un, unos, una, unas**)

Fill in the correct definite and indefinite articles. Form contractions when necessary.

1. Hay _____un_____ vaso en la cocina.
   (a)

2. El precio _____ libro no es alto.
   (of the)

3. No tenemos _____ dinero de Pedro.
   (the)

4. _____ libros están en la biblioteca.
   (the)

5. _____ fruta es roja.
   (the)

6. Quiero comprar _____ lámpara.
   (a)

7. Voy _____ la casa ahora.
   (to the)

8. Nueva York es _____ ciudad grande.
   (a)

9. El invierno es _____ estación fría.
   (the)

10. Deseo comprar _____ zapatos nuevos.
    (some)

11. El color _____ flores es bonito.
    (of the)

12. _____ padres de Anita trabajan en la oficina.
(the)

13. Son _____ lecciones más difíciles.
(the)

14. Llevo la medicina _____ hospital.
(to the)

15. María va al cine con _____ amigas.
(some)

B. Negative and Interrogative Sentences

Make the following sentences negative.

1. Mi mamá prepara la comida. _____

2. Carlos es un amigo de la familia. _____

3. Los abuelos son viejos. _____

4. Quiero comprar un periódico. _____

5. El dormitorio tiene dos camas. _____

Change the following sentences into questions.

1. El alumno contesta bien. _____

2. Usted habla francés. _____

3. Tú comprendes la lección. _____

4. La bandera es azul. _____

5. Ellos viven en Puerto Rico. _____

C. Subject Pronouns

Complete the following sentences with the appropriate Spanish subject pronouns.

1. _____ tengo zapatos negros.
(I)

2. _____ trabajamos en una fábrica.
(we, feminine)

3. _____ estudia todos los días.
   (*she*)

4. _____ son norteamericanas.
   (*they*, feminine)

5. ¿Habla _____ inglés?
   (*you*, formal singular)

6. _____ contestamos correctamente.
   (*we*, masculine)

7. ¿Sabemos _____ bailar?
   (*we*)

8. _____ no desean ir a la escuela.
   (*they*, masculine plural)

9. ¿Comprenden _____ las lecciones?
   (*you*, formal plural)

10. ¿No tienes _____ hambre?
    (*you*, informal singular)

D. Present Tense of Regular Verbs

Complete the sentences with the appropriate form of the verb in parentheses.

-AR Verbs

1. Yo _____ a mis abuelos en la ciudad.
   (visitar)

2. ¿Cuándo _____ tú en la clase?
   (entrar)

3. ¿No _____ Uds. mucha televisión?
   (mirar)

4. María _____ las lecciones.
   (practicar)

5. Nosotros no _____ la radio.
   (escuchar)

-ER Verbs

1. ¿ _____ el niño el ejercicio?
   (aprender)

2. Ellos _____ mucha soda.
   (beber)

3. ¿ _____ Ud. carne o pescado?
   (comer)

4. Yo _____ correctamente.
   (responder)

5. ¿ _____ tú la bicicleta?
   (vender)

-IR Verbs

1. ¿ _____ Uds. en español?
   (escribir)

2. La chica _____ en un apartamento.
   (vivir)

3. Nosotras _____ la puerta del garaje.
   (abrir)

4. Mi hermano _____ buenas notas.
   (recibir)

5. Los científicos _____ cosas importantes.
   (descubrir)

E. Preterit Tense of Regular Verbs

Complete the following sentences with the appropriate form of the verbs in the preterit tense.

-AR Verbs

1. Yo _____ a mis abuelos en la ciudad.
   (visitar)

2. ¿Cuándo _____ tú en la clase?
(entrar)

3. ¿No _____ Uds. mucha televisión?
(mirar)

4. María _____ las lecciones.
(practicar)

5. Nosotros no _____ la radio.
(escuchar)

-ER Verbs

1. ¿ _____ el niño el ejercicio?
(aprender)

2. Ellos _____ mucha soda.
(beber)

3. ¿ _____ Ud. carne o pescado?
(comer)

4. Yo _____ correctamente.
(responder)

5. ¿ _____ tú la bicicleta?
(vender)

-IR Verbs

1. ¿ _____ Uds. en español?
(escribir)

2. La chica _____ en un apartamento.
(vivir)

3. Nosotras _____ la puerta del garaje.
(abrir)

4. Mi hermano _____ buenas notas.
(recibir)

5. Los científicos _____ cosas importantes.
(descubrir)

F. Present Tense of Irregular Verbs

Complete each sentence with the appropriate form of the verb in parentheses.

1. Yo _____ pan en casa.
   (tener)

2. Nosotros _____ al aeropuerto.
   (ir)

3. ¿_____ Ud. comer ahora?
   (querer)

4. Yo siempre _____ la verdad.
   (decir)

5. ¿Me _____ Ud. el dinero para la cena?
   (dar)

6. ¿Qué _____ Uds. en el verano?
   (hacer)

7. Yo _____ la leche en el café.
   (poner)

8. Francisco _____ la respuesta.
   (saber)

9. ¿Cuándo _____ tú para México?
   (salir)

10. Yo _____ la música a la fiesta.
    (traer)

11. Mi papá _____ policía.
    (ser)

12. Yo _____ contento ahora.
    (estar)

13. ¿Cuántos años _____ Ud.?
    (tener)

14. Yo _____ a San Juan esta noche.
    (ir)

15. ¿Qué _____ Uds.?
             (decir)

16. Yo _____ el regalo a mi hermano.
            (dar)

17. Él no _____ estudiante.
            (ser)

18. ¿Cómo _____ (tú), Pablito?
            (estar)

19. Yo _____ de la escuela a las tres.
            (salir)

20. Yo no _____ la respuesta.
            (saber)

G. Uses of **ser** and **estar**

1. María _____ panameña.
            (es / está)

2. Yo _____ de los Estados Unidos.
            (soy / estoy)

3. ¿Cómo _____ Uds. hoy?
            (son / están)

4. Ellos _____ amigos.
            (son / están)

5. Madrid _____ en España.
            (es / está)

6. Tú no _____ pobre.
            (eres / estás)

7. El autor _____ escribiendo otro libro.
            (es / está)

8. Yo _____ triste.
            (soy / estoy)

9. Mis hermanas _____ altas.
     (son / están)

10. Nosotros _____ estudiantes.
      (somos / estamos)

H. Cardinal Numbers

Write out each number in Spanish.

1. Tengo _____ dólares.
             (50)

2. Hay _____ meses en un año.
          (12)

3. Una semana tiene _____ días.
                          (7)

4. En un minuto hay _____ segundos.
                          (60)

5. El día tiene _____ horas.
                    (24)

6. En un siglo hay _____ años.
                        (100)

7. Quince por dos son _____ .
                            (30)

8. Ochenta menos diez es _____ .
                               (70)

9. Una docena es más que _____ .
                               (11)

10. Mi padre tiene _____ años.
                        (40)

I. Telling Time

Complete each of the following time expressions in Spanish.

1. Es la _____ .
   (1:00)

2. Son las _____ .
   (2:30)

3. El tren llega a las _____ .
   (12:00 midnight)

4. Voy a casa a las _____ .
   (3:15 P.M.)

5. Miro la televisión a las _____ .
   (10:00 P.M.)

6. Salgo a la _____ .
   (1:30 P.M.)

7. ¿Qué hora es? — Son las _____ .
   (6:45 A.M.)

8. Las clases terminan a las _____ .
   (4:20)

9. Hay una película a las _____ .
   (8:00 P.M.)

10. Es _____ .
    (12:00 noon)

J. Weather Expressions

Complete all of the following sentences in Spanish.

1. ¿Felipe, _____ hoy?
   (how is the weather)

2. En marzo _____ .
   (it's windy)

3. ¿Cuándo _____ ?
   (*is it sunny*)

4. _____ en el invierno.
   (*It's cold*)

5. En el otoño _____ .
   (*it's cool*)

6. En Miami _____ .
   (*it's hot*)

7. _____ mucho en Alaska.
   (*It snows*)

8. Cuando _____ voy al cine.
   (*it rains*)

9. Generalmente _____ en la primavera.
   (*it's good weather*)

10. No salgo de la casa cuando _____ .
    (*it's bad weather*)

K. Descriptive Adjectives

Complete each sentence with the appropriate form of the adjective in parentheses.

EXAMPLE: Las rosas son plantas _____ .
            (bonito)

            Las rosas son plantas **bonitas**.

1. Yo conozco muchas canciones _____ .
   (popular)

2. Las lecciones no son _____ .
   (difícil)

3. Hay muchachas _____ en el equipo de básquetbol.
   (alto)

4. Nuestro presidente es _____ .

(joven)

5. Puerto Rico tienes muchas flores _____ .

(tropical)

6. La Casa _____ es un edificio importante.

(Blanco)

7. Los gatos son animales _____ .

(pequeño)

8. En la universidad hay estudiantes _____ .

(inteligente)

9. Es una actriz _____ .

(español)

10. Los abuelos son muy _____ .

(viejo)

L. Demonstrative Adjectives

Complete the following expressions using **este, esta, estos, estas,** or **ese, esa, esos,** and **esas**.

1. this book   _____ libro

2. that lamp   _____ lámpara

3. these houses   _____ casas

4. those desks   _____ escritorios

5. this kitchen   _____ cocina

6. that shoe   _____ zapato

7. these ties   _____ corbatas

8. those pages   _____ páginas

9. this song   _____ canción

10. that automobile   _____ automóvil

M. Possessive Adjectives

Complete the following expressions using **mi(s), tu(s), su(s),** or **nuestro(-a, -os, -as)**.

1. my mistake   _____ falta

2. your (*inf. sing.*) paper   _____ papel

3. his dentist   _____ dentista

4. her bicycle   _____ bicicleta

5. their teacher   _____ profesor

6. our dog   _____ perro

7. my classes   _____ clases

8. our beaches   _____ playas

9. your (*formal*) garden   _____ jardín

10. his pants   _____ pantalones

N. Gustar (to like)

Express the following English sentences in Spanish, using **me gusta(n), te gusta(n), le gusta(n), nos gusta(n),** or **les gusta(n)**.

1. I like the flowers.   _____ _____ las flores.

2. I like the food.   _____ _____ la comida.

3. Do you (*inf. sing.*) like to sing?   ¿ _____ _____ cantar?

4. She likes the winter.   _____ _____ el invierno.

5. You (*formal sing.*) like fresh air.   _____ _____ el aire fresco.

6. We like the mountains.   _____ _____ las montañas.

7. We like the country.   _____ _____ el campo.

8. They like the library.   _____ _____ la biblioteca.

9. Do you (*plural*) like the heat?   ¿ _____ _____ el calor?

10. He likes the furniture.   _____ _____ los muebles.

O. Prepositions

Change the English expression to Spanish, using the appropriate preposition. Use **al** and **del** when necessary.

1. near the house _____ la casa

2. around the park _____ el parque

3. under the tree _____ el árbol

4. in front of the cars _____ los automóviles

5. behind the garage _____ el garaje

6. on the table _____ la mesa

7. above the building _____ el edificio

8. far from the city _____ la ciudad

9. opposite the library _____ la biblioteca

10. through the factory _____ la fábrica

Primera Parte

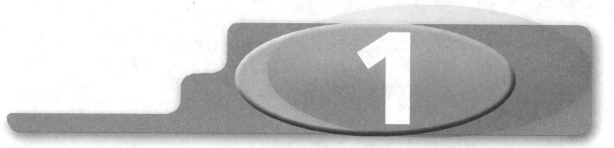

La naturaleza

Interrogative Words: CONOCER and SABER

1 Vocabulario

Consult the picture at the beginning of the lesson. Name some of the things found in nature and describe some of the activities that can be done at Villa Hermosa.

En Villa Hermosa la vida es buena. Venga a pasar sus vacaciones aquí, donde disfrutará

_____

_____

_____

_____

_____

A tour guide is talking to a group of visitors about a trip they're about to take. Read the dialog, paying special attention to the questions.

Did you notice the interrogative words **qué** and **cuál(es)** in the dialog between the tour guide and the tourists?

> *¿Qué* **cosas quieren ver?**
>
> *¿Qué* **sitios típicos . . .?**
>
> *¿Cuáles* **son los sitios . . .?**
>
> *¿Cuáles* **son sus intereses?**

Qué and **cuál(es)** both mean *what* or *which*.

Before a form of the verb **ser**, **qué** is used when asking for a definition and **cuál** when asking for a choice.

> NOTE: **Qué** never changes, but **cuál** has a plural form: **cuáles**, when referring to more than one.

Let's look at a few more examples:

> *¿Qué* **es la Casa Blanca?**   *What is the White House?* (definition)
>
> *¿Cuál* **es la Casa Blanca?**   *Which (one) is the White House?* (choice)

Before verbs other than **ser**, **qué** is used; unless choice (*which one, which ones*) is clearly indicated.

¿Qué pasa?	*What's going on?*
¿Qué dice Ud.?	*What are you saying?*
¿Qué quiere?	*What do you want?*
¿Cuál quiere?	*Which one do you want?*

Before a noun **qué** is used.

¿Qué libro quiere Ud.?	*What book do you want?*

3

¿Conoce Ud. a su marido?

MC: Buenas noches, amables televidentes. Yo soy su maestro de ceremonias, Baldomero Bocagrande. Bienvenidos a nuestro programa «*¿Conoce a sumarido?*» Las reglas del concurso son fáciles. Hacemos diez preguntas a una mujer. Ya sabemos las respuestas de su marido. Si las respuestas de los dos son iguales, el matrimonio puede ganarhasta un total de mil dólares, cien dólares por cada respuesta correcta.

Y ahora, vamos a comenzar con nuestra primera concursante, María López. ¿Cómo está, María? Tenemos una serie de preguntas para Ud. La primera pregunta es: ¿Sabe Ud. cuál es la actividad preferida de su marido?

MARÍA: Sí, él prefiere ir al campo.

MC: Muy interesante. ¿Por qué?

MARÍA: Porque le gustan la naturaleza, el sol, el aire fresco, la hierba, los árboles.

MC: ¿Cuáles son algunas de sus cosas favoritas en el campo?

MARÍA: A él le gustan las flores—las rosas y las violetas en particular.

MC: ¿Adónde van Uds. cuando no pueden ir al campo?

MARÍA: Vamos al Jardín Botánico o al parque.

el / la televidente TV *viewer*
el maestro de ceremonias *master of ceremonies*
bienvenidos *welcome*
el marido *husband*
el concurso *contest*
los dos *both*
igual(es) *the same*
el matrimonio *married couple*
el / la concursante *contestant*

MC: ¿Cuál es su parque preferido?

MARÍA: El Parque Bolívar en el centro.

MC: ¿Cuánto cuesta la entrada?

MARÍA: No cuesta nada. Es gratis.

MC: ¿Cuántas veces al año va al campo?

MARÍA: Dos o tres.

MC: Y, ¿cuándo van al parque?

MARÍA: Los fines de semana.

MC: ¿Quiénes van con Uds. generalmente?

MARÍA: Nuestros hijos.

MC: ¿Qué hacen Uds. después?

MARÍA: Vamos a un restaurante a comer, y luego, a casa.

MC: Damas y caballeros, esto es fantástico, sensacional. ¡Un aplauso para María! Sus diez respuestas son exactamente iguales a las de su marido. Felicitaciones, Uds. son un matrimonio perfecto. De veras, María, Ud. conoce muy bien a su marido, Manuel López.

MARÍA: ¿Cómo? Manuel López no es mi marido. Es el marido de la otra concursante.

damas y caballeros *ladies and gentleman* **felicitaciones** *congratulations* **de veras** *really* **¿cómo?** *eh?, what was that?*

Actividad B

Discusión

1. ¿Qué tipo de programa es «¿Conoce Ud. a su marido?»? ¿Cuáles son las reglas?

_____

2. ¿Cómo pueden ganar dinero? ¿Cuánto es el máximo?

_____

3. ¿Qué le gusta al marido de María?

_____

4. ¿Por qué gana Mario López?

_____

5. ¿Qué piensa Ud. de este tipo de programa? ¿Qué piensa Ud. de la televisión en general?

_____

Work with a partner. One student completes the questions with the word **qué** or **cuál(es)**. The other student answers the guest in a complete Spanish sentence.

1. ¿_____ flores le gustan a Ud.?

2. ¿_____ es su fruta favorita?

3. ¿_____ es un diccionario?

4. ¿_____ es la capital de España?

5. ¿_____ son las atracciones de una ciudad?

6. ¿_____ es un insecto beneficioso?

7. ¿_____ parque prefiere Ud.?

8. ¿En _____ ciudad vive Ud.?

9. ¿_____ son las mariposas?

10. ¿_____ son tres bebidas populares?

4 Did you notice all the interrogative expressions in the story in Section 3? What do all question words have in common? _____ If you answered an accent mark, you are correct. **Qué, por qué, cómo, cuándo, adónde,** and **dónde** never change. **Quién** has a plural form, **quiénes,** to ask about more than one person. **Cuánto** functions as an adjective and thus agrees in gender and number when a noun follows:

¿Cuánto dinero tienes?	_How much money do you have?_
¿Cuánta carne quieres?	_How much meat do you want?_

¿Cuántos libros lees? *How many books are you reading?*

¿Cuántas respuestas sabes? *How many answers do you know?*

Complete the following questions using the appropriate interrogative word.

1. ¿ _____ casas hay en la avenida?
   (Cuántas, Cuánto)

2. ¿ _____ de los dos quiere comprar Ud.?
   (Cuál, Qué)

3. ¿ _____ es un circo?
   (Cuál, Qué)

4. ¿ _____ está su papá?
   (Cómo, Por qué)

5. ¿ _____ hace mucho calor?
   (Dónde, Cuántos)

6. ¿ _____ van los autobuses?
   (Adónde, Dónde)

7. ¿ _____ personas viven en California?
   (Cuánta, Cuántas)

8. ¿ _____ dice Ud. eso?
   (Qué, Por qué)

9. ¿ _____ vas al cine?
   (Cuándo, Cuánto)

10. ¿ _____ quiere mirar el programa?
    (Quién, Cuál)

Work with a partner. One student completes the question with the proper interrogative word. The other student answers in a complete sentence.

1. ¿ _____ es el maestro/la maestra de la clase de español? (*who*)

   _____

2. ¿ _____ quiere ir Ud. después de las clases? (*where*)

   _____

3. ¿ _____ no come Ud. afuera? (*why*)

   _____

4. ¿ _____ dinero tiene Ud. en el banco? (*how much*)

   _____

5. ¿ _____ es un diccionario? (*what*)

   _____

6. ¿ _____ van a salir de la escuela? (*when*)

   _____

7. ¿ _____ hijos tienen tus padres? (*how many*)

   _____

8. ¿ _____ trabajan los sábados? (*who*)

   _____

9. ¿ _____ es la capital de Puerto Rico? (*what*)

   _____

10. ¿ _____ queda su restaurante favorito? (*where*)

   _____

5 Two other expressions to obtain information are formed with the word **quién(es)**: **a quién(es)** (whom?) and **de quién(es)** (whose?). Look at the following examples:

¿A quién ves?	*Whom do you see?*
Veo a Juan.	*I see Juan.*

¿De quién es el libro?	*Whose book is it?*
El libro es de Carlos.	*It is Carlos's book.*

Note that if you respond to the question **¿A quién(es) . . .?, a** must come after the verb in your answer. If you respond to the question **¿De quién(es) . . .?, de** must come after the verb **ser** in your answer.

Tell us about yourself by answering the following questions in Spanish.

1. ¿Quién prepara la comida en su casa?

_____

2. ¿Quiénes son sus actores favoritos?

_____

3. ¿De quién es la casa donde vive Ud.?

_____

4. ¿A quién quiere visitar Ud. en las vacaciones?

_____

5. ¿A quiénes va a invitar a su fiesta de cumpleaños?

_____

6. ¿De quién es Ud. amigo(-a) en su clase?

_____

6 The TV show you read about in Section 3 is called **¿Conoce Ud. a su marido?** (*Do you know your husband?*) One of the questions was **¿Sabe Ud. cuál es su comida favorita?** (*Do you know which is his favorite food?*) Both verbs, **conocer** and **saber**, mean *to know*. Both have an irregular **yo** form in the present tense.

yo	*conozco*	*sé*
tú	conoces	sabes
Ud., él, ella	conoce	sabe
nosotros, -as	conocemos	sabemos
Uds., ellos, ellas	conocen	saben

When do you use **conocer** and when do you use **saber**? Let's look at some examples:

> *Conozco* **a Miguel, pero no** *sé* **donde vive.**
>
> *I know (am acquainted with) Miguel, but I don't know where he lives.*

> **¿Conoces ese restaurante? ¿Sabes si es caro?**
>
> *Do you know (are you familiar with) that restaurant? Do you know if it's expensive?*

Can you see the difference? **Conocer** is always used in the sense of *to be acquainted with, to be familiar with something or somebody*. **Saber** means *to know facts, to have knowledge or information about something*. **Saber** can not be used with nouns that refer to people or places. When **saber** is followed by an infinitive, it means *to know how to*.

> **¿Sabes preparar comida mexicana?**
>
> *Do you know how to prepare Mexican food?*

Complete the following sentences with the correct form of **saber** or **conocer**.

1. Yo _____ que su mamá no está en casa.

2. ¿_____ Uds. a Felipe?

3. ¿_____ Ud. dónde vive Felipe?

4. Yo no _____ contestar la pregunta.

5. Yo _____ bien esta ciudad.

6. ¿_____ Ud. al señor Pérez?

7. ¿_____ Uds. a qué hora termina la clase?

8. Yo no _____ cómo se llama el profesor nuevo.

9. Nosotros no _____ esa novela.

10. ¿_____ tú si la puerta está cerrada?

Preguntas Personales

1. ¿Cuál es tu programa de televisión favorito? ¿Por qué te gusta?

_____

2. ¿Cuándo vas al cine?

_____

3. ¿Qué tipo de comida prefieres?

_____

4. ¿Cuáles son tus restaurantes preferidos?

_____

5. ¿Adónde vas generalmente cuando hace calor?

_____

Información personal

You have just been selected to serve as "**maestro de ceremonias**" for your class's TV quiz show. Prepare five questions you would ask one of the contestants.

1. _____

2. _____

3. _____

4. _____

5. _____

Composición

You are writing an article for the school paper profiling a "typical" student. What are some of the questions you might ask the students?

You are an investigator getting information from a client. Can you ask the right questions for the answers you are given?

Cápsula cultural

Los insectos son buenos para su salud (¡Y son deliciosos!)

¿Comería Ud. insectos? Antes de contestar, considere esto: en muchas partes de Hispanoamérica, y en el mundo entero, los insectos son considerados una golosina.

Por ejemplo, muchos bolivianos comen hormigas tostadas; en el norte del Perú los niños esperan las lluvias, que traen las sisapas, hormigas gigantes de casi dos pulgadas de largo y que se comen crudas. En las calles de la Ciudad de México, si ves a un vendedor con bolsitas de papel, gritando: —«chapulines, chapulines»— ¡él vende saltamontes fritos!

Muchos insectos tienen un alto valor nutritivo. Contienen vitaminas, minerales y pueden contener setenta por ciento de proteína. Muchos especialistas en nutrición dicen que es mejor recibir los nutrientes de un alimento fresco y natural que de un alimento artificial o de una píldora de vitaminas. ¿No está convencido? Pues, ¿le gustan los mariscos? ¿Ha comido langosta, camarones o cangrejos? Estos mariscos populares son crustáceos y pertenecen a la misma clase de animales que los insectos. A veces los llaman «insectos del mar». Entonces, comer una langosta no es muy diferente de comer un grillo o una oruga.

Discusión

1. ¿Cuáles son algunos insectos consumidos como alimentos?

2. Describa el valor nutritivo de los insectos.

3. ¿Qué son los crustáceos? Mencione algunos ejemplos.

4. ¿Qué diferencia hay entre un saltamontes y una langosta o un cangrejo?

5. ¿Serán los insectos una fuente de alimento en el futuro? ¿Por qué (no)?

Para investigar

Investiga en el Internet cuáles son algunas cosas (plantas, animales, reptiles, etc.) que se comen en el mundo.

VOCABULARIO

comería *would you eat*	**el camarón** *shrimp*
la golosina *delicacy*	**el cangrejo** *crab*
la pulgada *inch*	**pertenecer** *to belong*
crudo *raw*	**los llaman** *they are called*
la bolsita *small bag*	**la langosta** *lobster*
el saltamontes *grasshopper*	**el grillo** *cricket*
la píldora *pill*	**la oruga** *caterpillar*

En la playa

1 Vocabulario

la palmera

la gaviota

el faro

la salvavidas

la sombrilla de playa

el esquí acuático

el barco de vela

el salvavidas

las olas

silla de playa

el frisbee

el cubo

la pala

la toalla de playa

castillo de arena

las gafas de sol

la arena

LIFE GUARD

el traje de baño

el salvavidas

la loción bronceadora

las conchas

la manta

el colchón flotante de aire

Las seis diferencias   The following two pictures were taken at the beach. In the second one, there are six items missing. In Spanish, tell which items are missing.

1. _____

2. _____

3. _____

4. _____

5. _____

6. _____

Actividad B

Here's a happy beach scene. But there's a nasty rumor that *a shark* (**un tiburón**) has been seen in the vicinity. You've been sent a text message by the local TV news to warn you. Describe the scene and tell a story about what you see. You may use the following verbs or expressions: **leer, jugar, tomar el sol, ver, escuchar, dormir,** etc.

You are at the beach with a group of your friends. Read the dialog and see if you can find all forms of the verbs **querer** (*to want*) and **poder** (*to be able to, can*).

2 Now that you've seen **querer** and **poder** in action, can you fill in the correct forms of the verbs in the box below?

	querer	poder
yo	_____	_____
tú	_____	_____
Ud., él, ella	_____	_____
nosotros, -as	_____	_____
Uds., ellos, ellas	_____	_____

What happened to the stem of the verb **querer**? The **e** changed to _____ in all forms except for **nosotros**. What happened to the stem of the verb **poder**? The **o** changed to _____ in all forms except for **nosotros**.

3 There are other verbs that undergo the same changes. We identify them in the vocabulary at the end of the book like this: **empezar (ie)** *(to begin)*, **mover (ue)** *(to move)*. Now let's see some more examples. Can you complete the boxes below?

e to ie		pensar *(to think)*	perder *(to lose)*	mentir *(to lie)*
	yo	p**ie**nso	_____	_____
	tú	p**ie**nsas	_____	_____
	Ud., él, ella	p**ie**nsa	_____	_____
	nosotros, -as	pensamos	_____	_____
	Uds., ellos, ellas	p**ie**nsan	_____	_____

o to ue		almorzar *(to have lunch)*	volver *(to come back)*	dormir *(to sleep)*
	yo	alm**ue**rzo	_____	_____
	tú	alm**ue**rzas	_____	_____
	Ud., él, ella	alm**ue**rza	_____	_____
	nosotros, -as	almorzamos	_____	_____
	Uds., ellos, ellas	alm**ue**rzan	_____	_____

RULE: Stem changing **-ar** and **-er** verbs change **e** to **ie** and **o** to **ue** in all forms of the present tense, except **nosotros**.

Actividad **C**

Everyone likes to do something different. What do the students in the class prefer?

EXAMPLE: **Carlos *prefiere* nadar.**

1. Yo _____ dormir tarde.

2. Tú _____ ir al cine el sábado.

3. Ellos _____ comer comida rápida.

4. Miguel y yo _____ salir pronto.

5. Uds. _____ viajar en el verano.

6. Julia _____ estudiar en la biblioteca.

Actividad D

You are observing some children playing on the beach. Using a form of the stem-changing verb **encontrar (ue)**, tell what they find.

EXAMPLE: **Ellos *encuentran* una concha.**

1. Carlos _____ .

2. Yo _____ .

3. Ud. _____ .

4. Uds. _____ .

5. Nosotros _____ .

6. Tú. _____ .

4 There is one more important verb that has a similar change in the stem: in **jugar**, the **u** changes to **ue** in all forms except for **nosotros**.

yo	j**ue**go
tú	j**ue**gas
Ud., él, ella	j**ue**ga
nosotros, -as	jugamos
Uds., ellos, ellas	j**ue**gan

Actividad E

A **difference of opinion**   Work with a partner. One student reads the original statement. Another student changes the statement to agree with the new subject.

1. Los soldados **defienden** el país.

   Todos nosotros _____ .

2. Mi hermana no **miente**.

   Mis padres _____ .

3. Su gato **duerme** todo el día.

   Los leones _____ .

4. Los niños **juegan** en la playa.

   Yo _____ .

5. ¿No **encuentras** el traje de baño?

   Ud. _____ .

6. ¿**Entiendes** la lección?

   Uds. _____ .

7. Uds. **cierran** la puerta.

   María _____ .

8. ¿Qué **prefiere** Ud.?

   Tú _____ .

9. El pájaro **vuela** por el aire.

   Las mariposas _____ .

Summer plans   Work with a partner. One student asks a question using the correct form of the verb in parentheses. The other student answers in a complete sentence.

1. (jugar)   ¿A qué _____ Uds. en el campo?

Nosotros _____ .

2. (querer)   ¿Adónde _____ ir sus padres?

Ellos _____ .

3. (preferir)   ¿ _____ Ud. ir al Caribe?

Yo _____ .

4. (pensar)   ¿Dónde _____ (tú) pasar las vacaciones?

Yo _____ .

5. (almorzar)   ¿A qué hora _____ las personas en el trópico?

Ellas _____ .

6. (dormir)   ¿ _____ yo mucho?

No, tú no _____ .

7. (poder)   ¿ _____ nosotros viajar a una isla tropical?

Nosotros _____ .

8. (encontrar)   ¿ _____ el agente de viajes información sobre excursiones?

Sí, él _____ .

9. (costar)   ¿Cuánto _____ los billetes de avión?

Un billete _____ .

10. (volver)   ¿Cuándo _____ tú de Santo Domingo?

Yo _____ .

Actividad G

¿Qué hacen estas personas?

Work with a partner. One student poses the question:

¿Qué hace (haces, hacen, etc.)? The other student answers according to the verb clues.

EXAMPLE: (contar)   Juan y Pedro _____ hasta cien.

¿Qué hacen Juan y Pedro?   Juan y Pedro *cuentan* hasta cien en español.

1. (almorzar)   Los estudiantes _____ en la cafetería.

2. (empezar)   Yo _____ a trabajar.

3. (volver)   Nosotros _____ a casa.

4. (dormir)   Mi abuelo _____ la siesta.

5. (encontrar)   María y yo _____ el libro.

6. (perder)   Uds. _____ la paciencia.

7. (cerrar)   Ellas _____ la tienda.

En la playa de una isla tropical

Now let's read a story about an adventure at the beach. Look for the stem-changing verbs of another type.

Es un día de sol brillante. Estamos en una playa casi desierta de una isla tropical. Vemos las olas del mar y la arena blanca. Una brisa suave **mueve** las palmeras.

En la distancia, vemos a dos personas. **Siguen** las huellas de   **seguir (i)** *to follow*
su perro, caminando lentamente por la orilla del mar, y **sonríen** mientras hablan. ¿Qué dicen?

LA CHICA: Oh, Fernando. ¡Que contenta estoy! Esta isla es un paraíso. Ahora, el mundo no existe.

EL CHICO: Sí, tienes razón. Estamos lejos de los problemas del mundo. Pero, ¿quieres saber una cosa? Esta isla pacífica tiene una historia trágica, de violencia y de piratas.

LA CHICA: Oh, sí. ¡Qué romántico! Entonces, es seguro que hay tesoros debajo de la arena — perlas, diamantes, rubíes, monedas de oro . . .

EL CHICO: Quizás. Pero, ¿quién sabe dónde están?

La chica ve una cosa que brilla en la arena. Es una botella con un papel viejo adentro.

LA CHICA: (**ríe** alegremente) Mira, aquí hay un mapa. ¿Crees que **sirve**?

reír (i) *to laugh*
servir (i) *to serve, be useful*

EL CHICO: Sí, es un mapa de un tesoro. Pero eso es imposible. ¡Es ridículo!

LA CHICA: No es imposible, Fernando. Allí hay una piedra grande debajo de una palmera, como **muestra** el mapa. ¿Qué piensas? ¿Buscamos el tesoro allí?

mostrar (ue) *to show*

Los dos empiezan a **cavar** con las manos. Después de veinte minutos, Fernando grita, ¡Mira, Juanita! ¡Hay algo aquí! ¿Que encuentran los dos jóvenes en la arena?

cavar *to dig*

LOS DOS: ¡Ay, madre mía!

¿Qué encuentran los dos jóvenes en la arena?

Discusión

1. Describa la isla.

2. ¿Quiénes están en la playa? ¿Qué hacen?

_____

3. ¿Cuál es la opinión del chico?

_____

4. ¿Qué hay dentro de la botella?

_____

5. En su opinión, ¿qué encuentran los dos jóvenes? (Use su imaginación y escriba dos o tres conclusiones posibles.)

_____

 There were four verbs in the story that belong to a third class of stem-changing verbs:

reír   sonreír   seguir   servir

How are they different from the verbs we've already learned? These verbs are all -IR verbs. Let's see how they change:

	reír	sonreír	seguír	servír
yo	río	sonrío	sígo	sírvo
tú	ríes	sonríes	sígues	sírves
Ud., él, ella	ríe	sonríe	sígue	sírve
nosotros, -as	reímos	sonreímos	seguimos	servimos
Uds., ellos, ellas	ríen	sonríen	síguen	sírven

Now you know. Some -IR verbs change the **e** in the stem to i in all forms of the present tense except for **nosotros**. This change is indicated in the end vocabulary as follows: **reír(í)**. Other common verbs in this category are **pedir(i)** and **repetir(i)**.

You and your friends are ordering food in a Spanish restaurant. Everyone orders something different. Complete their orders with the correct form of the verb **pedir(i)**.

1. Yo _____ arroz con pollo.

2. Fernando _____ sopa.

3. Roberto y Carlos _____ una tortilla.

4. Doris y yo _____ una ensalada mixta.

5. Tú _____ bistec.

6. El mesero pregunta: —«¿Qué _____ Uds.?»

Now, let's try all the new verbs we've just learned.

1. (reír)   Carlos _____ en el cine.

2. (sonreír) ¿Por qué _____ (tú), ahora?

3. (servir)   Yo _____ la comida a mi familia.

4. (seguir)   Nosotros _____ las huellas del perro.

5. (repetir) Uds. siempre _____ lo que decimos.

6. (pedir)   Manuel y Jorge _____ un café.

At the beach. Let's see what these people are doing.

1. (querer)   Un niño _____ aprender a nadar.

2. (dormir)   La madre _____ bajo la sombrilla.

3. (encender) El padre _____ el fuego para la barbacoa.

4. (pedir)   Yo _____ una soda en el quiosco.

5. (preferir)   Mi hermanito _____ jugar en la arena.

6. (perder)   Tú _____ la pelota de playa.

7. (encontrar)   Mario y José _____ un caracol muy bonito.

8. (entender)   Yo no _____ lo que grita mi madre.

9. (repetir)   Ella _____ sus palabras.

10. (pensar, nevar)   Yo _____ : —«¡Qué bien que no
_____ en el verano!»

11. (sonreír)   El salvavidas _____ .

12. (seguir)   Dos perros _____ a mi hermanito.

You are in a hotel in Santo Domingo and want to say or ask the following in Spanish:

1. (entender)   Yo no _____ español muy bien.

2. (costar)   ¿Cuánto _____ un cuarto?

3. (dormir)   Generalmente nosotros _____ en cuartos diferentes.

4. (querer)   Mi familia _____ el cuarto para una semana.

5. (servir)   ¿A qué hora _____ Uds. el desayuno?

6. (pedir)   ¿Dónde _____ nosotros direcciones?

7. (cerrar)   ¿A qué hora _____ Uds. la cafetería?

8. (llover)   ¿ _____ mucho en el verano?

9. (preferir)   Mis hermanos _____ ir a la playa ahora.

10. (volver)   Mi mamá _____ al hotel a la una.

DIÁLOGO

José is calling Carmen on the phone. What is Carmen saying?

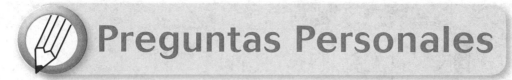

Preguntas Personales

1. ¿Qué haces en la playa?

_____

2. ¿Vives cerca de una playa? ¿De cuál?

_____

3. ¿Lees libros sobre piratas? ¿Por qué (no)?

_____

4. ¿Dónde puedes encontrar tesoros?

_____

5. ¿En qué islas del Caribe hablan español?

_____

Información Personal

Draw a treasure map. Write five sentences giving the clues necessary to find the treasure:

EXAMPLE:　**Hay una piedra grande debajo de una palmera.**

_____

1. _____

2. _____

3. _____

4. _____

5. _____

Cápsula cultural

Una playa diferente todos los días

¿Le gustaría pasar sus vacaciones en una playa en España? Pero, ¿cuál? ¡Hay más de dos mil! El país de España forma parte de la Península Ibérica, que tiene una costa de 1,698 (mil seiscientas noventa y ocho) millas con más de 2,000 playas y 200 balnearios.

Para identificar con precisión la localidad de cada área en el mapa, los españoles han dividido todo el territorio en siete secciones o costas. **la Costa Brava** es un área montañosa de la costa mediterránea que se extiende hasta la frontera de Francia.

Después viene **la Costa Dorada**, que pasa por Barcelona con sus playas de arena de color de oro. Después viene **la Costa del Azahar**, con sus grandes playas que pasan por Valencia. Sigue **la Costa Blanca**, que ofrece un invierno muy suave. Por fin, la última costa en el Mediterráneo es la popular **Costa del Sol**, que da a África.

Hay dos costas más en el Atlántico: En el sur está la **Costa de la Luz**, que se extiende hasta la frontera portuguesa.La costa al norte del Atlántico se llama **la Costa Verde**, a causa de su abundante vegetación verde.

A causa del gran volumen de turismo y construcción en la costa, voluntarios de la *Coastwatch* europea examinan cada año los desperdicios dejados en las playas españolas para inspeccionar el daño ambiental y preparar actividades de rehabilitación necesarias.

Discusión

1. Describa la costa de la Península Ibérica.

2. ¿Qué son las costas? ¿Por qué las han creado los españoles?

3. ¿Cuántas costas hay en España? ¿Cómo se llaman?

4. ¿Qué trabajo hace la *Coastwatch*?

Para investigar

Investiga en el Internet cuáles son algunos problemas causados por el exceso de turismo. ¿Qué podemos hacer para remediarlos?

VOCABULARIO

el balneario *beach resort*

bravo *wild*

dorado *golden*

la arena *sand*

el azahar *orange blossom*

por fin *finally*

dar a *to face*

a causa de *because of*

los desperdicios *waste, garbage*

dejado *left*

el daño ambiental *environmental damage*

En la joyería

Negative and Affirmative Expressions

1 Vocabulario

JOYERIA EL DIAMANTE

GRAN VENTA DE JOYAS

el collar de perlas

la esmeralda

el diamante

el reloj de pulsera

la cadena
el collar

el rubí

el brazalete
(la pulsera)

los aretes

el broche
(el prendedor)

la sortija

el anillo de diamantes

Juan has a job in a jewelry store. The manager has told him to place labels on all the articles in the showcase for the big sale. Can you help him?

cadena de oro $100   **collar de esmeraldas** $900

brazalete de plata $150   **aretes de perlas** $55

anillo de diamantes $500   **broche de rubíes** $300

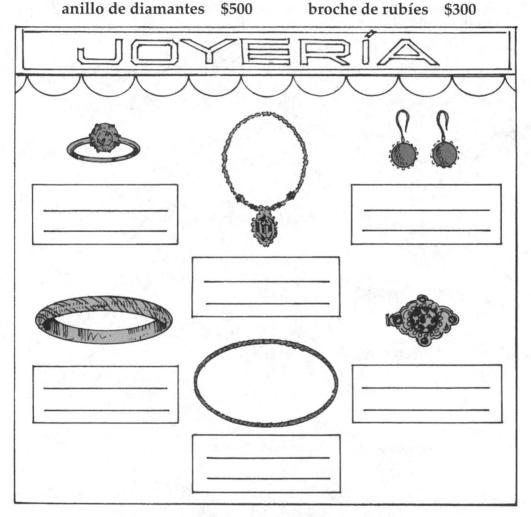

You are buying holiday presents in the jewelry department of a department store. What should you buy for these people on your list?

EXAMPLE: Tu padre: **Compro un reloj de pulsera para mi padre.**

1. Tu amigo Juan: _____

2. Tu amiga Carla: _____

3. Tu mamá: _____

4. Tu hermana Clarita: _____

5. Tu hermano Miguel: _____

You already know the most common negative word in the Spanish language: **no**. To make any sentence negative, simply put **no** before the verb. There are, however, other important negative expressions in Spanish. Read the following story and pay careful attention to the new negatives and to their corresponding affirmatives.

La magia

Un hombre está sentado en una silla delante de un grupo de personas, con las espalda hacia ellos. Tiene los ojos cubiertos.

hacia *towards*

No puede ver **nada**. Su ayudante toma una cosa y dice:

nada *nothing, anything*

    —Maestro. Ahora tengo algo en la mano. ¿Qué es?

algo *something*
ni . . . ni *neither . . . nor*
tampoco *either, neither*

Necesito saber. Dígame. Ahora, ¿sabe?
El hombre piensa un momento y contesta:

    —Veo algo. **No** es **ni** grande **ni** pesado. **Tampoco** es pequeño. Es . . . es . . . una cadena.

    —Estupendo, sensacional—grita el ayudante.—El maestro **nunca** comete un error, **no** falla **jamás**. Siempre tiene razón. Un aplauso, por favor.

nunca *never*
fallar *to fail*
jamás *never*
el mago *magician*

¿Pero, qué pasa aquí? ¿Es la magia de veras? ¿Es un mago el hombre? ¿Puede él ver cosas que **nadie** ve? ¿O es una simple ilusión? Si Ud. tiene buena memoria puede hacer lo mismo. Primero necesita una clave. Por ejemplo, en la clave del maestro, cada letra del alfabeto tiene una palabra equivalente. El maestro sabe de memoria esta tabla de equivalentes.

nadie *nobody*

la clave *key (to code)*

saber de memoria *to know by heart*

TABLA DE EQUIVALENTES

ahora	= a	seguramente	= h
vamos	= b	nombre Ud.	= i
maestro	= c	rápido	= j
¿qué?	= d	bueno	= l
necesito	= e	mire	= m
haga el favor	= f	dígame	= n
muy bien	= g		

Entonces, para descifrar el mensaje secreto, el mago toma simplemente la primera palabra de cada frase que dice el ayudante:

primero/a *first*

> —Maestro. Ahora tengo algo en la mano. ¿Qué es? Necesito saber. Dígame. Ahora, ¿sabe?

PRIMERA PALABRA	LETRA EQUIVALENTE
maestro	C
ahora	A
qué	D
necesito	E
dígame	N
ahora	A

¿Comprende ahora cómo el mago hace su magia? Ahora Ud. también puede sorprender a sus amigos con su «poder mental».

poder *power*

Actividad C

Answer the following questions about the store.

1. ¿Dónde está sentado el mago?

_____

2. ¿Por qué no puede ver nada?

_____

3. ¿Qué dice primero el ayudante del mago?

_____

4. ¿Qué hace el mago antes de contestar?

_____

5. ¿Qué tiene el ayudante en la mano?

_____

6. ¿En qué consiste la clave del mago?

_____

7. ¿Qué sabe de memoria el maestro?

_____

8. ¿Qué palabra de cada frase es importante?

_____

9. ¿Cuántas letras tiene la palabra «cadena»?

_____

10. ¿Cuántas frases usa el ayudante del mago?

_____

2   Notice the following negative expressions in the preceding story.

Nadie ve.	_No one sees._
Tampoco es pequeño.	_He is not small either._
No puede ver _nada_.	_He/She can't see anything._
Nunca comete un error.	_He/She never makes a mistake._
No es _ni_ grande _ni_ pesado.	_He is neither big nor heavy._
No falla jamás.	_He is never wrong._

Now read the following expressions.

No puede ver _nada_. _Nada_ **puede ver.**	_He can't see anything._
No comete _nunca_ **un error.** _Nunca_ **comete un error.**	_He never makes a mistake._
No es pequeño _tampoco_. _Tampoco_ **es pequeño.**	_He is not small either._

cosas que no ve *nadie*	}	*things that no one sees*
cosas que *nadie* ve		

No miente jamás.	}	*He never lies.*
Jamás miente.		

Look at the first sentence in each pair. Where is the negative word placed? Directly before the verb. Now look at second sentence in each pair.

What word is placed directly before the verb? _____ Where is

the negative word placed? _____

RULE: There are two ways of negating a sentence in Spanish:

   (a) **no** + verb + negative word

   (b) negative word + verb

Work with a partner. One student reads a negative expression. The partner changes the expression to the positive.

EXAMPLE: *Nadie* **ve el programa de TV.**   *Alguien* **ve, el programa de TV.**

1 También es pequeño.   _____

2. Siempre comete un error.   _____

3. Puede ver algo.   _____

4. Siempre miente.   _____

5. Es grande y pesado.   _____

María likes to do what her older sister, Rosa, does. What does María say?

EXAMPLE: **Yo no compro joyas. ¿Y tú?**
           Yo *tampoco* compro joyas.   OR   **Yo *no* compro joyas *tampoco*.**

1. Yo no quiero el dinero. ¿Y tú?

_____

2. Yo no uso anteojos. ¿Y tú?

_____

3. Yo no encuentro el reloj. ¿Y tú?

_____

4. Yo no sé cocinar. ¿Y tú?

_____

5. Yo no puedo ir al restaurante. ¿Y tú?

_____

Actividad **F**

Say that you don't ever do the following things:

EXAMPLE: **comer chocolate**
            Yo _nunca_ (_jamás_) **como chocolate.**
            Yo no como _nunca_ (_jamás_) **chocolate.**

1. trabajar los domingos

_____

2. comprar joyas

_____

3. tomar el sol

_____

4. decir mentiras

_____

5. comer afuera

_____

Fernando doesn't like certain foods. What does he tell his mother?

EXAMPLE: **las frutas . . . las legumbres**
            No me gustan ni las frutas ni las legumbres.

1. el maíz . . . el arroz

_____

2. la leche . . . el jugo

_____

3. el pollo . . . el rosbif

_____

4. los tacos . . . las enchiladas

_____

5. las naranjas . . . las manzanas

_____

NOTE: When the object of a verb is a negative or an affirmative word referring
         to a person, the personal **a** is used:

         Veo _a_ alguien.   _I see someone._
         No veo _a_ nadie.   _I don't see anyone._

Actividad H

Miguel takes great pleasure in saying the opposite of what his twin brother Marcos says. Give Miguel's negative statements. Work with a partner.

EXAMPLE: **Yo oigo** *algo.* **¿Y tú?**   **Yo no oigo** *nada.*

1. Yo veo a alguien. ¿Y tú?   _____

2. Yo escribo algo. ¿Y tú?   _____

3. Yo busco a alguien. ¿Y tú?   _____

4. Yo tomo algo. ¿Y tú?   _____

5. Yo quiero a alguien. ¿Y tú?   _____

Actividad I

Your mother is asking you some questions. Answer them negatively.

1. ¿Haces algo ahora?

    _____

2. ¿Conoces a alguien en México?

    _____

3. ¿Dices siempre la verdad?

    _____

4. ¿Quieres comer algo?

    _____

5. ¿Vas al cine con tus amigos?

    _____

6. ¿Llamas a alguien por teléfono?

    _____

There is one more negative word (**ninguno, -a, -os, -as** *none, not any, no*) and one more affirmative word (**alguno, -a, -os, -as** *any, some*) that need your special attention. Look at the following examples:

¿Quieres algunas frutas?

¿Quieres hacer *alguna* **pregunta?**	*Do you want to ask any question?*
No, no quiero hacer *ninguna* **pregunta.**	*No, I don't want to ask any question.*
¿Necesitas *algún* **consejo?**	*Do you need some advice?*
No, no necesito *ningún* **consejo.**	*No, I don't need any advice.*
¿Ves *algunos* **libros aquí?**	*Do you see some books here?*
No, no veo *ningunos* **libros aquí.**	*No, I don't see any books here.*
¿Puedes comprar *algunas* **cosas?**	*Can you buy some things?*
No, no puedo comprar *ningunas* **cosas.**	*No, I can't buy any things.*

Did you observe that both **alguno** and **ninguno** agree in gender and number with nouns they accompany? What's more, they become **algún** and **ningún** before a masculine singular noun:

¿Tienes *algún* **amigo español?**	*Do you have any Spanish friend?*
No, no tengo *ningún* **amigo español.**	*No, I don't have any Spanish friend.*

Actividad J

Your friend is offering you different things. Say that you don't want any:

EXAMPLE: **¿Quieres** *algún* **postre?**   **No, gracias. No quiero** *ningún* **postre.**

1. ¿Quieres alguna torta?   _____

2. ¿Quieres algunos discos? _____

3. ¿Quieres alguna fruta? _____

4. ¿Quieres algún libro? _____

5. ¿Quieres algún plato típico? _____

You are in a contrary mood today. Answer the following questions negatively.

1. Carlos va a la fiesta. ¿Y tú?

_____

2. ¿Sabes algo sobre el Paraguay?

_____

3. ¿Va tu hermana siempre al cine por la noche?

_____

4. ¿Conocen tus padres a alguien en España?

_____

5. ¿Vale algún libro mil dólares?

_____

6. ¿Qué exámenes tienes los sábados?

_____

7. ¿Está abierta alguna tienda hoy?

_____

8. ¿Tienes algún trabajo para mañana?

_____

9. ¿Quieres comer un pastel o un sándwich?

_____

10. ¿Ves algo interesante en la joyería?

_____

In this conversation, you have the role of Javier Jalapeño, an assistant to a great magician.

Preguntas Personales

1. ¿Por qué le gusta ver a mucha gente las ilusiones?

_____

2. ¿Qué significa la expresión «la mano es más rápida que el ojo»?

_____

3. ¿Qué regalos prefieres dar (o recibir)?

_____

4. ¿Generalmente, quiénes usan joyas?

_____

5. ¿Qué clase de joyas usa una chica (un chico)?

_____

Información Personal

Tell us about yourself by completing the following paragraph.

Los fines de semana yo prefiero _____ pero no me gusta _____ .
　　　　　　　　　　　　　　　　　　1.　　　　　　　　　　　　　　　　　2.
Mis platos favoritos son _____ y _____ . Nunca como ni
　　　　　　　　　　　　　　3.　　　　　　　　4.
_____ ni _____ . Generalmente paso mis ratos libres _____ ,
　　5.　　　　　　　　6.　　　　　　　　　　　　　　　　　　　　　　7.
pero nunca _____ .
　　　　　　　8.

Composición

You want to put on a comedy skit as *El Gran Fandango*, the world's greatest mind reader, before your Spanish class. To demonstrate your abilities, think of an object. Make up a

key and write the sentences that your assistant will use to enable you to "read minds."
Then get into pairs and try it with your partner.

_____

_____

_____

_____

_____

_____

_____

Cápsula cultural

El oro: el metal deseado

A través de los siglos, la gente ha viajado a tierras desconocidas y peligrosas en busca de oro. La mayoría de los exploradores europeos que vinieron a Las Américas buscaban oro en los territorios de los aztecas de México y los incas del Perú. Siglos después, durante las famosas «fiebres del oro», miles de personas fueron a California y a Alaska con la esperanza de encontrar oro y hacerse ricos. Muchos de ellos murieron en el esfuerzo.

¿Por qué existe este deseo tan fuerte de poseer este metal? El oro siempre ha sido valioso, parcialmente a causa de su escasez. Pero el oro es también un metal hermoso y lustroso. Además es blando y fácil de moldear en muchas formas. Se ha usado para hacer monedas y joyas por su propiedad de no oxidarse. El oro está medido en quilates: 24 quilates es el oro puro.

En Bogotá, Colombia, está el Museo del Oro, donde se exhiben más de 30,000 piezas de oro, incluso máscaras, pendientes y adornos de toda clase. Para los indígenas que fabricaban estas obras de arte, el oro era «el sudor del sol».

Discusión

1. ¿Qué ha hecho mucha gente para adquirir el oro?

2. ¿Qué pasó durante la «fiebre del oro»?

3. ¿Por qué ha sido valioso el oro?

4. ¿Qué es El Museo del Oro y dónde está?

Para investigar

¿Cuáles son algunos problemas causados por la extracción de minerales de la tierra?

VOCABULARIO

a través de *through*
la fiebre del oro *gold rush*
el esfuerzo *attempt, effort*
la escasez *shortage*
oxidarse *to rust*

el quilate *carat*
donde *where*
incluso *including*
el indígena *native*
sudor *sweat*

El fin de semana

Formal and Informal Commands

1 Vocabulario

What can we do for fun on a weekend?

ir de compras

ir a un concierto de rock

ver una película

hacer ejercicio

jugar a los bolos

patinar

ir al teatro

patinar en el hielo

ver una exhibición en el museo

nadar en la piscina

montar a caballo

Do you enjoy any of the activities at the beginning of this lesson? How about inviting one or more of your friends to join you? It's very simple. Look at the following examples.

¡Vamos **a la fiesta!**	*Let's go to the party!*
¡Vamos **a jugar al monopolio!**	*Let's play monopoly!*

Vamos is used to express *let's go*. **Vamos a** + infinitive is used to express *let's*.

NOTE: Did you notice the inverted exclamation mark (¡) before each sentence starting with **vamos**? In Spanish, sentences that have a normal exclamation mark at the end also have an inverted exclamation mark at the beginning.

Tell your friend to do the following activities with you.

EXAMPLE: dance   **Vamos a bailar.**

1. skate   _____

2. see a horror movie   _____

3. play soccer   _____

4. go bowling   _____

5. visit the museum   _____

6. swim in the swimming pool   _____

A friend of the family is flying in this weekend. Tell him/her to join you in five different activities.

EXAMPLE: **¡Vamos a un concierto de rock!**

Cierre los ojos y abra la boca: el hipnotismo

Read the following story about a hypnotist to see how he commands people to do things.

Es sábado por la noche y la familia Colón está sentada delante de su televisor mirando un programa especial sobre los ilusionistas. Esta noche van presentar al hipnotista Mandrako el Maravilloso.

CHITO: Papá, ¿qué es un hipnotista?

SR. COLÓN: Es un hombre que vive de la ignorancia de la gente.

SRA. COLÓN: ¡Carlos, no **digas** eso! El hipnotismo es el arte de crear en una persona un estado similar al sueño y así la persona acepta órdenes sin resistir.

SR. COLÓN: Sí, especialmente si la persona es un individuo débil y no tiene inteligencia.

PILAR: ¡Miren! La función empieza ahora.

La función toma lugar en un teatro oscuro. Mandrako, un hombre alto y flaco vestido todo de negro, está en el escenario. Mandrako escoge a un miembro del auditorio.

MANDRAKO: ¡Ud., señor! **Suba** por favor.

SR.COLÓN (a su   Voy a demostrar que todo esto es una estupidez.
familia):

MANDRAKO: **Tome** asiento, por favor. Ahora **mire** mi reloj. Ud. tiene sueño, mucho sueño. **Cierre** los ojos.

                  (El señor Colón parece dormirse bajo dormirse bajo la influencia del mago y cae en un trance profundo.)

Ahora, **abra** la boca y **ladre** como un perro. **Meta** su dedo en el oído y **salte** como un mono, **corra** como un gato. Muy bien. Ahora voy a contar hasta diez y puede abrir los ojos. No va a recordar nada.

El hombre en el teatro se despierta. El señor Colón parece despertarse también y dice:

SR. COLÓN: ¡Qué estupidez! ¿No ves que un hombre inteligente como yo no es susceptible a sus sugerencias y mandatos?

SRA. COLÓN: Claro, mi amor. ¿Pero, por qué no sacas el dedo de tu oído ahora?

Discusión

1. ¿Qué hace la familia Colón por la noche?

   _____

2. ¿Qué es el hipnotismo, según la señora de Colón?

   _____

3. ¿Qué dice el mago para hipnotizar al señor?

   _____

4. ¿Cuáles son sus mandatos?

   _____

5. ¿Qué opina Ud. del valor del hipnotismo?

   _____

 Mandrako gave a number of commands to Mr. Colón. In some he used the pronoun **Ud.** and in others he didn't. That's because the use of the pronoun is optional. Let's list some of Mandrako's commands.

-AR VERBS	-ER VERBS	-IR VERBS
Tome Ud. asiento.	*Meta* su dedo en el oído.	*Suba* ahora.
Mire mi reloj.	*Corra* como un gato.	*Abra* la boca.

These are called formal commands. They are used when addressing people as **Ud.** or **Uds.** In the formal command forms, **-AR** verbs end in **-e**, **-ER** and **-IR** verbs end in **-a**. To give a formal command, drop the **-o** of the **yo**-form of the present tense and add the appropriate endings.

INFINITIVE	PRESENT TENSE YO-FORM	FORMAL COMMAND	MEANING
hablar	habl-	Hable	*Speak*
comer	com-	Coma	*Eat*
dormir	duerm-	Duerma	*Sleep*

To make a formal command plural, add the letter **n** to the singular command.

SINGULAR	PLURAL
Cierre (Ud.) la ventana.	*Cierren* (Uds.) la ventana.
No *sirva* (Ud.) el café ahora.	No *sirvan* (Uds.) el café ahora.
Repita (Ud.) la lección.	*Repitan* (Uds.) la lección.

Work with a partner. One student makes up a command. The other student acts it out.

EXAMPLE: STUDENT 1   STUDENT 2
               mirar la televisión   **Mire la televisión.**

1. leer el periódico
2. comprar una revista
3. subir al autobús
4. entrar en la clase
5. beber un café
6. estudiar la lección
7. montar a caballo
8. dormir la siesta
9. comer un pedazo de pizza
10. nadar en la piscina

Now you be the teacher for the day. Tell your students to do the following.

EXAMPLE: entrar en la clase   *Entren* **en la clase.**

1. cerrar las ventanas   _____
2. abrir el libro de español   _____
3. no dormir en clase   _____
4. repetir las palabras   _____
5. aprender un poema   _____

 Some verbs in Spanish have an irregular **yo** form. These verbs also follow the same rule to form the formal command.

INFINITIVE	PRESENT TENSE YO-FORM	FORMAL COMMAND	
		SINGULAR	PLURAL
decir (*to say*)	**digo**	**Dig***a*	**Dig***an*
hacer (*to do*)	**hago**	**Hag***a*	**Hag***an*
oír (*to hear*)	**oigo**	**Oig***a*	**Oig***an*
poner (*to put*)	**pongo**	**Pong***a*	**Pong***an*
salir (*to go out*)	**salgo**	**Salg***a*	**Salg***an*
tener (*to have*)	**tengo**	**Teng***a*	**Teng***an*
traer (*to bring*)	**traigo**	**Traig***a*	**Traig***an*
venir (*to come*)	**vengo**	**Veng***a*	**Veng***an*

NOTE: There are three important verbs that do not follow the rule for formal commands: **dar, ir,** and **ser.** You will have to memorize the following forms:

(**dar**)   *Dé* **(Ud.) un ejemplo.**   } *Give an example.*
            Den (Uds.) un ejemplo.

| (ir) | *Vaya* **(Ud.) a casa.** | } | *Go home.* |
| | *Vayan* **(Uds.) a casa.** | | |

| (ser) | **No** *sea* **(Ud.) tonto.** | } | *Don't be foolish.* |
| | **No sean (Uds.) tontos.** | | |

Actividad F

Give a formal command using the following phrases.

EXAMPLE: decir la verdad   (Ud.)   *Diga* **la verdad.**

1. dar la información   (Ud.)   _____
2. oír la explosión   (Uds.)   _____
3. poner el libro sobre la mesa   (Ud.)   _____
4. no salir   (Uds.)   _____
5. tener mucho cuidado   (Ud.)   _____
6. venir mañana   (Ud.)   _____
7. ser bueno con su hermanita   (Ud.)   _____
8. decir la verdad   (Uds.)   _____
9. no ir al centro   (Uds.)   _____
10. hacer el trabajo   (Ud.)   _____

Actividad G

Express the following formal commands in Spanish.

EXAMPLE: Write the answer.   *Escriba* **la respuesta.**

1. Give an example.   (Ud.)   _____
2. Bring a Spanish film.   (Ud.)   _____
3. Don't leave now.   (Uds.)   _____
4. Say something.   (Ud.)   _____
5. Go to the cafeteria now.   (Uds.)   _____

5 You now know how to give formal commands (**Ud., Uds.**). But what happens if you want to tell a friend or somebody you address as **tú** to do something? You must use the INFORMAL COMMAND.

To form an informal command, use the **Ud./él/ella** form of the present tense.

PRESENT TENSE Ud./él/ella	INFORMAL COMMAND	MEANING
Ud./él/ella *lee* el libro.	¡*Lee* el libro!	*Read the book!*
Ud./él/ella *compra* los discos.	¡*Compra* los discos!	*Buy the records!*
Ud./él/ella *abre* la ventana.	¡*Abre* la ventana!	*Open the window!*

NOTE: To make the informal command plural, use the **Uds.**-form of the formal command.

(**Tú**)   *Habla* despacio.   ⎫
(**Uds.**)   *Hablen* despacio. ⎬   *Speak slowly.*

Work with a partner. Tell one of your friends to do the following activities.

1. (visita) el museo conmigo.

_____

2. (escribir) la tarea en español

_____

3. (comprar) entradas para nosotros

_____

4. (jugar) a los bolos este sábado

_____

5. (patinar) en el parque el fin de semana

_____

6. (almorzar) en mi casa

_____

7. (hablar) conmigo después de la clase

_____

8. (comer) en la cafetería conmigo

_____

9. (ayudar) a tus amigos

_____

10. (volver) a mi casa temprano

_____

 If you want to tell a friend *not* to do something, you must go back to the *formal* command form and add an **-s.**

¡*Salga* (Ud.)!	¡No *salgas* (tú)!
¡*Abra* (Ud.) la ventana!	¡No *abras* (tú) la ventana!
¡*Mire* (Ud.) ese programa!	¡No *mires* (tú) ese programa!

Express the following commands in the **tú**-form in Spanish.

EXAMPLE: Write all the words. Don't write only the first word.

Escribe **todas las palabras.** *No escribas* **solo la primera palabra.**

1. Eat all your lunch. Don't eat only the dessert.

_____

2. Speak with your father. Don't speak with your mother.

_____

3. Study the lesson. Don't study only the vocabulary.

_____

4. Listen to the teacher. Don't listen to your friend.

_____

5. Call Monday. Don't call Tuesday.

_____

7 Many verbs have irregular familiar command forms. Here are some of the most common:

decir: *di*	salir: *sal*
hacer: *haz*	ser: *sé*
ir: *ve*	tener: *ten*
poner: *pon*	venir: *ven*

The negative forms of those commands are regular:

No *digas*	No *salgas*
No *hagas*	No *seas*
No *vayas*	No *tengas*
No *pongas*	No *vengas*

Complete the following informal commands to your friend with the correct form of the verb in parentheses.

1. (poner)   ¡No _____ la mesa allí!

2. (ir)   ¡No _____ a la tienda ahora!

3. (comprar)   ¡ _____ las entradas hoy!

4. (comer)   ¡ _____ temprano para salir después!

5. (hacer)   ¡ _____ las tareas esta noche!

6. (decir)   ¡ _____ siempre la verdad!

7. (venir)   ¡ _____ temprano! ¡No _____
tarde!

8. (salir)   ¡ _____ del cuarto!

9. (vender)   ¡ _____ tu carro!

10. (ir)   ¡ _____ a ver la película!

Work with a partner. Your mother and you tell your little sister to do certain things and not do others. Express your commands in the informal form in Spanish.

EXAMPLE: *Ve(te)* **a la biblioteca.** *No vayas* **al cine.**

Go to the library. Don't go to the movies.

1. Do your homework. Don't watch television.

_____

2. Be good. Don't tell lies.

_____

3. Be careful. Don't run.

_____

4. Go to your room. Don't close the door.

_____

5. Read a good book. Don't listen to your Ipod.

_____

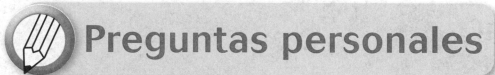

1. ¿Generalmente, qué haces por la noche los días de escuela?

_____

2. ¿Qué tipo de películas te gusta ver?

_____

3. ¿Qué tipo de música prefieres escuchar?

_____

4. ¿Practicas algunos deportes o prefieres ser espectador(-a)?

_____

5. ¿Qué opinas de la televisión moderna?

_____

DIÁLOGO

You are talking with a friend about plans for the weekend.

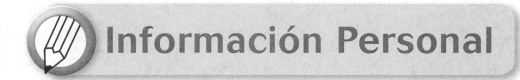

Información Personal

You have been selected to play the part of "El Gran Fandango," the world's greatest hypnotist. Using some of the commands you have just learned, tell a subject what you wish him/her to do.

1. _____
2. _____
3. _____
4. _____
5. _____
6. _____

Cápsula cultural

«¿Papá, me das mi domingo?»

En la mayoría de los países hispanoamericanos el domingo es el día de la familia, cuando todos se reúnen y comparten juntos. Pero el domingo es también un día importante para los niños. ¿Por qué? Porque los domingos los niños les preguntan a sus padres: —«¿Me das mi domingo?» Así es como piden su dinero.

El domingo es el día cuando los adultos dan dinero a los niños. Los chicos pueden comprar lo que quieran o necesiten o lo pueden ahorrar. Ellos deciden qué comprarán, no sus padres. Realmente es el día cuando los adultos les dedican tiempo a los hijos, llevándolos al parque, a la feria, o a otros lugares divertidos e interesantes. Y es el día en que los niños se divierten comprándose cosas que quizás los adultos no les comprarían.

Discusión

1. ¿Cómo pasan los domingos las familias en los países hispanoamericanos?

2. ¿Por qué es importante el domingo para los niños en México?

3. ¿Qué significa «¿me das mi domingo»?

4. ¿Qué pueden hacer los niños con el dinero que reciben?

5. ¿Por qué es importante para los miembros de una familia pasar tiempo juntos?

VOCABULARIO

compartir *to share*

Comunicándose

Adjectives and Adverbs

1 Vocabulario

la estampilla/el sello

el correo aéreo

EL CORREO

el cartero
la cartera

el buzón

el encabezamiento

Sr. Daniel Rivera
Banco Central
Calle D #5
Managua, Nicaragua

la carta

$25

el giro postal

la despedida

Hasta luego
José Noa

el
cuerpo

la tarjeta postal

el portacartas

la firma

la dirección

el/la dependiente

Sr. José Pérez
Calle Acosta, #23
Naguabo, PR 00178

el sobre

el paquete
postal

Sr. Daniel Rivera
Banco Central
calle D #5
Managua, Nicaragua

Querida Ana

el
saludo

echar una
carta al correo

Actividad Ⓐ

Picture story. Mario is sending a letter to his friend Marta in Ponce, Puerto Rico. These are the steps he takes.

Mario compra , y . Entonces, escribe la . Primero,

pone la , el y el . Luego, escribe el ,

la y la .

Mario mete la carta en el , escribe el , el y

pone el . Mario el , lo lleva al y lo mete

en el .

El toma el sobre y lo pone en un . Otro lleva el portacartas

al aeropuerto. Todas las llegan a su destino por avión. Cuando la carta de

Mario llega al en Ponce, el lleva la a la casa de Marta.

Finalmente Marta recibe su carta. ¡Está contentísima!

2 When we speak about someone or something, we use adjectives to describe that person or thing. You already know that adjectives in Spanish agree in gender (masculine or feminine) and number (singular or plural) with the noun they describe. Do you remember how to make an adjective feminine?

Él es *simpático*.   Ella es _____ .

Él es *inteligente*.   Ella es _____ .

Él es *joven*.   Ella es _____ .

Adjectives ending in **o** change the **o** to **a** in the feminine form. Other adjectives remain unchanged. Remember, however, that there is an exception: adjectives of nationality ending in a consonant add an **a** for the feminine form. Look at the following examples.

Carlos es *español* y María es *española*.   *Carlos is Spanish and María is Spanish.*

Paul es *francés* y Monique es *francesa*.   *Paul is French and Monique is French.*

How do we describe more than one person or thing?

Él es *pequeño*.   Ellos son _____ .

Ella es *pequeña*.   Ellas son _____ .

Él / ella es *fuerte*.   Ellos/ellas son _____ .

Él / ella es *popular*.   Ellos/ellas son _____ .

The rules are very simple:

RULES: If the singular adjective ends in a vowel, add **s** to form the plural.
If the singular adjective ends in a consonant, add **es** to form the plural.

You also know that descriptive adjectives usually follow the noun:

Compro un sobre *azul*.   *I buy a blue envelope.*

Leo un periódico *argentino*.   *I read an Argentinean newspaper.*

One of your classmates describes some people or objects to you. You want to know about other people or things.

EXAMPLE: YOUR CLASSMATE: **Miguel es mexicano. (Isabel)**
            YOU: **¿Es *Isabel mexicana* también?**

1. YOUR CLASSMATE: La nueva profesora es española.   (el director)

   YOU: _____

2. YOUR CLASSMATE: El español es fácil.   (la biología)

   YOU: _____

3. YOUR CLASSMATE: El carro de Eduardo es amarillo.   (su casa)

   YOU: _____

4. YOUR CLASSMATE: Mi perro es grande y gordo.   (tus gatos)

   YOU: _____

5. YOUR CLASSMATE: El padre de Raúl es alto y rubio.   (la madre)

   YOU: _____

6. YOUR CLASSMATE: Mis hermanas son simpáticas.   (tus hermanos)

   YOU: _____

3   Do you remember **alguno** and **ninguno**? They stand before the noun and drop the final **o** before a masculine singular noun:

¿Conoces a *algún* periodista?   *Do you know any newspaperman?*
No, no conozco a *ningún* periodista.   *No, I don't know any newspaperman.*

There is a special group of adjectives that may stand before or after the noun. Look at the following examples:

Luis es un chico *bueno*.   **Luis es un *buen* chico.**   *Luis is a good boy.*
José es un alumno *malo*.   **José es un *mal* alumno.**   *José is a bad student.*

Leo el capítulo *primero*.   **Leo el *primer* capítulo.**   *I read the first chapter.*
Vivo en el piso *tercero*.   **Vivo en el *tercer* piso.**   *I live on the third floor.*

The sentences in both Spanish columns mean the same thing. What happened to the adjectives in the right column? _____ . They dropped the final **o**. The adjective was shortened. What is the gender of the nouns described by those adjectives? _____ . Are they singular or plural? _____ .

4   Now look at these sentences:

El español es mi *tercera* clase.   *Spanish is my third class.*
Ellas son *malas* alumnas.   *They are bad students.*
Los *primeros* capítulos son largos.   *The first chapters are long.*
Luis y Carlos son *buenos* chicos.   *Luis and Carlos are good boys.*

Were the adjectives shortened in the above sentences? _____ . Here's the easy rule:

RULE: **Bueno, malo, primero,** and **tercero** are shortened only before a masculine singular noun.

Actividad **C**

Complete the following sentences with the correct form of the adjective in parentheses.

1. Siempre saco _____ notas en álgebra. (malo)

2. ¿Tienes _____ preguntas? (alguno)

3. Cuando hace _____ tiempo, leo un _____ libro. (malo, bueno)

4. Es la _____ vez que repito la palabra. (tercero)

5. Me gustan las _____ semanas del verano. (primero)

6. El _____ mes del año es marzo. (tercero)

7. La _____ página de la lección es fácil. (primero)

8. _____ día voy a hablar bien el español. (alguno)

9. Yo no tengo _____ examen. (ninguno)

10. Quiero comer un _____ desayuno. (bueno)

Actividad D

Francisco is always saying the opposite of his twin brother Fernando:

EXAMPLE: **Carlos es un buen amigo.**   **No, Carlos es un *mal* amigo.**

1. María es una mala estudiante.   _____

2. Hoy hace buen tiempo.   _____

3. El hijo del Sr. Pérez es un mal chico.   _____

4. Ella saca buenas notas en español.   _____

5. Leer es un mal hábito.   _____

5 The adjective **grande** can also stand before or after the noun. But look what happens:

Buenos Aires es una ciudad *grande*.	*Buenos Aires is a large city.*
Buenos Aires es una *gran* ciudad.	*Buenos Aires is a great city.*
El general era un soldado *grande*.	*The general was a large soldier.*
El general era un *gran* soldado.	*The general was a great soldier.*

How do you express great before a singular noun (masculine or feminine)? _____ . Before a plural noun (masculine or feminine)? _____ .

What does the adjective **grande(s)** mean when placed after a noun?

RULES: After a noun, **grande(-s)** means *large* or *big*.
Before a noun, **gran (grandes)** means *great*.

Describe five large or great people, places, things, using a form of **grande.**

EXAMPLE: Simón Bolívar: **un gran general**

1. _____

2. _____

3. _____

4. _____

5. _____

Here are some statements taken from a newspaper. Look at the following index and tell in what section they would be found.

Anuncios	60
Consultorio Sentimental	24
Deportes	55
Editorial	5
Espectáculos	27
Noticias internacionales y nacionales	23
Noticias locales	30
Personales	62
Televisión	48

EXAMPLE: un nocaut en el último round *la sección deportiva*

1. ¡Gran venta de ropa de verano! _____

2. Hombre roba varias tiendas. _____

3. Necesitamos más policías para combatir el crimen. _____

4. Tienes que tener más confianza en tus relaciones. _____

5. Carro negro, en buenas condiciones, precio bajo. _____

6. Anotación final: Yanquis 7, Atléticos 3 _____

7. Pérez-Carvajal anuncian matrimonio. _____

8. *Ataque de los Monstruos del Espacio* estrena en el Teatro Capri. _____

9. Mundo Latino (Variedades) Canal 7 _____

10. Joven de 25 años busca persona atractiva para una relación seria _____

Conecciones sociales

Es sábado por la noche y Paco Pérez, matando el tiempo sin nada que hacer, está revisando su cuenta de Facebook para ver si encuentra a un viejo amigo. Paco se graduó de la escuela **hace poco** y ahora se encuentra en la universidad y no conoce a nadie.

Luego de una hora sin tener éxito, de repente parece reconocer a alguien. —«Sí, es ella, Laura Zapata»— pensó Paco. — «Estaba en una de mis clases en la escuela. Laura era alta y delgada, de ojos negros y pelo largo. Era muy bonita y un poco tímida y callada. Recuerdo que sonreía **tímidamente**.»

Paco siempre quería salir con ella pero nunca tuvo el valor de hablar con ella para pedirle una cita. Quizás ésta será su oportunidad.

Paco escribió: «Hola, Laura. Es Paco. Hace casi un año que nos graduamos de la escuela y ahora estoy en la universidad. ¿Cómo van las cosas?».

Poco después, Paco recibe una respuesta: «Hola, Paco. ¿Estás en la universidad? ¡Qué bueno! Estoy muy contenta de tener noticias de ti. Yo también estoy en la universidad, pero las cosas no son

exactamente a pedir de boca. Necesito mucha ayuda en mis clases de matemáticas y en las de computadoras.

matar el tiempo *to kill time*
revisar *to check out*
la cuenta *the account*
hace poco *a short time ago*

¿Cómo van las cosas? *How's everything?*

a pedir de boca *without a hitch*

Y tú, Paco Páez, ¿todavía eres capitán del equipo de futbol? Todas las chicas te admiramos tanto . . . ¡Eras nuestro héroe!» Paco lee el mensaje de Laura y le responde: «Mira, Laura. No soy Paco Páez, soy Paco Pérez, y estuve en tu clase de computadores en la escuela. Ahora soy miembro del "Geek Squad" y trabajo como tutor. Iba a preguntarte si querías salir conmigo, pero veo que te impresionan los atletas . . . »

Minutos después, Laura responde: «¡Oh no, Paco! Al contrario, admiro mucho a los chicos intelectuales como tú. En efecto, tengo un examen importantísimo la semana que viene y estudia con un miembro del *Geek Squad* es **precisamente** lo que quiero. ¡Vamos a juntarnos lo más pronto posible!»

Paco, muy contento, piensa: «¡Lo digo, pero no lo creo!»

¡Lo digo, pero no lo creo!
Unbelievable!

Discusión

1. ¿Por qué revisaba Paco su cuenta de Facebook?

2. ¿Quién era Laura Zapata?

3. ¿Cómo iban los estudios de Laura en la universidad?

4. ¿Quién era Paco Páez y por qué era tan popular? ¿Cómo se siente Paco Pérez cuando Laura lo llama Paco Páez?

5. Escriba un mensaje para un amigo (una amiga) que no ha visto en mucho tiempo. Dígale lo que hace actualmente.

6   In the previous story there are various words ending in **mente**. Do you recall them? Words like **exactamente**, **tímidamente**, and **precisamente** are called adverbs, words that describe a verb, and adjective, or another adverb. How are adverbs formed? Very simply, **muy facilmente**: just add the ending **mente** to the feminine singular from of an adjective. (**Mente** is usually the Spanish equivalent to English *ly*.)

FEMININE FORM OF ADJECTIVE	ADVERB
rápida	rápida*mente*
seria	seria*mente*
fácil	fácil*mente*

Note: Many Spanish adjectives are the same in both the masculine and feminine forms, so just ad **mente**:

dulce + mente = dulcemente

triste + mente = tristemente

Can you continue giving the adverbs formed from the following adjectives? Use them in a complete sentence.

EXAMPLE: **atento**   *attentive*   **Yo siempre escucho *atentamente* en clase.**

1. **constante**   *constant*   El niño habla _____ .

2. **loco**   *crazy*   Mi primo conduce su auto _____ .

3. **fácil**   *easy*   El atleta completa el maratón _____ .

4. **dulce**   *sweet*   Gloria canta _____ .

5. **hábil**   *skillful*   El mecánico repara el motor _____ .

Salu2: Txtng en español

Ola Laura, ¿ktal? ¿Qacs? Toy en la un tudiando. ¡Q plomo!

M1ml b7s

Armando

Armando tas en la uni? Mdr mim probal tas en kf ymm HL

aki npn bss chau.

Laura

Vocabulario

ENGLISH	ESPAÑOL	NETSPEAK EN ESPAÑOL
I am (**estar**)	**estoy**	**toy**
you are (**ser**)	**eres**	**rs**
call me	**llámame**	**ymm**
café; coffee	**café**	**kf**
kisses, love	**besos**	**b7s, bss**
greetings	**saludos**	**salu2**
hi	**hola**	**hla**
it doesn't matter	**da igual**	**d=**
mission impossible	**misión imposible**	**mi**
text me later	**mándame un mensaje luego**	**m1ml**
see you later, bye	**chao**	**chao**
what's new?, what's up?	**¿qué tal?**	**ktal?**
nothing's happening	**no pasa nada**	**npn**
what are you doing?	**¿qué haces?**	**qacs?**
see you later	**hasta luego**	**hl**
what a drag!	**¡qué plomo!**	**q plomo!**
dying of laughter, lol	**muerto(a) de risa**	**mdr**
please	**por favor**	**xfa**
wait	**espera**	**pera**

Actividad H

Describe how some of your friends do certain things.

EXAMPLE: **Víctor participa** *activamente* **en los deportes.**

1. Rosa habla _____ el francés. (perfectly)

2. Fernando estudia _____ las matemáticas. (seriously)

3. Carlos siempre entra _____ en la clase. (quickly)

4. Tomás habla _____ . (intelligently)

5. Miguel trabaja _____ . (precisely)

7 There are other common adverbs that are not formed from adjectives. Here is a list of the most important ones:

ahora *now*

bastante *enough*

bien *well*

casi *almost*

cerca *near, nearby*

demasiado *too (much)*

despacio *slowly*

después *later, afterwards*

hoy *today*

lejos *far, far away*

mal *badly, poorly*

mañana *tomorrow*

más *more*

menos *less*

mucho *a lot, much*

muy *very*

poco *little*

pronto *soon*

siempre *always*

tarde *late*

temprano *early*

ya *already*

Margarita always says the opposite of what her mother says. What does Margarita say? Work with a partner:

EXAMPLE: **Tu padre baila bien.**   **No, mi padre baila *mal*.**

1. Tu hermanito come poco. _____

2. Tú vas a llegar tarde. _____

3. Tu hermana debe trabajar menos. _____

4. Tus abuelos viven cerca. _____

5. Tú debes salir ahora. _____

Work with a partner. One student asks the question: **¿Cuándo vas a . . . ?** The other student answers using a Spanish adverb.

EXAMPLE: **hacer la tarea de español** (tomorrow)
¿Cuándo vas a hacer la tarea de español?
Voy a hacer la tarea de español *mañana*.

1. ir al cine (today)

_____

_____

2. escribir una carta (afterwards)

_____

_____

3. salir de la clase (soon)

_____

_____

4. leer el periódico (now)

_____

_____

5. dormir (early)

_____

_____

 **Bien** and **bueno; mal** and **malo**

Remember that **bien** and **mal** are adverbs. They describe actions and don't change their form. **Bueno** and **malo** are adjectives. They describe nouns and agree with them in gender and number.

As with other descriptive adjectives, **bueno** and **malo** agree with the noun and usually follow it.

María es _buena._   **Pablo es** _malo._

Jorge es _bueno._   **Rosa es** _mala._

María y Jorge son buenos.   **Pablo y Rosa son** _malos._

But:

María escribe _bien._   **Pablo escribe** _mal._

María y Jorge escriben _bien._   **Pablo y Rosa escriben** _mal._

Complete with the correct word: **bien** or **bueno (buena, buenos, buenas)**.

1. La película es _____ .

2. Roberto es un amigo _____ .

3. Yo estoy _____ , gracias.

4. Tú cantas y bailas muy _____ .

5. Leo una novela _____ .

6. Dan películas _____ en el Teatro Colón.

7. Ricardo es un niño _____ .

8. El bebé duerme _____ .

Repeat **Actividad L**, using **mal** or **malo (mala, malos, malas)**.

1. La película es _____ .

2. Roberto es un amigo _____ .

3. Yo estoy _____ .

4. Tú cantas y bailas muy _____ .

5. Leo una novela _____ .

6. Dan películas _____ en el Teatro Colón.

7. El bebé duerme _____ .

 # Composición

You see someone on Facebook that you haven't seen for some time. Write to him (her) and tell what you have done in the mean time. Ask about your friend's activities

Querido (-a) _____:

_____

_____

_____

_____

_____

_____

_____

_____

_____

_____

_____

Un cordial saludo de

_____

Cápsula cultural

¡Noticias de última hora!

Hay miles de periódicos y revistas publicados diariamente en el mundo de habla española. Estas publicaciones tratan de una variedad de asuntos: noticias internacionales y locales, deportes, cine, comida, moda, automóviles, televisión, salud, negocios, dinero, etc.

En España e Hispanoamérica hay kioscos o puestos de periódicos y revistas en casi cada esquina importante. Estos kioscos ofrecen una gran selección de periódicos, revistas, libros de bolsillo y otros materiales de lectura. Algunas de las publicaciones más populares son para los adolescentes y jóvenes.

Si echamos una mirada al índice de una de estas revistas, vemos secciones de «gente», «belleza», «moda», «chismes», «salud», «consultorio sentimental» y «humor».

A veces, hay una tira cómica con dibujos o una «fotonovela». Las fotonovelas son muy populares entre los jóvenes. Son cuentos cortos románticos, ilustrados con fotografías.

De esta manera, el lector puede leer un cuento mientras mira las fotos de las personas. ¡Es como mirar una telenovela!

Discusión

1. ¿Dónde se venden los periódicos y las revistas?

2. ¿De qué materias tratan?

3. ¿Qué se lee en la sección del horóscopo?

4. ¿Si necesitas consejo sobre relaciones románticas, qué sección consultas?

Para investigar

Investiga en el Internet cuáles son los periódicos y las revistas en español más populares.

VOCABULARIO

el asunto *matter*
casi *almost*
el bolsillo *pocket*

el índice *table of contents*
el chisme *gossip*
la telenovela *soap opera*

Repaso I

Lección 1

a. Spanish interrogatives

¿**a quién(-es)?** *whom?*   ¿**de quién(-es)?** *whose?*

¿**adónde?** *where (to)?*   ¿**dónde?** *where?*

¿**cómo?** *how?*   ¿**por qué?** *why*

¿**cuál(-es)?** *what? which one(s)?*   ¿**qué?** *what?, which?*

¿**cuándo?** *when?*   ¿**quién(-es)?** *who?*

¿**cuánto (-a, -os, -as)?** *how much (many)?*

b. **Conocer** and **saber** mean *to know*. **Conocer** is used in the sense of *to be acquainted, to be familiar with*; **saber** means *to know facts, to have information about something*:

Conozco **ese libro.**   *I know (I am familiar with) that book.*

Sé **que ella viene mañana.**   *I know that she's coming tomorrow.*

Saber followed by an infinitive means *to know how to*.

El *sabe hablar* **español.**   *He knows how to speak Spanish.*

Lección 2

Some Spanish verbs have stem changes in all forms of the present tense, except for **nosotros**. There are three types of changes:

(1) **-AR, -ER**, and **-IR** verbs that change **e** to **ie**.

pensar	pienso, piensas, piensa, pensamos, piensan
perder	pierdo, pierdes, pierde, perdemos, pierden
mentir	miento, mientes, miente, mentimos, mienten

(2) **-AR**, **-ER**, and **-IR** verbs that change **e** to **ue**.

almorzar	almuerzo, almuerzas, almuerza, almorzamos, almuerzan
volver	vuelvo, vuelves, vuelve, volvemos, vuelven
dormir	duermo, duermes, duerme, dormimos, duermen

NOTE: **Jugar** changes **u** to **ue: j**uego, juegas, juega, jugamos, juegan

(3) **-IR** verbs that change **e** to **i**.

repetir	repito, repites, repite, repetimos, repiten

Lección 3

a. Spanish negatives and their corresponding affirmative expressions:

NEGATIVE	AFFIRMATIVE
nada *nothing* **nadie** *no one, nobody* **ni . . . ni** *neither . . . nor* **nunca** ⎱ **jamás** ⎰ *never* **tampoco** *neither* **ninguno (-a, -os, -as)** *no, none*	**algo** *something* **alguien** *someone, somebody* **o** *or* **siempre** *always* **también** *also, too* **alguno (-a, -os, -as)** *any, some*

b. There are two ways of negating a sentence in Spanish.

no + verb + negative word: *No* quiero *nada.* ⎱
negative word + verb: *Nada* quiero.   ⎰ *I don't want anything.*

c. When the object of a verb is a negative or an affirmative word referring to a person, the personal **a** is used.

Llamo a alguien.   *I call someone.*

No llamo a nadie. } *I don't call anyone.*
A nadie llamo.   } *I call no one.*

Lección 4

a. **Vamos a** + infinitive is used in Spanish to express *let us*.

Vamos a jugar **al tenis.**   *Let's play tennis.*

Vamos is used to express *let's go*:

Vamos a **la fiesta.**   *Let's go to the party.*

b. Singular formal commands are formed by changing the ending **-o** of the **yo-**form of the present tense to **-e** for **-AR** verbs and to **-a** for **-ER** and **-IR** verbs. Plural formal commands are formed by adding **-n** to the singular command.

	REGULAR COMMANDS		
INFINITIVE	PRESENT TENSE YO-FORM	FORMAL COMMAND	
		SINGULAR	PLURAL
hablar	habl*o*	habl*e*	habl*en*
comer	com*o*	com*a*	com*an*
dormir	duerm*o*	duerm*a*	duerm*an*

IRREGULAR COMMANDS		
INFINITIVE	SINGULAR	PLURAL
dar	dé	den
ir	vaya	vayan
ser	sea	sean

c. Informal commands in the singular (**tú**-form) are identical with the **Ud./él/ella**-form of the present tense.

INFINITIVE	UD./ÉL/ELLA-FORM	INFORMAL COMMAND
habl**ar**	habl*a*	habl*a*
com**er**	com*e*	com*e*
dorm**ir**	duerm*e*	duerm*e*

d. Negative informal commands in the singular (**tú**-form) are formed by adding **s** to the singular formal command.

FORMAL COMMAND	NEGATIVE INFORMAL COMMAND
salga	no salga*s*

e. Many verbs have irregular informal command forms:

decir: di	ir: ve	salir: sal	tener: ten
hacer: haz	poner: pon	ser: sé	venir: ven

Lección 5

a. Adjectives agree in gender and number with the nouns they describe. Adjectives that end in **o** change the **o** to **a** in the feminine form. Other adjectives remain unchanged, except for adjectives of nationality, which have feminine forms in **-a: el alumno español, la alumna española**.

To form the plural of adjectives, add **s** to an adjective ending in a vowel and **es** to an adjective ending in a consonant.

inteligent*e* **inteligentes**
azu*l* **azul*es***

Descriptive adjectives in Spanish usually follow the noun.

una mujer *fuerte*

b. The adjectives **alguno** and **ninguno** stand before the noun and drop the final **o** before a masculine singular noun.

¿Tienes *algún* periódico?

No, no tengo *ningún* periódico.

c. **Bueno, malo, primero,** and **tercero** may stand before or after the noun. They are shortened before a masculine singular noun.

Voy a un *buen* hotel. / Voy a un hotel *bueno*.

Es un *mal* consejo. / Es un consejo *malo*.

Lean el *primer* capítulo. / Lean el capítulo *primero*.

Vivo en el *tercer* piso. / Vivo en el piso *tercero*.

d. **Grande** means *large* when it stands after the noun. It means great when it stands before the noun. **Grande** becomes **gran** before a singular noun.

Madrid es una gran ciudad.   *Madrid is a great city.*

Mi abuelo es un hombre grande.   *My grandfather is a large man.*

e. Adverbs describe another adverb, an adjective, or a verb. Adverbs are usually formed by adding **-mente** to the singular feminine form of the adjective.

rápida   rápida*mente*

Some common adverbs are not formed from adjectives.

f. The adverbs **bien** and **mal** do not charge form. The adjectives **bueno** and **malo** agree in gender and number with the noun they describe.

Ella habla *bien* (*mal*). / Ellas hablan *bien* (*mal*).

Ella es *buena* (*mala*). / Ellas son *buenas* (*malas*).

Here are ten pictures of people doing various activities. Complete the description below each picture by using the correct for of one of the following verbs.

almorzar	costar	jugar	preferir	servir
comenzar	dormir	pensar	querer	sonreír

1. El bebé _____ la siesta.

2. Los alumnos _____ en la cafetería.

3. La Sra. Gómez _____ empanadas.

4. Anita y Juanita _____ .

5. La mamá pregunta: «¿Qué traje de baño _____ ?»

6. Jorge _____ en Rosita.

7. ¿Cuánto _____ esta cadena?

8. Los muchachos _____ a los bolos.

9. Carlitos _____ las gafas de sol.

10. La película _____ pronto.

Actividad **B**

¿Quién es Mandrako el mago? Read the following sentences and then decide which one of the five men they describe. Put an X in the correct circle.

No lleva nunca sombrero.   **Usa un arete en una oreja.**

No lleva corbata tampoco.   **También lleva una cadena de oro.**

Lleva gafas.   **Jamás lleva traje.**

Sonríe mucho.   **No tiene mucho pelo pero tiene barba.**

Actividad C

How many of these words do you remember? Fill in the Spanish words, then read down the boxed column of letters. What do Miguel and Rosa see at the beach?

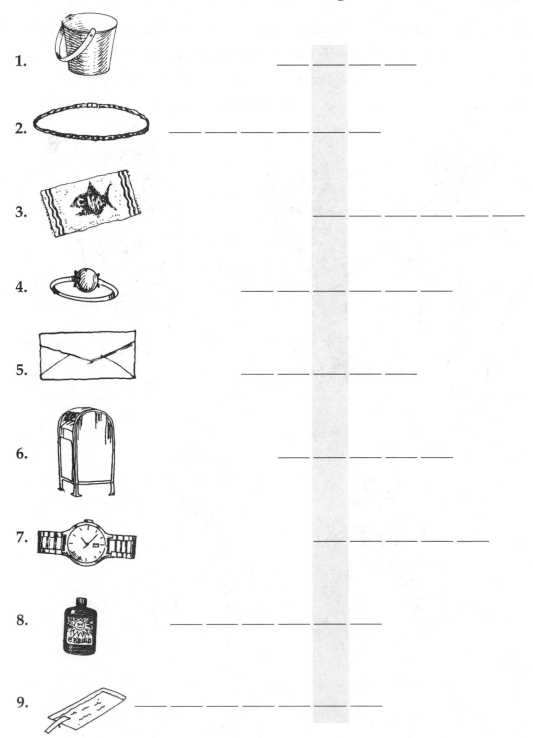

1. ___ ___ ___ ___

2. ___ ___ ___ ___ ___ ___

3. ___ ___ ___ ___ ___

4. ___ ___ ___ ___ ___

5. ___ ___ ___ ___

6. ___ ___ ___ ___

7. ___ ___ ___ ___ ___

8. ___ ___ ___ ___

9. ___ ___ ___ ___

Hidden in the puzzle below are

8 ADJECTIVES   16 ADVERBS

_____   _____   _____

_____   _____   _____

_____   _____   _____

_____   _____   _____

_____   _____   _____

_____   _____   _____

_____   _____   _____

Find the hidden words, circle them in the puzzle, and then write them in the space above. The words may read from left to right, right or left, up or down, or diagonally.

C	A	S	I	E	M	P	R	E	E
H	F	S	O	N	E	M	R	T	L
U	O	C	Á	Ñ	B	U	E	N	A
O	I	Y	U	M	I	C	E	I	M
G	R	A	N	D	E	H	D	S	N
E	E	S	U	O	N	O	R	G	O
I	S	L	C	E	R	C	A	U	J
C	C	O	D	I	M	Í	T	N	E
E	P	R	O	N	T	O	C	O	L
H	Á	B	I	L	M	E	N	T	E

Actividad E

Here are eight pictures. Write an appropriate command under each of the pictures, using the following verbs.

cerrar	ir	poner	traer	volver
comprar	mirar	salir	venir	

1. ¡No _____ la televisión ahora!

2. ¡Manuela, _____ Ud. a la pizarra!

3. ¡ _____ Ud. el televisor allí!

4. ¡No _____ el vestido rojo,

_____ el azul!

5. ¡ _____ a jugar afuera!

6. ¡ _____ a la tienda y _____ pan!

7. ¡No _____ a casa tarde!

8. ¡ _____ Ud. la ventana, por favor!

Actividad F

Let's do something special this weekend. What? To find the answer, write the letters in the blanks below:

1. Podemos ir al museo para ver la ___ ___ ___ ___ ___ ___ ___ ___ ___ de arte.
   1   2   3

2. Hay un ___ ___ ___ ___ ___ ___ ___ ___ de música clásica.
   4   5   6

3. En el cine dan una ___ ___ ___ ___ ___ ___ ___ ___ de ciencia ficción.
   7   11   8   9

4. ¿Quieres ir a ___ ___ ___ ___ ___ esta noche?
   12

5. En el estadio hay un ___ ___ ___ ___ ___ ___ ___   ___ ___
   13 10   14

___ ___ ___ ___ ___ ___
15 16

¡Vamos a ___ ___ ___ ___ ___ ___ ___   ___ ___   ___ ___
7 12 13 10 4 9 6   11 3   5 8

___ ___ ___ ___ ___ !
1   2   14 16 15

Actividad H

Crucigrama de la naturaleza

1				2 H		3		4				
		5		O	6					7		
				R		8						
				M								
				I	9							
		10		G				11		12		
13				A								
								14				
						15						
			16	17								
	18											
			19									
	20											

HORIZONTALES

3. leaves
5. river
8. rock, stone
9. spider
11. flower
13. grasshopper
15. earth, soil
18. bird
19. sun
20. lake

VERTICALES

1. butterfly
2. ant
4. bee
6. worm
7. tree
8. plant
10. rain
12. frog
14. grass
16. field
17. fly (insect)

Picture Story   Can you read this story? Whenever you come to a picture, read it as if it were a Spanish word.

Jorge Luis Pérez tiene 13 años. Hoy es y está en la con

sus . Su le pone en todo el porque hace mucho .

A Jorge Luis le gustan la , el 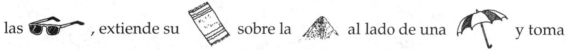 y las . Él quiere vivir en una

 tropical, tener un y pasar los días en . La Sra. Pérez se pone

las , extiende su sobre la al lado de una y toma

el . El Sr. Pérez prepara la para la . Mientras tanto,

Jorge Luis juega con sus 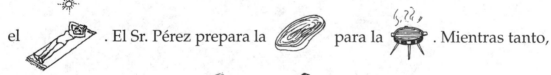 , por la con su ,

 en el  , busca  y hace un  con su y su

 . Un perfecto.

Segunda Parte

6

Por la mañana / Por la noche

Reflexive Verbs; Passive SE

1 Vocabulario

The new words that follow are all verbs. They belong to a special family of verbs called REFLEXIVE VERBS. See if you can guess their meanings.

despertarse (ie)

levantarse

bañarse

lavarse

cepillarse los dientes

vestirse (i)

peinarse

cepillarse el pelo

afeitarse

quitarse la ropa /devestirse (i)

acostarse (ue)

dormirse (ue)

Actividad **A**

Match the descriptions with the pictures:

Él se peina.	Nosotras nos acostamos.
Ellas se visten.	Uds. se cepillan los dientes.
Tú te despiertas.	Carlos se levanta.
Yo me lavo.	Mi papá se afeita.

1. _____

2. _____

3. _____

4. _____

5. _____ 6. _____

7. _____ 8. _____

 A verb is reflexive when the subject does something to itself. To use a verb "reflexively," we add a special pronoun, called a *reflexive pronoun*, to indicate that the subject and object of the verb refer to the same person or thing. You probably noticed, however, that some English verbs do not seem to be reflexive while their Spanish equivalents are.

For example, *to get up* is **levantarse**. The verb **levantar** by itself, without the reflexive pronoun, means simply *to raise or to lift*:

Él *levanta* **la mesa.**   *He lifts the table.*

But:

Él *se levanta.*   *He gets up.* (literally, *He lifts himself.*)

Let's look at some more reflexive verbs in Spanish that are not reflexive in English. Just remember that the reflexive pronoun in Spanish REFLECTS the action expressed by the verb on the subject:

La abuela *divierte* **a los niños.**   *The grandmother amuses the children.*

La abuela *se divierte.*   *The grandmother has fun (amuses herself).*

El papá *acuesta* **al bebé.**   *The father puts the baby to bed.*

El papá *se acuesta.*   *The father goes to bed (puts himself to bed).*

Llamo **a Luis.**   *I call Luis.*

Me llamo **Luis.**   *My name is Luis (I call myself Luis)*

Actividad B

In each group, select the sentence with a reflexive verb:

1. (a) Se lava con agua fría.
   (b) Lava el carro con agua fría.

2. (a) La muchacha mira la televisión.
   (b) La muchacha se mira en el espejo.

3. (a) Mi madre viste a mi hermana.
   (b) Mi madre se viste.

4. (a) Ud. se despierta temprano.
   (b) Ud. despierta a su mamá temprano.

5. (a) José pone el abrigo en la silla.
   (b) José se pone el abrigo.

El ciclismo

Let's read a story about a very popular sport— bicycle racing. How many reflexive verbs can you identify?

En España y en muchos países hispanoamericanos, el ciclismo es más que un deporte—es una pasión. En Colombia, por ejemplo, cada año más de sesenta ciclistas participan en una carrera de varios días. El ganador es un héroe nacional y recibe mucho dinero y regalos.

la carrera *race*
el ganador *winner*

Escuchemos una entrevista con el joven Víctor Veloz, un ciclista muy popular.

PERIODISTA: Buenos días, Víctor. Queremos saber cómo vive un campeón. ¿Puedes describir un día típico de tu vida?

VÍCTOR: Bueno. Por lo general, me despierto muy temprano, a las cinco de la mañana. Me gusta practicar cuando no hace mucho calor.

PERIODISTA: Sí, claro. ¿Qué haces para comenzar el día?

VÍCTOR: Después de levantarme, me lavo la cara y las manos, me afeito y me cepillo los dientes.

PERIODISTA: Sí, sí, comprendo. Eso hacemos todos. ¿Pero, haces algo especial para hacerte campeón?

hacerse *to become*

VÍCTOR: Tomo un desayuno ligero. Me visto, me pongo los zapatos, me peino y salgo a practicar dos o tres horas. Luego vuelvo a casa, me baño y almuerzo. Después del almuerzo, que es bastante grande, me acuesto.

ligero *light*

PERIODISTA: ¿Y después, qué haces por la tarde?

VÍCTOR: Hago ejercicios y monto en bicicleta dos o tres horas más. Me siento a comer a las siete y media y me acuesto antes de las diez. Necesito mucho descanso y no tengo tiempo para divertirme.

sentarse (ie) *to sit down*

PERIODISTA: Muy interesante. Veo que no haces nada excepcional. Todos los jóvenes tienen la misma oportunidad de hacerse campeones. Todos son iguales. A propósito, tienes una bicicleta bonita. ¿Cuánto vale?

valer *to be worth, to cost*

VÍCTOR: Diez mil dólares.

Actividad C

Answer each question using complete sentences.

1. ¿Qué es el ciclismo para muchos hispanoamericanos?

   _____

2. ¿Qué recibe generalmente el ganador?

   _____

3. ¿Qué quiere saber el periodista sobre Víctor Veloz?

   _____

4. ¿Por qué se levanta Víctor tan temprano?

   _____

5. ¿Qué hace Víctor después de levantarse?

_____

6. ¿Qué clase de desayuno toma Víctor?

_____

7. ¿Qué hace Víctor después del almuerzo? ¿Por qué?

_____

8. Según el periodista, ¿qué oportunidades tienen todos los jóvenes?

_____

9. ¿Cómo es la bicicleta de Víctor?

_____

10. ¿Qué necesita Ud. para hacerse campeón en un deporte?

_____

Sí o no. Víctor Veloz is talking about himself. If a statement is incorrect, change it to make it correct. Work with a partner.

EXAMPLE: **Me desvisto después de acostarme.**
            No. Ud. _se desviste antes de acostarse._

1. Me despierto a las siete de la mañana.

_____

2. Me lavo antes de levantarme.

_____

3. Me visto antes del desayuno.

_____

4. Me siento a descansar después del almuerzo.

_____

5. Me baño cuando me levanto por la mañana.

_____

6. Me afeito después del desayuno.

_____

7. Me acuesto a medianoche.

_____

8. Necesito acostarme tarde.

_____

Actividad E

You are the person in the picture. What do you do in the morning?

EXAMPLE:

Me despierto.

1. _____

2. _____

3. _____

4. _____

5. _____

6. _____

Actividad  F

What do you do in the evening?

1. _____

2. _____

3. _____

4. _____

5. _____

6. _____

3   Look at the following sentence: **Yo me lavo.** Whom am I washing? _____ Is the action being performed on the subject or on someone else? _____ Do the subject (**yo**) and the reflexive pronoun (**me**) refer to the same person or to two different people?

NOTE: Different subjects require different reflexive pronouns.

yo *me* **lavo**	**nosotros** *nos* **lavamos**
tú *te* **lavas**	
Ud. *se* **lava**	**Uds.** *se* **lavan**
él *se* **lava**	**ellos** *se* **lavan**
ella *se* **lava**	**ellas** *se* **lavan**

RULE: In a sentence using a reflexive verb, the subject is also the object of the action. The reflexive pronoun is placed before the conjugated verb.

What is Gerardo's routine? Look at the picture and say what Gerardo does at the time indicated.

EXAMPLE:

Gerardo se despierta a las seis y media de la mañana.

1. _____

2. _____

3. _____

4. _____

5. _____

Complete each sentence with the correct reflexive pronoun.

1. Yo _____ despierto a las seis.

2. Ellos siempre _____ levantan tarde.

3. ¿A qué hora _____ acuestan Uds.?

4. Nosotros _____ vestimos antes de salir.

5. ¿Cuándo _____ baña Ud.?

6. Tú _____ lavas las manos antes de comer.

7. Marta _____ peina tres veces al día.

8. Nosotras _____ cepillamos el pelo todas las noches.

What are all these people doing? Complete the sentences with the correct form of the verb in parentheses:

1. (acostarse)   Yo _____ _____ temprano.

2. (bañarse)   Ella _____ _____ con agua fría.

3. (sentarse)   Tú _____ _____ cuando estás cansado.

4. (peinarse)   Rosa _____ _____ antes de ir a la fiesta.

5. (dormirse)   Los niños _____ _____ después de mirar la televisión.

6. (ponerse)   Ud. _____ _____ el suéter que compró.

7. (despertarse) Nosotros _____ _____ tarde los domingos.

8. (vestirse)   Uds. _____ _____ rápido.

9. (quitarse)   Yo _____ _____ los zapatos cuando llego

a casa.

10. (afeitarse)   Mis hermanos _____ _____ dos veces al

día.

4   In Spanish reflexive constructions, we do not use the possessive adjective (**mi, tu, su,** etc.) with parts of the body or wearing apparel, since the reflexive pronoun obviously refers to the subject. The definite article is used instead.

Tú te lavas *el* **pelo.**	*You wash your hair.*
	(literally; *You wash yourself the hair*)
Él se pone *los* **zapatos.**	*He puts on his shoes.*
Yo me cepillo *los* **dientes.**	*I brush my teeth.*
Ud. se quita *el* **abrigo.**	*You take off your coat.*

Actividad J

Work with a partner. One student asks: **¿Qué haces ahora?** The other student describes what he/she is doing.

EXAMPLE: get up   **¿Qué haces ahora?**   *Yo me levanto.*

1. wash face   _____

2. brush teeth   _____

3. brush hair   _____

4. take off pajamas   _____

5. put on shoes and socks _____

5 In all the sentences up to this point, the reflexive pronoun came directly before the conjugated verb: **Yo me lavo con agua fría**. In a negative sentence, the reflexive pronoun is not separated from the verb. The word **no** stands before the reflexive pronoun.

Yo *no me lavo* **con agua y jabón.**   *I don't wash myself with water and soap.*

Tú *no te acuestas* **a las seis.**   *You don't go to bed at six o'clock.*

Say that one of the persons listed doesn't do any activity at a certain time.

EXAMPLE: tú / no peinarse / a medianoche
Tú *no te peinas* **a medianoche.**

Carlos	no acostarse	las siete de la mañana
Yo	no despertarse	las once de la noche
Mis padres	no peinarse	las doce de la noche
Tú	no dormirse	medianoche
Uds.	no levantarse	las cuatro de la tarde
Ud.	no sentarse	las dos de la tarde
Mi madre	no cepillarse los dientes	mediodía

1. _____

2. _____

3. _____

4. _____

5. _____

6. _____

 **6** How are reflexive verbs used to give a command? Look at this short game of **Simón dice** and then answer the questions that follow.

Simón dice (al Sr. López):   **¡Levánte*se* (Ud.)!**   **¡No *se* levante (Ud.)!**
                                                ¡Láve*se* (Ud.)!   **¡No *se* lave (Ud.)!**
                                                ¡Vísta*se* (Ud.)!   **¡No *se* vista (Ud.)!**

Simón dice (a sus amigos):	¡Levánten*se* (Uds.)!	¡No *se* levanten (Uds.)!
	¡Láven*se* (Uds.)!	¡No *se* laven (Uds.)!
	¡Vístan*se* (Uds.)!	¡No *se* vistan (Uds.)!
Simón dice (a Josefina):	¡Levánta*te*!	¡No *te* levantes!
	¡Láva*te*!	¡No *te* laves!
	¡Víste*te*!	¡No *te* vistas!

Where is the reflexive pronoun in relationship to the verb? In the affirmative (yes) command, the reflexive pronoun is AFTER the verb and attached to it. Note also that all the affirmative commands of reflexive verbs have an accent mark to retain the original stress. In a negative (no) command, the reflexive pronoun is BEFORE the verb; **no** is placed BEFORE the reflexive pronoun.

Actividad L

Tell a friend to do the following.

1. Wake up! _____

2. Take a bath! _____

3. Brush your teeth! _____

4. Have fun! _____

5. Go to bed! _____

6. Comb your hair! _____

Actividad M

Make the commands in Actividad L negative.

1. _____

2. _____

3. _____

4. _____

5. _____

6. _____

Actividad N

Tell the students (**Uds.**) in the class to do the following.

1. Wake up early! _____
2. Take off your coat(s)! _____
3. Wash your hands! _____
4. Sit down now! _____
5. Have fun! _____
6. Comb your hair! _____

Actividad O

Make the commands in Actividad N negative.

1. _____
2. _____
3. _____
4. _____
5. _____
6. _____

Actividad P

You be the teacher. Tell a student to do or not to do the following.

1. Don't take off your hat! _____
2. Put on your coat! _____
3. Get up from the chair! _____
4. Don't wash your face! _____

5. Don't sit down! _____

6. Don't fall asleep! _____

What happens when the reflexive verb is used as an infinitive?
Look at the following examples:

Voy a *bañarme* **ahora.**   *I'm going to take a bath now.*

El bebé no quiere *acostarse.*   *The baby doesn't want to go to bed.*

No debes *dormirte* **en clase.**   *You shouldn't fall asleep in class.*

Where is the reflexive pronoun placed? It is placed after the infinitive and attached to it.

Complete the following sentences, using the correct Spanish form of the verb in parentheses.

1. Él no quiere _____ las manos con jabón.   (*to wash*)

2. Felipe y yo queremos _____ allí.   (*to sit down*)

3. ¡ _____ Ud. ahora mismo!   (*to bed*)

4. El niño no puede _____ .   (*to fall asleep*)

5. Nosotros vamos a _____ en las vacaciones.   (*to have fun*)

6. No tengo tiempo de _____ ahora.   (*to take a bath*)

7. El ciclista debe _____ temprano.   (*to get up*)

8. ¡ _____ (tú) el pelo bien!   (*brush*)

9. ¡ _____ Ud. aquí, por favor!   (*sit down*)

10. Cuando hace frío tengo que _____ un suéter.   (*to put on*)

Actividad R

You are writing a text message to a friend. Include some of the following information: When you get up on weekends, your usual routine to get ready for school, what you do on weekends, what you do for fun, etc.

Querida Lupe:

¿Qué haces generalmente durante la semana? En una semana típica, yo _____

_____

_____

_____

Mi madre me dice _____

_____

_____

_____

Tu amigo de siempre,

Eduardo

8 Passive or impersonal **se**

The pronoun **se** has another important use in Spanish. It is used when there is no particular person doing the action. (There is no specific subject mentioned.) In English we can say a variety of things: one, you, we, people, it is etc. In Spanish we just use **se**. Here are some examples:

SPANISH	ENGLISH EQUIVALENT
Aquí *se* **habla español.**	*Spanish is spoken here.* *One speaks Spanish here.* *You, we, they, people* (in general) *speak Spanish here.*
Se **dice que hace calor en el trópico.**	*They say that it's hot in the tropics.* *It is said that it's hot in the tropics*

SPANISH	ENGLISH EQUIVALENT
¿Cómo *se* va al centro? }	*How do you get downtown?* *How does one get downtown?*
***Se* come bien en París.** }	*You eat well in Paris.* *One eats well in Paris.*
***Se* prohibe fumar.** }	*No smoking.* *It is forbidden to smoke.*

NOTE: The verb following se is usually in the singular. However, if there is a plural noun immediately following the verb, the verb is used in the thirdperson plural form:

Se habl*an muchas lenguas* en Sudamérica.

No se permit*en coches* en la avenida.

Se cierr*an los bancos* a las dos.

¿Por dónde se sale? Everything is new to you in Madrid and you are asking for information. Follow the example.

EXAMPLE: **por dónde / salir del museo**
           ¿Por dónde se sale del museo?

1. cuándo / abrir las tiendas   _____

2. qué / poder comprar en esta tienda   _____

3. por dónde / entrar en el teatro   _____

4. cómo / subir al autobús   _____

5. cuándo / permitir visitas   _____

6. en qué / ir al jardín botánico   _____

7. qué / hacer para divertirse   _____

8. cómo / llegar a la estación   _____

Actividad T

The construction **se** is very often seen on signs. See if you can match the expressions with the corresponding sign.

1. SE PROHÍBE FUMAR

2. SE VENDE CASA

3. SE NECESITA SECRETARIA

4. SE CAMBIA DINERO

5. SE SIRVE COMIDA CRIOLLA

6. SE ABRE A LA UNA

7. NO SE PERMITE APARCAR

8. SE ALQUILAN CUARTOS

9. SE INSTALAN TELEVISORES

10. NO SE ACEPTAN CHEQUES

(a) we open at 1:00
(b) rooms for rent
(c) no parking
(d) we do not accept checks
(e) TVs installed

(f) currency exchange
(g) house for sale
(h) home style cooking
(i) secretary wanted
(j) no smoking

Ud. es un(a) ciclista famoso(a). Un periodista quiere escribir un artículo para un periódico y le hace varias preguntas.

Preguntas Personales

1. ¿Cómo te diviertes en las vacaciones?

_____

2. ¿Cómo te vistes durante el verano?

_____

3. ¿A qué hora te despiertas los domingos?

_____

4. ¿Cuántas veces al día te cepillas los dientes?

_____

5. ¿Qué deportes se practican en tu escuela?

_____

Información Personal

List five things you do in the morning before leaving for school.

1. _____

_____

2. _____

_____

3. _____

_____

4. _____

_____

5. _____

_____

 # Cápsula cultural

La bicicleta: el automóvil de los niños

El automóvil en Hispanoamérica es todavía un artículo de lujo para muchos. Debido a su alto costo, las familias con autos por lo general tienen sólo uno. Con ese único auto se hace todo: llevar a los niños a la escuela, hacer las compras semanales, ir al trabajo y pasear los fines de semana.

No es como en los Estados Unidos, donde muchas veces cada miembro mayor de edad tiene su propio automóvil. Los jóvenes adolescentes norteamericanos esperan comprarse y conducir su propio auto. En Hispanoamérica los jóvenes pueden sacar la licencia de conducir, pero en general no obtienen un automóvil hasta muchos años después.

Como nota curiosa, en Hispanoamérica se dice que el primer automóvil que uno tiene es un triciclo, que luego se convierte en una bicicleta. Cuando los niños reciben por primera vez una bicicleta con ruedas de entrenamiento, dicen: "Ahora yo también tengo mi carro".

Discusión

1. ¿Por qué muchas de las familias de Hispanoamérica tienen sólo un carro?

2. ¿Qué cosas hacen con el automóvil?

3. ¿Qué esperan los adolescentes de los Estados Unidos?

4. Para un niño hispano, ¿cómo es su bicicleta?

5. ¿Cuáles son algunos de los problemas de una sociedad que depende del automóvil?

VOCABULARIO

lujo *luxury*
debido a *due to*

sacar la licencia *to get a license*
las ruedas de entrenamiento *training wheels*

Una historia policíaca

Preterit Tense

1 Vocabulario

Vocabulario

¿Quiénes son? Complete the sentences with the appropriate words.

el (la) abogado(-a) defensor(-a)
el (la) cómplice
una pistola
el (la) fiscal
el (la) fugitivo(a)

el (la) juez(-a)
el jurado
las víctimas
la celda
el (la) testigo

1. Vio el incidente; es _____ .

2. Defiende al acusado; es _____ .

3. Es el lugar donde ponen al sospechoso; es _____ .

4. Representa al público; es _____ .

5. Es un criminal que se escapó; es _____ .

6. Es un arma de fuego; es _____ .

7. Deciden si un acusado es inocente; es _____ .

8. Está encargado(-a) de la corte; es _____ .

9. Personas que son víctimas de criminales; son _____ .

10. Participa en la comisión de un crimen; es _____ .

¿**Qué pasa?** Use the following verbs and express what's going on in the picture.

robar   levantar   dar   llevar   llegar

1. _____

_____

2. _____

_____

3. _____

_____

4. _____

_____

5. _____

_____

Actividad **B**

Las cinco diferencias There are two crimes scenes illustrated below, according to two different witnesses. They look similar, but there are five differences between them. Tell what they are.

2 Up to now we have talked about things happening **ahora** (now), **hoy** (today), and even **mañana** (tomorrow). How do you express actions or events that took place **anoche** (last night), **ayer** (yesterday), **las semana pasada** (last week), or **el año pasado** (last year)? Of course, you need to use verbs in a past tense. One such past tense in Spanish is the preterit.

Here's a story about a theft and a smart detective. Pay special attention to the verbs in bold type. They are in the preterit (past) tense.

El testigo mentiroso

Dejó de llover a las dos de la tarde. El inspector Delgado **abrió** la ventana de su oficina y **miró** hacia la calle. En ese momento **sonó** el teléfono. La señora Laura Moreno, muy nerviosa, **preguntó:**

dejar de *to stop*

sonar *to sound, to ring*

—¿Puede Ud. venir a mi casa inmediatamente?

El inspector salió y **llegó** veinte minutos más tarde a la casa de la señora Moreno. **Tocó** a la puerta. Laura **abrió** y dijo:

—Pase, pase, Inspector Delgado. ¡**Ocurrió** algo terrible! **Salí** temprano esta mañana para visitar a mi amiga Fernanda y cuando **regresé** una hora después, **encontré** la puerta de la casa abierta. **Entré** y **vi** la sombra de un hombre en el estudio de mi marido. Estaba solo; no tenía cómplice. En ese momento el hombre me **vio** y **saltó** por la ventana. **Corrió** por el jardín y yo **corrí** detrás de él, pero él **entró** rápidamente en un carro y **se escapó**. En el estudio encontré abierta la caja fuerte y **descubrí** que el ladrón **robó** mis joyas. Valen una fortuna, casi un millón dólares. Afortunadamente están aseguradas».

la sombra *shadow*

la caja fuerte *safe*

asegurado *insured*

—¿**Reconoció** Ud. al hombre, señora?

—No estoy completamente segura porque no vi su cara, pero creo que el ladrón puede ser Juan, un empleado que **despedimos** la semana pasada. Él sabe dónde tengo mis joyas. Además, **encontré** esta gorra en el jardín. Es de Juan.

despedir *to dismiss, to fire*

El inspector **escuchó** todo con mucha atención, **examinó**, los muebles en desorden, y **salió** al jardín. **Vio** las huellas de unos zapatos de hombre en la tierra mojada.

mojado *wet*

—Inspector Delgado, ¿quiere más información sobre Juan? Puedo darle toda la ayuda necesaria para atrapar al ladrón.

—¡Señora, quiero saber la verdad y no las mentiras que **contó** Ud.!

Mi consejo (para Ud.) es buscar un buen abogado porque es seguro que va a tener que defenderse en la corte por tratar de defraudar a su compañía de seguros.

SOLUCIÓN:

Según Laura, ella **corrió** detrás del ladrón por el jardín. Pero en el jardín el inspector encontró solamente las huellas de un hombre. Laura robó las joyas para colectar el dinero del seguro.

Actividad C

Discusión

1. ¿Quién llamó al inspector Delgado? ¿Por qué?

   _____

2. Según Laura, que vio ella en el estudio de su marido?

   _____

3. ¿Cómo reaccionó el hombre cuando vio a Laura?

   _____

4. ¿Qué encontró Laura en el jardín?

   _____

5. ¿Qué vio el inspector en el jardín?

   _____

6. ¿Por qué son populares las historias policíacas?

   _____

To form the preterit tense of regular verbs, simply remove the **-ar, -er,** or **-ir** ending of the verb and substitute another ending:

	robar to steal	**correr** to run	**descubrir** to discover
yo	rob*é*	corr*í*	descubr*í*
tú	rob*aste*	corr*iste*	descubr*iste*
Ud., él, ella	rob*ó*	corr*ió*	descubr*ió*
nosotros, -as	rob*amos*	corr*imos*	descubr*imos*
Uds., ellos, ellas	rob*aron*	corr*ieron*	descubr*ieron*

There is one **-ar** verb (**dar**) that takes the **-er** endings in the preterit tense instead of the regular **-ar** endings.

dar　to give			
yo	*di*	nosotros, -as	*dimos*
tú	*diste*		
Ud., él, ella	*dio*	Uds., ellos, ellas	*dieron*

You were a witness to a bank robbery and are testifying in court. Complete the sentences with the preterit form of the verb in parentheses.

1. Yo _____ en el banco a las once de la mañana.
　　　(entrar)

2. Dos hombres _____ detrás de mí y _____ la puerta.
　　　　　　　(entrar)　　　　　　　　　　　　(cerrar)

3. Una señora y yo _____ a gritar.
　　　　　　　(comenzar)

4. El director del banco _____ los gritos y _____ a la policía.
　　　　　　　　　(escuchar)　　　　　　　　(llamar)

5. La policía _____ pronto.
　　　　　(llegar)

6. Los ladrones no _____ nada.
   (robar)

7. El director del banco _____ las gracias a la policía.
   (dar)

On Monday morning, your teacher wants to know what the students did on Sunday. Complete the sentences with the preterit form of the verb in parentheses.

1. Yo _____ hasta las diez.
   (dormir)

2. Manuel _____ en casa de sus abuelos.
   (comer)

3. Jorge y Raúl _____ una película de horror.
   (ver)

4. Tú _____ de compras con tus padres.
   (salir)

5. Mis hermanos y yo _____ amigos en el aeropuerto.
   (recibir)

6. Uds. _____ un paseo por el parque.
   (dar)

7. Rosario _____ tres millas.
   (correr)

8. Pablo y María _____ cartas.
   (escribir)

You have just returned from a weekend at a friend's house and your little brother wants to know what you did. Answer the questions.

1. ¿Saliste a comer a un restaurante?

_____

2. ¿Qué comiste?

_____

3. ¿Viste alguna película buena?

_____

4. ¿Compraste el regalo para mamá?

_____

5. ¿A qué hora te despertaste el domingo?

_____

6. ¿Nadaste en la piscina?

_____

7. ¿Diste un paseo por el centro de la ciudad?

_____

8. ¿Te divertiste mucho?

_____

9. ¿Conociste a los padres de tu amigo?

_____

10. ¿Invitaste a tu amigo a venir a nuestra casa?

_____

4 -AR and -ER verbs with stem changes in the present tense have regular forms in the preterit. -IR verbs with stem changes in the present tense (**e** to **ie, o** to **ue,** and **e** to **i**) change **e** to **i** and **o** to **u** in the third-person singular and plural of the preterit. Let's look at some examples.

	PRESENT TENSE YO-FORM	PRETERIT
encontrar (ue)	encu*e*ntro	encontré, encontraste, encontró, encontramos, encontraron
pensar (ie)	p*ie*nso	pensé, pensaste, pensó, pensamos, pensaron
perder (ie)	p*ie*rdo	perdí, perdiste, perdió, perdimos, perdieron
volver (ue)	v*ue*lvo	volví, volviste, volvió, volvimos, volvieron
But:		
mentir (ie)	m*ie*nto	mentí, mentiste, *mintió*, mentimos, *mintieron*
dormir (ue)	d*ue*rmo	dormí, dormiste, *durmió*, dormimos, *durmieron*
pedir (i)	p*i*do	pedí, pediste, *pidió*, pedimos, *pidieron*
servir (i)	s*i*rvo	serví, serviste, *sirvió*, servimos, *sirvieron*

You went with some friends to a restaurant last night. Using the verb **pedir**, say what each of you ordered.

1. Yo _____ un bistec con papas fritas.

2. Manuel _____ el pollo frito.

3. Rosa y yo _____ una limonada.

4. Tú _____ la sopa del día.

5. Los hermanos Gómez _____ hamburguesas.

6. María _____ sopa y una hamburguesa.

 There are many verbs in Spanish with irregular preterit forms that change their stem completely.

tener *to have*			
yo	tuve	nosotros	tuvimos
tú	tuviste		
Ud., él, ella	tuvo	Uds., ellos, ellas	tuvieron

The following verbs also have stem changes.

estar	est*u*ve	poner	p*u*se	venir	v*i*ne
poder	p*u*de	querer	qu*i*se	hacer	h*i*ce

NOTE: The stem of the verb **hacer** changes from **hac** to **hiz** in the third-person singular to keep the **c** sound: **hizo**

Read the following dialog that contains many stem changes in the preterit tense.

The common endings of these verbs are:

> e
> iste
> o
> imos
> ieron

Complete the table below:

	estar to be	hacer to do, make	poder to be able	poner to put	querer to want	tener to have	venir to come
	est-	hic-	pud-	pus-	quis-	tuv-	vin-
yo	estuve	hice	_____	_____	_____	_____	_____
tú	estuviste	hiciste	_____	_____	_____	_____	_____
Ud., él, ella	estuvo	hizo	_____	_____	_____	_____	_____
nosotros -as	estuvimos	hicimos	_____	_____	_____	_____	_____
Uds., ellos, ellas	estuvieron	hicieron	_____	_____	_____	_____	_____

Actividad H

Complete each sentence with the correct form of the verb in parentheses.

1. El sábado pasado yo no _____ ir a la fiesta.
(querer)

2. Mis abuelos _____ a visitarnos ayer.
(venir)

3. Esta mañana Ud. _____ los jeans nuevos.
(ponerse)

4. ¿Dónde _____ tú el verano pasado?
(estar)

5. Nosotros no _____ terminar las tareas anoche.
(poder)

6. El verano pasado ellas _____ que trabajar.
(tener)

7. ¿Qué _____ Uds. el fin de semana pasado?
(hacer)

8. ¿Quién _____ ausente el lunes pasado?
(estar)

9. ¿Donde _____ tú los periódicos que compré?
(poner)

Actividad

The following things are happening today. How would you say they happened yesterday? Work with a partner.

EXAMPLE: **Mis primos vienen a visitarme.**
              Mis primos *vinieron* a visitarme.

1. Yo no puedo ver esa película.   _____

2. Ellos hacen todo el trabajo.   _____

3. Mi mamá pone la comida en las mesa.   _____

4. Los ladrones pueden escaparse.   _____

5. Nosotros tenemos que ir a la escuela.   _____

6. Tú no quieres comer afuera.   _____

7. María hace un viaje a México.   _____

8. Yo no tengo tiempo.   _____

9. ¿Dónde ponen Uds. los periódicos?   _____

10. Ud. viene por la mañana.   _____

 There are two verbs that share the same irregular forms in the preterit, **ser** and **ir**. Only the context makes clear what the meaning is.

	ser *to be*	ir *to go*
yo	fui	fui
tú	fuiste	fuiste
Ud., él, ella	fue	fue
nosotros, -as	fuimos	fuimos
Uds., ellos, ellas	fueron	fueron

Mi hermano *fue* testigo del robo.   *My brother was a witness to the robbery.*

Él *fue* a declarar al cuartel de policía.   *He went to testify at the police station.*

After the summer vacation, you and your friends ask each other where you went.

1. ¿Adónde _____ tú, Javier?

2. ¿Y Uds., Margarita y Rosario, adónde _____ ?

3. ¿Adónde _____ Roberto?

You are on a school trip to Madrid and are keeping a diary. Complete the following entries with the correct form of the verb in parentheses.

Ayer nosotros _____ muchas cosas. Por la mañana nosotros _____
            (hacer)   (ir)
al Museo del Prado y _____ varias exhibiciones. Jorge y Darío no
                               (ver)
_____ ir con nosotros y _____ de compras. Por la tarde
     (querer)   (ir)
yo _____ a dar un paseo con María por el Parque del Retiro. Ella _____
   (salir)   (ponerse)
zapatos nuevos y no _____ caminar mucho. Nosotros _____
                          (poder)   (tener)
que tomar un taxi para regresar al hotel. Por la noche un amigo español _____
                                                                (venir)
al hotel y nosotros dos _____ a comer afuera. En el restaurante mi amigo
                                 (salir)
_____ una comida típica española. El mesero _____ muy despacio.
   (pedir)   (servir)
Nosotros _____ en el restaurante hasta muy tarde y yo _____
               (estar)   (acostarse)
después de medianoche.

Verbs with roots ending in a vowel + **-ER** or **-IR** share some common irregularities in the preterit. Let's look at two of them.

	creer	oír
yo	creí	oí
tú	creíste	oíste
Ud., él, ella	creyó	oyó
nosotros, -as	creímos	oímos
Uds., ellos, ellas	creyeron	oyeron

Note that the **i** has an accent mark in the **yo, tú,** and **nosotros** forms. In the other two forms, the **i** changes to **y**. Can you complete the table below?

	leer	caerse
yo	leí	me caí
tú	_____	te _____
Ud., él, ella	_____	se _____
nosotros, -as	_____	nos _____
Uds., ellos, ellas	_____	se _____

You have heard rumors about a trip to Mexico during the holiday break. Complete the sentences with the correct preterit tense form of the verb **oír**.

1. Yo _____ que la escuela planea un viaje a México.

2. ¿ _____ tú lo mismo?

3. Yo no, pero Juan _____ eso también.

4. Y Julia y Mercedes _____ que no va a costar mucho.

5. ¿Qué _____ Uds.?

6. Nosotros _____ que el viaje va a ser en diciembre.

8 Remember the endings shared by some irregular verbs? **-e, -iste, -o, -imos, -ieron**. There are two verbs (**decir** [to say] and **traer** [to bring]) with similar irregular stems that have the same endings except for the third-person plural (**-eron** instead of **-ieron**).

	decir	traer
yo	dij*e*	traj*e*
tú	dij*iste*	traj*iste*
Ud., él, ella	dij*o*	traj*o*
nosotros, -as	dij*imos*	traj*imos*
Uds., ellos, ellas	dij*eron*	traj*eron*

Somebody organized a surprise party for you and you want to know who brought the different foods. Complete the sentences with the correct preterit form of **traer**.

1. ¿Qué _____ tú, Daniel?

2. Yo _____ los sándwiches.

3. Y Ud., Srta. López, ¿qué _____ ?

4. Margarita y yo _____ las sodas.

5. Rosa _____ la torta.

6. José y su hermano _____ los globos (balloons).

Answer the following questions in complete Spanish sentences. Work with a partner who will ask you the question.

1. ¿Leyó Ud. el periódico ayer?

_____

2. ¿Quién fue el primer presidente de los Estados Unidos?

_____

3. ¿Dónde estuvo Ud. el domingo pasado?

_____

4. ¿Qué tiempo hizo el fin de semana pasado?

_____

5. ¿Quién vino tarde a la clase hoy?

_____

6. ¿Quién oyó las noticias en su casa anoche?

_____

7. ¿Para qué clase tuvo Ud. que hacer tareas anoche?

_____

8. ¿Qué dijo la professora a la clase de matemáticas?

_____

Preguntas Personales

1. ¿Adónde fuiste el sábado pasado por la noche?

_____

2. ¿Qué hiciste anoche?

_____

3. ¿A qué hora saliste de casa esta mañana?

_____

4. ¿A qué hora te acostaste anoche?

_____

5. ¿Trabajaste la semana pasada?

_____

DIÁLOGO

You were found at night near the scene of a crime, and the next day a policeman wants to question you. Here are your answers. What are the questions?

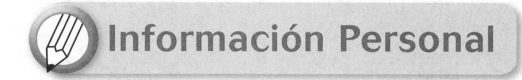

Información Personal

Make a list of five things you did yesterday:

1. _____

2. _____

3. _____

4. _____

5. _____

Composición

You witnessed a robbery. Fill out the following police report.

INFORME DEL TESTIGO

Apellido: _____   **Nombre:** _____   **Edad:** _____

Dirección: _____   **Teléfono:** _____

_____

1. ¿Qué vio Ud.?

   _____

   _____

2. ¿Dónde tuvo lugar el incidente?

   _____

   _____

---

3. ¿Qué hicieron los ladrones?

_____

_____

4. Describa a los ladrones.

_____

_____

5. ¿Adónde fueron los ladrones después?

_____

_____

 # Cápsula cultural

¡Auxilio, policía!

Si estás en un apuro en un país extranjero, ¿adónde vas por ayuda? A un policía, por supuesto. Pero, ¿a qué tipo? En España, por ejemplo hay tres tipos diferentes de policía:

La _Policía Nacional_ se encuentra en las ciudades. Llevan uniforme marrón, están armados y guardan los edificios oficiales. Otro grupo que se emplea por todo el país es la _Guardia Civil_. Sus miembros patrullan en autos o motocicletas y se encuentran generalmente en las áreas rurales. Llevan uniforme verde y un sombrero distinto llamado el _tricornio_. Un tercer grupo es la _Policía Municipal_ (los Urbanos). Estos oficiales trabajan para los varios gobiernos municipales y son, básicamente, policías de tránsito, aunque tienen jurisdicción en asuntos de orden pública. Generalmente, llevan uniformes azules en el invierno y blancos en el verano.

Una nota curiosa: Costa Rica es el sólo país de habla hispana sin fuerzas armadas. El presidente abolió el ejército y hoy este país de Centroamérica es el único país que tiene sólo su policía para defenderse.

Discusión

1. ¿Cuáles son los diferentes tipos de policía de España?

2. ¿Cómo se llama el sombrero de los miembros de la Guardia Civil?

3. ¿Qué trabajo hacen básicamente los Urbanos?

4. ¿Cómo es diferente Costa Rica de los otros países hispanoamericanos?

5. ¿Qué piensas de la idea de abolir las fuerzas armadas de un país?

Para investigar

Busca en el Internet fotos de policías de varios países hispanoamericanos y compártelas con la clase.

VOCABULARIO

estar en un apuro *to be in trouble*
encontrarse *to be found*
marrón *brown*

patrullar *to patrol*
jurisdicción *jurisdiction*

8

Las vacaciones

Imperfect Tense

1 Vocabulario

montar a caballo

dar una caminata por la montaña

montar en bicicleta

sacar fotos en un sitio pintoresco

pescar en el río

navegar

remar en el lago

jugar al golf

jugar al tenis

tirar el frisbee

jugar al ping pong

jugar al voleibol

descansar en el campo

hacer jogging

hacer ejercicios aeróbicos

jugar a los dominós

jugar a las cartas

Actividad A

Here's a picture of a wonderful resort. Can you describe some of the things people can do here? Use some of the verbs suggested below to complete your description.

pescar	sacar fotos	subir
jugar	respirar	tomar el sol

EXAMPLE: **Dos jóvenes están remando en el lago.**

_____

_____

_____

_____

_____

_____

_____

Actividad B

Sometimes you need the right equipment to be able to enjoy an activity. Can you name the activities in which you would use these pieces of equipment?

1. _____

2. _____

3. _____

4. _____

5. _____

6. _____

7. _____

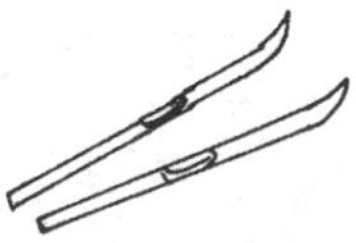

8. _____

9. 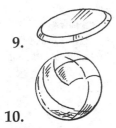 _____

10. _____

Doctor, tengo muchos problemas.

Let's read a one-act play about a man with a lot of problems.
Pay attention to the verbs in bold type. These verbs are in the
imperfect, another past tense in Spanish.

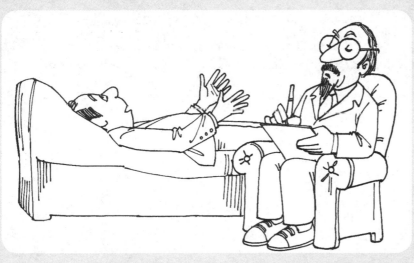

Escena: El consultorio del famoso psiquiatra Sergio Sesogrande. El
paciente está acostado en el sofá mientras el doctor toma notas.

el consultorio
doctor's office

DOCTOR: Dígame, Sr. Comequeso, ¿desde cuándo tiene esos
sentimientos de inseguridad?

desde *since*

PACIENTE: Toda mi vida, doctor.

DOCTOR: ¿De veras? Pero, ¿qué relación **tenía** con sus amiguitos
cuando era niño.

el amiguito *little
(young) friend*

PACIENTE: No me **interesaban** los otros niños. **Eran** muy
superficiales. **Prefería** pasar el tiempo en casa con mis dos
compañeros Gerardo y Geraldo. **Eran** muy amables; yo siempre
hablaba con ellos.

DOCTOR: ¿Ah, sí? ¿Qué tipo de persona **eran**?

PACIENTE: No **eran** personas. **Eran** peces dorados, muy
inteligentes y cariñosos. La gente no sabe que un pez puede ser
un amigo sincero y leal.

el pez dorado
goldfish
cariñoso
affectionate

DOCTOR: ¡Me imagino! (Dice para sí: «Este tipo es realmente extraño.») ¿Y nunca **tenía** ganas de divertirse con otras personas, de jugar a la pelota, ir al cine, etc.?

PACIENTE: No. esas cosas nunca me **interesaban**.

DOCTOR: Señor Comequeso, no necesito oír más. Veo bien su problema. Necesita más experiencia, tener interacción con otros seres humanos. Voy a hacer un programa para convertirlo en un hombre interesante y popular como yo; un hombre que puede tener éxito en nuestra sociedad moderna. A propósito, supongo que Ud. no trabaja y que no gana dinero.

PACIENTE: ¡Al contrario! Escribo programas para videojuegos y gano más de cien mil dólares al año.

DOCTOR: Entonces, ¿cuál es el problema?

PACIENTE: El problema es que todo el mundo quiere ser mi amigo y no tengo tiempo para compartir con Gerardo y Geraldo.

¡Me imagino! *I can imagine!*
para sí *to himself / herself*
tener ganas de *to feel like*

compartir *to share*

Discusión

1. ¿De qué sufre el paciente?

2. De niño, ¿con quiénes pasaba la mayor parte del tiempo?

3. ¿Cuál es el consejo del doctor?

4. ¿Qué hace un psiquiatra?

2 In Spanish, there are different ways to express actions in the past. You have already learned one tense, the preterit. Now let's learn another, the imperfect. Later on, we'll see the differences in use between the two. Look at the following examples:

Yo *jugaba* al tenis todos los días.	*I played (was playing, I used to play) tennis every day.*
Tú *descansabas* en el campo.	*You used to rest, etc. in the country.*

Ud. *remaba* **en el lago.**	*You used to row, etc. in the lake.*
Ella *nadaba* **en la piscina.**	*She used to swim, etc. in the swimming pool.*
Nosotros *montábamos* **a caballo.**	*We used to go, etc. horseback riding.*
Uds. *sacaban* **muchas fotos.**	*You used to take, etc. a lot of pictures.*
Ellos *pescaban* **en el río.**	*They used to fish, etc. in the river.*

All the above verbs are **-AR** verbs. What endings were added to the stem to form the imperfect?

yo	*-aba*
tú	*-abas*
Ud., él, ella	*-aba*
nosotros, -as	*-ábamos*
Uds., ellos, ellas	*-aban*

Actividad D

You are reminiscing with a friend about your early childhood. Complete the sentences with the correct form of the imperfect of the verb in parentheses.

1. Yo _____ todos los días en el parque.
   (jugar)

2. Mi madre _____ por las mañanas.
   (trabajar)

3. Mi hermanito y yo _____ a los abuelos los domingos.
   (visitar)

4. Mis padres _____ las vacaciones en la playa.
   (pasar)

5. Nuestros abuelos nos _____ muchos dulces.
(comprar)

6. Yo _____ muy temprano.
(despertarse)

7. Por las tardes tú y yo _____ la televisión.
(mira)

8. Mi hermana _____ por teléfono todo el tiempo.
(hablar)

9. Tú _____ el almuerzo en mi casa.
(tomar)

10. En el invierno _____ mucho.
(nevar)

 Now let's look at these examples of **-ER** and **-IR** verbs.

-ER	-IR
Yo *comía* en la cafetería.	Yo *salía* temprano.
Tú *corrías* rápido.	Tú nunca *mentías*.
Ud. *quería* ser dentista.	Ud. *dormía* mucho.
Él *hacía* bien las tareas.	Ella *vivía* en Nueva York.
Nosotros *teníamos* mucho dinero.	Nosotras *decíamos* siempre la verdad.
Uds. *leían* en español.	Uds. se *reían* mucho.
Ellas *sabían* la lección.	Ellos *servían* la comida

Note that the endings are the same for both **-ER** and **-IR** verbs. Write them in the space provided.

yo _____   nosotros _____

tú _____   _____

Ud. / él / ella _____   Uds. / ellos / ellas _____

Actividad **E**

Here's a description of what's going on in the classroom now. Say that the same thing used to happen last year by changing the sentences to the correct form of the imperfect. Work with a partner who will read these sentences in the present tense.

EXAMPLE: La maestra dice: «Buenos días».
            El año pasado la maestra decía: «Buenos días».

1. Un alumno abre las ventanas.

_____

2. Yo quiero hablar en español.

_____

3. Los alumnos saben contestar bien.

_____

4. Nosotros tenemos muchas tareas.

_____

5. Tú lees y escribes en español.

_____

6. El director viene a nuestra clase.

_____

7. Uds. se duermen en clase.

_____

8. Yo entiendo la lección.

_____

9. Ud. cree todo lo que dice la maestra.

_____

10. Los alumnos conocen a todos los profesores.

_____

Using the construction **hace** + *time expression* + *imperfect tense*, write five things you used to do two years ago. You may use the following verbs:

dormir	leer	trabajar	escribir
vivir	hacer	pasar	nadar

EXAMPLE: **Hace dos años yo vivía en otra ciudad.**

1. _____

2. _____

3. _____

4. _____

5. _____

There are only three verbs with irregular forms in the imperfect tense. One of them, **ver,** keeps the **e** of the **-ER** ending in all forms; **ser** and **ir** are irregular. Memorize their forms.

	ser	ir
yo	*era*	*iba*
tú	*eras*	*ibas*
Ud., él, ella	*era*	*iba*
nosotros, -as	*éramos*	*íbamos*
Uds., ellos, ellas	*eran*	*iban*

ver			
yo	*veía*	nosotros, -as	*veíamos*
tú	*veías*		
Ud., él, ella	*veía*	Uds., ellos, ellas	*veían*

Actividad G

You are talking with some friends about the past. Complete the sentences with the correct forms of the imperfect of **ser**.

1. Tú _____ bueno en matemáticas.

2. Javier _____ mi mejor amigo.

3. Yo _____ capitán del equipo de fútbol.

4. La maestra _____ muy estricta.

5. Tú y yo _____ los campeones de tenis.

6. María y Rosa _____ las muchachas más bonitas de la clase.

7. Uds. _____ malos estudiantes.

Actividad H

Where did the following people go when you were little?

EXAMPLE: mi hermana / a la universidad
            Cuando yo era niño, mi hermana iba a la universidad.

1. mis padres / al campo   _____

2. yo / a la escuela   _____

3. mi abuelo / a la plaza   _____

4. Ud. / al cine   _____

5. tú / al parque   _____

6. Uds. / al supermercado   _____

You want to ask your mother questions about her life when she was a child. Here are the answers. Make up your questions. Work with a partner.

EXAMPLE: Yo jugaba en el parque.
Mami, ¿dónde jugabas cuando eras niña?

1. Yo vivía en una ciudad muy grande.

¿Dónde _____?

2. En las vacaciones mis padres y yo íbamos a las montañas.

¿Adónde _____?

3. Yo tenía muchos amigos.

¿Cuántos _____?

4. Yo veía a mis abuelos todos los domingos.

¿Cuándo _____?

5. Yo iba a la escuela en bicicleta.

¿Cómo _____?

6. Los fines de semana yo salía al parque con Luisa.

¿Con quién _____?

Preguntas Personales

1. ¿Qué hacías cuando eras niño(a)?

_____

2. ¿Dónde vivías hace cinco años?

_____

3. ¿A qué escuela ibas entonces?

_____

4. ¿Qué tipo de alumno(a) eras?

_____

5. ¿Quién era tu mejor amigo(a)?

_____

Información Personal

You are a psychiatrist who just opened a new office. Your first client is lying on the couch. Think of five questions you want to ask about his or her childhood. You may want to use some of the following verbs:

vivir	jugar	hacer	saber
ir	ser	tener	querer

1. _____

2. _____

3. _____

4. _____

5. _____

Composición

The school nurse is trying to set up a summer program and needs some information from the students about how they spent their vacations as children. Tell the following:

1. where you used to go

2. how you traveled there

3. what the weather was like

4. what usually did there

5. why you liked or disliked the vacation

EXAMPLE: **Yo siempre viajaba con mis padres a Puerto Plata.**

Because of the problems he's been having lately, Mr. Moreno is undergoing psychoanalysis. What does he tell the psychiatrist?

# Cápsula cultural

Las vacaciones en Hispanoamérica

El concepto de vacaciones en Hispanoamérica es diferente al de los Estados Unidos o los países europeos. En realidad, los días de fiesta son las vacaciones para la mayoría de la gente en Hispanoamérica. Debido a las condiciones sociales y económicas, en la mayoría de los países del mundo hispano los beneficios laborales, por ejemplo las vacaciones pagadas, no son tan buenos como en otros países del mundo. Y en los casos en donde ofrecen vacaciones, la gente no gana lo suficiente como para viajar al extranjero. Quizás es por eso que los hispanoamericanos generalmente no posponen sus vacaciones, como es común en los Estados Unidos.

La recreación es parte de la vida diaria. Y si se ha trabajado toda la semana, entonces se toma el fin de semana para descansar y divertirse. Familias enteras van en excursiones a balnearios o a la playa, con comida, juegos y baile.

Discusión

1. ¿Cómo compara el concepto de vacaciones en Hispanoamérica y en los Estados Unidos?

2. ¿Cómo son los beneficios laborales en Hispanoamérica, comparados con otros países?

3. ¿Por qué los hispanoamericanos no viajan generalmente al extranjero?

4. ¿Qué hacen las familias hispanoamericanas durante los fines de semana?

5. ¿Por qué es importante tener la oportunidad de divertirse?

VOCABULARIO

debido a *due to*
los beneficios laborales
   employment benefits

ganar *to earn*
diario *daily*

¿Cuándo?

Imperfect and Preterit Tenses Compared

MEDIDAS DE TIEMPO

un minuto = 60 segundos	un mes = 30/31 días (4 semanas)
una hora = 60 minutos	un año = 12 meses
un día = 24 horas	un siglo = 100 años
una semana = 7 días	la eternidad = tiempo infinito

Actividad A

Work with a partner. Match each time expression in the left column with its equivalent in the right column and then definite it.

EXAMPLE: 60 minutos   una hora   **Hay sesenta minutos en una hora.**

1. 60 segundos   a. una semana

2. 12 meses   b. un siglo

3. 7 días   c. un mes

4. 4 semanas   d. un año

5. cien años   e. un minuto

Commonly Used Time Expressions

hoy	*today*
de hoy en ocho días	*a week from today*
de hoy en quince días	*two weeks from today*
mañana	*tomorrow*
pasado mañana	*one week from tomorrow*
la semana pasada }	*next week*
la semana que viene }	

Note how the following vocabulary words (**mañana, ayer**, etc.) relate to each other.

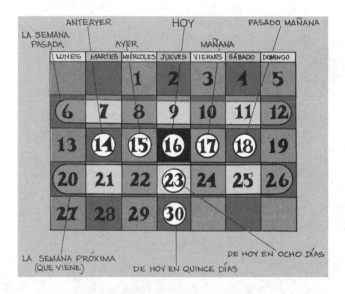

Complete each Spanish sentence with the appropriate time expression:

EXAMPLE: *Today* I'm leaving for Spain.   *Hoy* **salgo para España.**

1. *A week* from today I will be on the   _____ salgo para España.
   Costa del Sol.

2. Are you going shopping *tomorrow*?   ¿Vas de compras _____?

3. My sister arrived *last week*.   Mi hermana llegó _____.

4. *Yesterday* I didn't feel well.   _____ no me sentí bien.

5. Next week we have a test.   _____ tenemos un examen.

La adivina

Since we are learning about time expressions and the past, let's read a story about a fortune teller (**una adivina**).

ROSANA: Josefina, ¿quieres venir conmigo a consultar a la vieja adivina, doña Matilde? Todas nuestras amigas dicen que ella puede ver el pasado y predecir el futuro.

JOSEFINA: ¡Me sorprendes! Tú eres inteligente y racional. Y sin embargo crees en esas cosas. Yo no voy a gastar mi dinero así. Pero, si insistes, como eres mi mejor amiga, te acompaño.

sin embargo
nevertheless

ROSANA: Bien. Vamos **pasado mañana**, el viernes por la tarde.

Llega el viernes y las dos amigas están sentadas alrededor de una mesa. En el centro de la mesa hay una bola de cristal. La adivina habla.

MATILDE: Voy a comenzar con.el pasado de la Srta. Rosana. Cuando Ud. era niña, Ud. contaba con los dedos de las manos y de los pies. Sólamente **hace poco** aprendió Ud. a calcular.

hace poco *a little while ago*

ROSANA: Al contrario. Yo era muy buena en matemáticas. Gané mi primer premio en matemáticas cuando tenía diez años.

MATILDE: Cuando Ud. tenía 16 años decía mentiras de sus amigas.

ROSANA: ¡Jamás!

MATILDE: Finalmente, en su clase de español, Ud. escribía notas anónimas a los muchachos guapos.

ROSANA: Todos esto es ridículo. No quiero escuchar más. Vamos, Josefina. Tú tenías razón. ¡Qué estúpida soy! ¡Ella no sabe nada!

MATILDE: Un momento. Veo algo interesante sobre su amiga Josefina en la bola de cristal.

JOSEFINA: ¿Oh? ¿Qué ve Ud.?

MATILDE: Veo a una muchacha tímida y nerviosa.

JOSEFINA: Cierto.

MATILDE: Estaba enamorada secretamente de Antonio, el atleta más popular de la escuela.

JOSEFINA: Sí, sí, es verdad. Siga, siga. Es increíble, Ud. sabe muchísimo.

MATILDE: Eso es todo por hoy. Si quieren saber más, vengan la semana que viene.

Las dos jóvenes salen a la calle.

JOSEFINA: No comprendo cómo ella sabía esas cosas de mi pasado. ¡Es realmente una maravilla!

ROSANA: ¡Qué va! Tu hermana la visitó la semana pasada y tú sabes la boca grande que tiene ella.

¡qué va! *no way!*

Discusión

Answer each question in a complete sentence.

1. ¿Cómo se llama la adivina?

_____

2. Según Rosana, ¿qué puede hacer doña Matilde?

_____

3. ¿Qué cree Josefina de esas cosas?

_____

4. ¿Qué sabía la adivina del pasado de Rosana?

_____

5. En su opinión, ¿por qué creen algunas personas en los adivinos?

_____

 You have now learned two very important past tenses in Spanish. Let's look at them:

Siempre *llegaba* tarde, pero ayer *llegó* temprano.

Iba a la escuela en carro, pero un día *tuve* que ir en bus.

Todos los sábados *venía* mi tío, pero el sábado pasado *no vino*.

What time expressions are used in the clauses on the left? What do they tell us about the actions described?

RULE: In Spanish we use the imperfect to express what used to happen or happened over and over again — that is, repeated or habitual actions in the past. That's why the imperfect is often used with expressions like **por lo general** (*in general*), **a menudo** (*often*), **siempre** (*always*), **todos los días** (*every day*).

What time expressions are used in the clauses on the right?

Un día, ayer, or **el sábado pasado** imply that the action happened at a specific time.

In Spanish, we use the preterit to express specific events that are not habitual, that started and ended within a specific time frame. That's why the preterit is often used with expressions that determine a specific time, like **anoche** *(last night)*, **ayer** *(yesterday)*, **esta mañana** *(this morning)*, **el lunes pasado** *(last Monday)*, and others.

Actividad D

The preterit and imperfect forms of the verb are given in each of the following sentences. Select the correct choice.

1. _____ al cine a menudo.
    (Iban, Fueron)

2. ¿Quién _____ las tareas anoche?
    (hizo, hacía)

3. Me _____ a las ocho el lunes pasado.
    (desperté, despertaba)

4. Ella _____ de casa temprano esta mañana.
    (salía, salió)

5. ¿Dónde _____ siempre el autobús?
    (tomabas, tomaste)

6. ¿Dónde _____ el autobús ayer?
    (tomabas, tomaste)

7. Por lo general, yo _____ en el parque.
    (corría, corrí)

8. Los domingos Juan _____ a sus abuelos.
    (visitaba, visitó)

9. Todos los viernes _____ temprano a casa.
    (llegábamos, llegamos)

10. El viernes pasado _____ tarde.
    (llegábamos, llegamos)

Actividad E

You are at a party where everyone is talking about the past. Using the cues provided, make statements about the way it was. Be careful, some verbs have to be used in the preterit and some in the perfect.

1. yo / ir todos los sábados al cine

_____

2. nosotros / estar una vez en Nueva York

_____

3. yo / salir a dar un paseo todas las noches

_____

4. Juan / leer dos novelas el verano pasado

_____

5. nosotros / nadar el sábado pasado en la piscina

_____

6. mis padres / viajar a Europa hace un año

_____

7. Uds. / ir a la playa todos los veranos

_____

8. tu hermana / trabajar por lo general hasta tarde

_____

9. mi tío / venir de España hace cinco años

_____

10. tú / llegar siempre tarde a la escuela

_____

3 There is still more to learn about the past. Look carefully at these sentences:

Yo *dormía* **cuando** *sonó* **el teléfono.** *I was sleeping when the telephone rang.*

Ud. *estaba* **en casa cuando** *llamé.* *You were at home when I called.*

Rosa *escribía* **una carta cuando** *Rose was writing a letter when her*
**   *llegó* su amiga.** *   friend arrived.*

Hacía **sol cuando** *salimos.* *The sun was shining when we left.*

How many actions are described in each sentence? _____ How many

verb tenses are used in each sentence? _____ Which tenses are they?

_____ and _____ . Which word combines the two clauses

describing the two actions? _____ .

Let's summarize: The IMPERFECT describes an ongoing or continuous past action

lasting an unspecified amount of time. In English, we can say *was (were) + . . .* ing,

or *used to . . .* The PRETERIT expresses a specific past action that happened at one

point while the other action was in progress. Imagine two cameras—an instant

and a video camera. Which one would represent the imperfect? _____

the preterit? _____ .

Complete the sentence with the correct form of the preterit or the imperfect of the verb in parentheses.

1. Eran las cuatro de la tarde cuando tú _____ a casa.
   (llegar)

2. El sábado pasado Juan _____ al fútbol con sus hermanos.
   (jugar)

3. Yo siempre _____ temprano.
   (levantarse)

4. Mi padre _____ cuando mi madre _____ .
      (leer)   (llamar)

5. El año pasado ellas _____ a Colombia.
                       (ir)

6. Cuando yo _____ a Luis, él _____ un traje muy elegante.
          (ver)   (llevar)

7. Por lo general, ellos _____ las tareas juntos.
                   (hacer)

8. Tú siempre _____ muchas cartas.
           (recibir)

9. Yo _____ cuando alguien _____ a la puerta.
   (lavarse)   (tocar)

10. Cuando mi hermano _____ , nosotros _____ en Miami.
              (nacer)   (vivir)

Actividad G

Your neighbor's window was broken in a ball game, and she complained to your father. Answer his questions.

1. ¿Dónde estabas esta tarde cuando yo entré en casa?

_____

2. ¿Con quién jugabas cuando te llamé?

_____

3. ¿A qué jugaban Uds.?

_____

4. ¿Qué hiciste al ver que la pelota caía en otra casa?

_____

5. ¿Qué hacía la vecina (*neighbor*) cuando la pelota cayó en su casa?

_____

6. ¿Dónde estaba tu madre cuando Uds. terminaron de jugar?

_____

7. ¿Qué le dijiste a tu mamá sobre la ventana?

_____

4 Read this short description of a little girl's holiday:

Era el diez de junio y **eran** las siete de la mañana. El sol **brillaba** y **hacía** un tiempo precioso. **Estábamos** en un hotel al lado de la playa y por la ventana se **veía** el mar. En la playa **había** otra muchacha. **Era** alta y **llevaba** un traje de baño rojo. Yo **quería** jugar con ella, pero **tenía** que esperar a mis padres porque yo **tenía** solamente ocho años. Mis padres **dormían** . . .

Which tense did the girl use? _____ She used the IMPERFECT to describe circumstances and conditions in the past. The circumstances and conditions may refer to time, dates, weather, attitudes, states of mind, physical descriptions, age, or locations. All circumstances described in the imperfect happened over an unspecified amount of time.

What happens if the narrator wants to tell about actions that occurred at a specific point in time? Let's pick up the story from the last sentence.

Mis padres **dormían** y **decidí** despertarlos. **Abrí** su puerta y **grité**: «¡Levántense! ¡Vamos a la playa!»

Which tense is used to describe the narrator's actions? _____ Why?

Actividad H

Write a short paragraph describing your early years. Complete each sentence with the imperfect of the verb in parentheses.

Cuando yo _____ niño, mi familia _____ en Chicago, en un
         (ser)   (vivir)

apartamento pequeño. Mi padre _____ de mecánico en un garaje. Él
                          (trabajar)

siempre _____ temprano a casa y él y yo _____ a jugar pelota al
      (llegar)   (salir)

parque. En invierno mi madre _____ chocolate caliente y _____ a
                              (preparar)   (sentarse)

contarme cuentos. Yo _____ a una escuela cerca de casa.
                     (ir)

Actividad I

You are telling what you saw this morning on your way to school. Complete the paragraph with the correct form of the preterit or the imperfect of the verb in parentheses.

Esta mañana _____ cuando yo _____ de casa. Yo _____
             (llover)   (salir)   (caminar)

rápidamente cuando yo _____ a un señor que _____ en la
                         (oír)   (gritar)

calle. _____ un hombre que _____ detrás de un perro muy
           (ser)   (correr)

grande. Aparentemente el hombre _____ a un amigo en la calle y el
                                (encontrar)

perro _____ mientras los dos amigos _____ .
       (escaparse)   (hablar)

Actividad J

Imagine that you spent last summer in Mexico. Tell you friends in Spanish about a special excursion you took one day. Be careful! You have to decide when to use the imperfect and when to use the preterit.

1. It was August and I was in Mexico City.

   _____

2. I was living in a hotel.

   _____

3. One day I woke up early.

_____

4. I was going to take a trip.

_____

5. I opened the window and saw that the sun was shining.

_____

6. We were going by bus.

_____

7. I dressed quickly.

_____

8. We were going to see the pyramids (_las pirámides_).

_____

9. They were very beautiful.

_____

10. I enjoyed myself.

_____

5   Remember the verbs **saber** and **conocer**? They have special meanings in the preterit tense, different from their meanings in the imperfect. Let's first conjugate both in the preterit. **Conocer** is regular, but **saber** is irregular:

	conocer	saber
yo	conoc*í*	sup*e*
tú	conoc*iste*	sup*iste*
Ud., él, ella	conoc*ió*	sup*o*
nosotros, -as	conoc*imos*	sup*imos*
Uds., ellos, ellas	conoc*ieron*	sup*ieron*

Now look at these examples:

¿*Conocías* a Juan?   _Did you know Juan?_

Sí, lo *conocí* hace dos meses.   _Yes, I met him two months ago._

¿Sabías que tenemos un examen hoy?   *Did you know that we have a test today?*

Sí, pero lo supe muy tarde ayer.   *Yes, but I found out late yesterday.*

RULE: In the imperfect tense, **conocer** means "knew (someone or something)"; in the preterit, it means "met."

In the imperfect tense, **saber** means "knew (something or how to do something)"; in the preterit, it means "found out."

Actividad K

Work with a partner. Have the following conversation in Spanish.

1. Do you know María?

_____

Yes, I met María at a party yesterday.

_____

2. Do you know where she lives?

_____

Yes, I found out that she lives near my house.

_____

3. Did you also meet her sister, Rosa?

_____

Yes, I met Rosa last week.

_____

4. Did you know that they are Cuban?

_____

No, I didn't know.

_____

Play the role of a telephone psychic. Tell the person on the line some things that he/she used to do in the past.

EXAMPLE: **De niño, *vivía* en una ciudad grande.**

You went to a fortune teller. To find out if she's any good, you asked her to tell you some things about your past. React to what she says.

Preguntas Personales

1. ¿Cuando eras niño(a), qué hacías para divertirte?

_____

2. ¿Qué aprendías en la escuela elemental?

_____

3. ¿Cómo era tu familia?

_____

4. ¿Qué hacías durante las vacaciones?

_____

5. ¿Te gustaba tu vida? ¿Por qué (no)?

_____

Información Personal

You have been asked to "tell about yourself." Describe some interesting or important facts or events from your past. (You don't have to tell the truth. No one is going to check. So, go ahead, be outrageous!)

_____

_____

_____

_____

_____

_____

_____

_____

_____

Cápsula cultural

La Víspera de San Juan

En varios países de habla hispana existe una tradición muy interesante relacionada con el 23 de junio, el Día de San Juan. Este día anuncia la llegada del verano; y en la víspera, la gente se reúne para celebrar y practicar varios rituales, con la esperanza de recibir buena suerte.

En Puerto Rico, por ejemplo, la gente va a la playa y se tira tres veces. Según la tradición, eso les dará buena suerte. El ritual termina con una fiesta donde se sirven platos y bebidas tradicionales.

En las Islas Canarias de España también existe una tradición similar. En este caso las personas recogen ropa vieja, muebles rotos y otros artículos que no sirven. También hacen una lista de las cosas negativas que quieren cambiar en sus vidas. Entonces hacen una hoguera, casi siempre en la playa, y tiran al fuego las cosas que ya no quieren y la lista. Después de eso, las personas se tiran al mar inmediatamente. De esta manera dan la bienvenida al verano y esperan buena suerte y cosas positivas en el futuro.

Discusión

1. ¿Qué hace mucha gente para tener buena fortuna?

2. ¿Adónde va la gente de Puerto Rico y las Islas Canarias la Víspera de San Juan?

3. ¿Qué escriben en la lista?

4. ¿Por qué hacen las hogueras?

5. ¿Qué beneficios psicológicos tienen las tradiciones?

VOCABULARIO

la víspera *eve*
se tiran *throw themselves*
la hoguera *bonfire*

10

Los deportes

Demonstrative Adjectives and Pronouns

1 Vocabulario

el fútbol

el béisbol

el boxeo

el básquetbol / el baloncesto

el ciclismo

el fútbol americano

la natación

levantar pesas

la lucha libre

el voleibol

el esquí

el patinaje

la carrera

la esgrima

el tenis

la gimnasia

las artes marciales

el guante de béisbol

el guante de boxeo

el bate

el casco

la cesta

la pelota de béisbol

el balón de fútbol

la raqueta

la espada

las gafas

el monopatín

el uniforme

la red

el balón de fútbol americano

los patines de rueda

los patines de hielo

Actividad A

Mr. González needs sports equipment for his gym classes. Can you help him choose some items?

Para jugar al béisbol necesita _____ .

Para jugar al básquetbol necesita _____ .

Para esquiar necesita _____ .

Para jugar al fútbol americano necesita _____ .

Para la natación necesita _____ .

Para el tenis necesita _____ .

Para el voleibol necesita _____ .

Para el boxeo necesita _____ .

Actividad B

What sports activities are these people engaged in?

1. _____

2. _____

3. _____

4. _____

5. _____ 6. _____

¡Kiai! El grito del alma (en japonés)

Let's read about another popular sport, **el karate**:

Kiai es la palabra japonesa que expresa el grito antes de dar un golpe o una patada.

Con un simple golpe de pie o de mano, una persona puede romper una tabla de madera o un ladrillo. ¿Imposible? No. Es muy posible si Ud. sabe **ese** antiguo arte japonés llamado karate. La palabra karate significa «mano vacía». **Eso** significa que no se usan armas.

el golpe *blow*
la patada *the kick*
romper *to break*
la tabla *board*
el ladrillo *brick*
vacío *empty*

Para combatir se utilizan solamente ciertas partes del cuerpo como las manos, los pies, los codos y las rodillas. **Estas** partes del cuerpo son come armas.

el codo *elbow*
la rodilla *knee*

El karate nació en la India hace más de dos mil años. En aquellos tiempos, unos budistas usaban una forma similar de combate para defenderse de los animales salvajes. **Este** sistema pasó a China, Japón y Corea, y se convirtió en un método de defensa personal. Hoy día, además, de ser un arte marcial, el karate es un deporte de competición que se practica en todos los países del mundo.

Los estudiantes avanzan desde el grado de principiantes hasta el de expertos. Estos grados corresponden a cinturones de colores diferentes. Los principiantes, por ejemplo, llevan cinturón blanco y los expertos, negro. Muchas de las asociaciones de karate tienen reglas estrictas para evitar la violencia. Algunas de **estas** reglas son!

(1) dedicarse a la educación intelectual y física.

(2) ser corteses y modestos.

(3) respetar a todos, superiores e inferiores, amigos o enemigos.

(4) utilizar el karate sólo en emergencias.

(5) ser buenos.

El estudiante que quiere tener éxito tiene que pasar muchos años de práctica. Por ejemplo, tiene que demostrar su fuerza rompiendo dos o tres ladrillos con un solo golpe de pie o de otra parte del cuerpo. ¿Todavía está Ud. interesado en aprender? Buena suerte pero, ¡tenga cuidado con los dolores de la cabeza!

tener éxito *to succeed*

Discusión

Answer the following questions with complete sentences.

1. ¿Qué puede hacer con un golpe una persona que sabe karate?

   _____

2. ¿Qué quiere decir la palabra «karate» en japonés?

   _____

3. ¿Qué partes del cuerpo se usan en el karate?

   _____

4. ¿Quién usó originalmente el karate?

   _____

5. ¿Qué es el karate hoy día?

   _____

In the previous reading selection, you saw the following expressions:

ese **antiguo arte**   *that ancient art*
eso **significa**   *that means*
estas **partes del cuerpo** *these parts of the body*

en *aquellos* tiempos	*in those (distant) times*
este sistema	*this system*
esto es un arte marcial	*this is a martial art*
estos grados	*these grades*
estas reglas	*these rules*

2 The demonstratives *this, these, that*, and *those* are used in English to point out specific persons or things. In Spanish, there are many more demonstratives. Let's take a look.

How many possibilities are there in Spanish to point out things? _____

Este (this) refers to a person or thing that is *here* (**aquí**), next to you. **Ese** (that) refers to a person or thing that is *there* (**ahí**), away from you or close to the person you are talking to. **Aquel** *(that)* refers to a person or thing that is *over there* (**allí**), far from you and the person you are talking to. **Este, ese**, and **aquel** are demonstrative adjectives agreeing in number and gender with the noun they accompany.

Let's look at the forms of **este**:

est*e* **hombre**	*this man*	**est***os* **hombres**	*these men*
est*a* **mujer**	*this woman*	**est***as* **mujeres**	*these women*

Now write the appropriate form of **este** for the following words:

_____ traje   _____ guantes

_____ camisa   _____ medias

The forms of **ese** have the same endings:

es*e* **árbol**	*that tree*	**es***os* **árboles**	*those trees*
es*a* **casa**	*that house*	**es***as* **casas**	*those houses*

Write the appropriate form of **ese** for the following words:

_____ caballo   _____ gatos

_____ vaca   _____ gallinas

Finally, forms of **aquel** also have the same endings, but an extra **l** is placed before them.

aquel chico	*that boy*	**aquellos chicos**	*those boys*
aquella chica	*that girl*	**aquellas chicas**	*those girls*

Now write the appropriate form of **aquel** for the following words:

_____ disco   _____ cuadros

_____ ventana   _____ puertas

Note that in Spanish demonstrative adjectives have to be repeated before each noun.

Quiero comprar *esos* **periódicos y**   *I want to buy those newspapers and*
  esas revistas.   *magazines.*

Actividad D

You are in a sports store and want to find out how much various items cost. Ask questions using the appropriate form of **este**.

EXAMPLE: **esquíes**   **¿Cuánto cuestan *estos* esquíes?**

1. guante   _____

2. bate   _____

3. balones   _____

4. raqueta   _____

5. cestas   _____

6. cascos   _____

7. pelota   _____

8. bicicletas _____

Actividad E

You're showing your friend what you would like for your birthday. Form sentences using the appropriate form of **ese**.

EXAMPLES: **camisa**   **Me gusta** *esa* **camisa.**
            suéteres   **Me gustan** *esos* **suéteres.**

1. abrigo _____

2. sortija _____

3. gafas de sol _____

4. zapatos _____

5. reloj de pulsera _____

6. perfume _____

7. traje de baño _____

8. cadena de oro _____

Actividad F

You are watching a parade with your friend and are calling each other's attention to things you see: Use a the appropriate form of **aquel**.

EXAMPLE: **caballo**   **¡Mira** *aquel* **caballo!**

1. gigante _____

2. músicos _____

3. muchacha _____

4. banderas _____

5. banda _____

6. soldados _____

7. coche _____

8. flores _____

You are going shopping at the supermarket. Say what you are going to buy.

EXAMPLES: **pan (aquí)**   **Voy a comprar** *este* **pan.**
            torta (ahí)   **Voy a comprar** *esa* **torta.**
            frutas (allí)   **Voy a comprar aquellas frutas.**

1. helado (aquí)   _____

2. sodas (allí)   _____

3. pollo (ahí)   _____

4. carne (aquí)   _____

5. manzanas (ahí)   _____

6. huevos (allí)   _____

7. crema (ahí)   _____

8. legumbres (aquí)   _____

9. jugo (allí)   _____

 Now look at the following sentences:

Me gusta esta camisa pero no *aquella.*	*I like this shirt but not that one.*
¿Qué película vas a ver, *esta* **o** *esa***?**	*Which film are you going to see, this one or that one?*
Quiero comprar *ese* **libro, no** *este.*	*I want to buy that book, not this one.*
¿Quieres escuchar *estos* **discos o** *esos***?**	*Do you want to listen to these records or those ones?*

When **aquel, este**, and **ese** are used by themselves (without nouns), they are called demonstrative pronouns. The form of the demonstrative pronoun depends on the gender and number of the noun it represents. Demonstrative pronouns have the same forms as demonstrative adjectives.

este esta	} this one	estos estas	} these
ese esa	} that one	esos esas	} those
aquel aquella	} that one	aquellos aquellas	} those

Actividad H

Marcos went to summer camp and found signs telling him what to do everywhere. Select the demonstrative pronoun that completes the sentence correctly.

1. Ponga su ropa en esta silla, no en _____.   (a) este   (b) esos   (c) aquella

2. Entre por esa puerta, no por _____.   (a) aquel   (b) esta   (c) este

3. Duerma en aquel cuarto, no en _____.   (a) ese   (b) esos   (c) aquella

4. Abra estas ventanas, no _____.   (a) aquellos   (b) estos   (c) esas

5. Use esos zapatos, no _____.   (a) estas   (b) aquellos   (c) ese

6. Báñese en este baño, no en _____.   (a) esa   (b) aquellas   (c) ese

7. Siga esas reglas, no _____.   (a) esos   (b) estas   (c) aquel

8. Corra por aquel patio, no por _____.   (a) esa   (b) este   (c) estas

Actividad I

Complete the following sentences in Spanish.

1. Quiero _____ sombrero, no _____ .
              (this)   (that one)

2. Necesito _____ libros, no _____ .
     (those)   (those over there)

3. Prefiero _____ flores rojas.
     (these)

4. _____ lección no es difícil, pero _____ sí.
  (that)   (this one)

5. Abre _____ ventana y cierra _____ .
    (this)   (that one over there)

6. _____ papeles son importantes.
 (those over there)

7. _____ soldados son españoles; _____ son franceses.
  (those)   (these)

8. _____ niño es mi hermano; _____ es su amigo.
  (that)   (that one over there)

Preguntas Personales

1. ¿Practicas algún deporte? ¿Cuál(es)?

_____

2. ¿Qué equipos de deporte hay en tu escuela?

_____

3. ¿Sabes algún arte marcial? ¿Cuál(es)?

_____

4. ¿Cuáles son algunos deportes populares hoy día?

_____

5. ¿Deben participar las muchachas en todos los deportes? ¿Por qué (no)?

_____

DIÁLOGO

Rafael wants to join a team at school. He's talking with the head of the Physical Education Department.

Información Personal

You want to convince the coach of your favorite sport that you would be a good addition to the team. Complete the sentences that follow.

1. A mí me gusta mucho _____ .

2. Ese deporte es _____ .

3. Yo creo que soy _____ .

4. El año pasado _____ .

5. Quiero _____ .

Composición

A group of visitors from different countries have come to your school. You are explaining to them the ways Americans spend their leisure time. Talk about some popular activities.

Los fines de semana, muchos norteamericanos _____

_____

_____

_____

_____

_____

_____

_____

_____

 Cápsula cultural

El juego más rápido (y más peligroso) del mundo

Algunos lo llaman el juego más rápido; otros dicen que es el más peligroso, a causa de la velocidad en que la pelota va por el aire (150 millas por hora). El juego se llama *Jai Alai* o *Pelota Vasca*. Este juego antiguo se originó en el País Vasco, pero ahora se juega por toda España y el mundo entero.

Jai Alai es similar a la pelota de mano, pero hay mayores diferencias. Hay una competencia entre dos equipos, con dos jugadores en cada equipo. Se juega en una cancha larga y ancha de tres paredes, llamada el *frontón*. El objeto del juego es lanzar la pelota contra una de las paredes. Se gana un punto si el otro equipo no puede devolver la pelota.

La pelota es un poco más pequeña que una pelota de tenis y no parece peligrosa, pero está cubierta de cuero y es tan dura como una piedra. Las manos de los jugadores nunca tocan la pelota. Emplean un guante grande y curvo llamado *cesta* o *chistera*. Esta chistera es más de un pie de largo y tiene una ranura para atrapar y luego tirar la pelota; está atada a la muñeca del jugador con correas de cuero.

Una pared protectora de alambre separa a los jugadores de los espectadores. ¡Cuando ven la velocidad con que la pelota viaja, están muy contentos de estar detrás de esa protección!

Discusión

1. ¿Qué es el Jai Alai? ¿Dónde se originó?

2. ¿Cómo se juega este deporte?

3. ¿Qué se necesita para jugar el juego?

4. ¿Qué juegos son similares? ¿Cómo son diferentes?

Para investigar

En el Internet, investiga el Jai Alai en los Estados Unidos.

VOCABULARIO

la pelota de mano *handball*
el equipo *team*
la cancha *court*
devolver *to return*
peligroso *dangerous*
dura *hard*

la ranura *groove*
atrapar *to trap, catch*
la muñeca *the wrist*
la correa *strap*
el cuero *leather*
el alambre *wire*

Repaso II

Lección 6

a. Reflexive verbs have a special pronoun, called a reflexive pronoun, to indicate that the subject and object of the verb refer to the same person or thing.

lavar*se*	dormir*se*	acostar*se*

b. Some Spanish reflexive verbs have nonreflexive English equivalents.

levantarse *to get up*
divertirse *to have fun*
acostarse *to go to bed*

c. Different subjects require different reflexive pronouns.

yo	*me* visto	nosotros, -as	*nos* vestimos
tú	*te* vistes		
Ud., él, ella	*me* visto	Uds., ellos, ellas	*se* visten

d. In Spanish reflexive constructions, the definite article is used instead of the possessive adjective with parts of the body or wearing apparel.

Tú te lavas *la* **cara.**	*You wash your face.*
Tú te pones *el* **sombrero.**	*You put your hat on.*

e. The reflexive pronoun normally stands directly before the verb.

> Yo *me* acuesto temprano.
> Tú no *te* vistes rápido.

The reflexive pronoun follows the verb and is attached to it in affirmative commands and when the reflexive verb is used as an infinitive.

AFFIRMATIVE COMMAND	INFINITIVE
Levánta*te*. Levánte*se*. Levánten*se*.	No queremos levantar*nos*. ¿Por qué quieres acostar*te* temprano?

Lección 7

a. The preterit tense of regular verbs is formed by dropping the -AR, -ER, or -IR ending of the infinitive and adding preterit endings.

b. **Dar** takes -ER verb endings in the preterit tense: **di, diste, dio, dimos, dieron**.

c. -AR and -ER verbs with the stem changes in the present tense (**e** to **ie** and **o** to **ue**) have regular stems in the preterit:

	PRESENT TENSE		PRETERIT	
pensar (ie)	*pi*enso	pensamos	pensé	pensamos
	*pi*ensas	*pi*ensan	pensaste	pensaron
	*pi*ensa	*pi*ensan	pensó	pensaron
volver (ue)	*vu*elvo	volvemos	volví	volvimos
	*vu*elves	*vu*elven	volviste	volvieron
	*vu*elve	*vu*elven	volvió	volvieron

-IR verbs with stem changes in the present tense (**e** to **ie**, **o** to **ue**, and **e** to **i**) change **e** to **i** in the third-person singular and plural of the preterit.

	PRESENT TENSE		PRETERIT	
sentir (ie)	*siento*	*sentimos*	*sentí*	*sentimos*
	sientes	*sienten*	*sentiste*	*sintieron*
	siente	*sienten*	*sintió*	*sintieron*
dormir (ue)	*duermo*	*dormimos*	*dormí*	*dormimos*
	duermo	*duermen*	*dormiste*	*durmieron*
	duermo	*duermen*	*durmió*	*durmieron*

d. Many Spanish verbs have irregular preterit forms. **Estar, hacer, poder, poner, querer, tener**, and **venir** have irregular stems and irregular endings common to all these verbs.

yo	estuv	*e*
tú	hic	*iste*
Ud.	pud	*o*
él, ella	pud	*o*
nosotros, -as	quis	*imos*
Uds.	tuv	*ieron*
ellos, ellas	vin	*ieron*

The preterit stem of **hacer** changes **c** to **z** in the third-person singular to keep the original sound: **hizo**.

e. **Ser** and **ir** share the same irregular forms in the preterit. Only the context makes the meaning clear.

ser	fui, fuiste, fue, fuimos, fueron

Yo *fui* **al cine.**   *I went to the movies.*

Yo *fui* **víctima de un robo.**   *I was the victim of a robbery.*

f. Verbs ending in a vowel + **-er** or **-ir** change **i** to **y** in the third-person singular and plural. In the other forms, the **i** has an accent:

leer	leí, leíste, leyó, leímos, leyeron

g. **Decir** and **traer** have irregular preterit tense forms.

	decir	traer
yo	*dije*	traje
tú	*dijiste*	trajiste
Ud., él, ella	*dijo*	trajo
nosotros, -as	*dijimos*	trajimos
Uds., ellos, ellas	*dijeron*	trajeron

Lección 8

a. The imperfect of regular verbs is formed by dropping the -AR, -ER, and -IR ending of the infinitive and adding imperfect endings.

b. There are only three verbs with irregular forms in the imperfect tense.

	ir	ser	ver
yo	*iba*	*era*	*veía*
tú	*ibas*	*eras*	*veías*
Ud., él, ella	*iba*	*era*	*veía*
nosotros, -as	*íbamos*	*éramos*	*veíamos*
Uds., ellos, ellas	*iban*	*eran*	*veían*

Lección 9

a. Uses of the preterit and the imperfect tenses.

IMPERFECT	PRETERIT
Describes repeated or habitual actions (equivalent to English *used* to):	Describes specific events that are not habitual:
Iba al cine todos los sábados.	*Fui* **al cine el sábado pasado.**
Describes an ongoing or continuous action (equivalent to English *was (were)* + . . . *ing*):	Describes a particular action that happened while another action was in progress:

Miguel *dormía* profundamente cuando Jorge *llegó* a su casa.

Lección 10

a. Demonstrative adjectives.

este / esta	*this*	**estos / estas**	*these*
ese / esa	*that*	**esos / esas**	*those*
aquel / aquella	*that*	**aquellos / aquellas**	*those*

b. Demonstrative pronouns.

este / esta	*this one*	**estos / estas**	*these*
ese / esa	*that one*	**esos / esas**	*those*
aquel / aquella	*that one (over there)*	**aquellos / aquellas**	*those*

Actividad A

Here are nine pictures showing what Pepito did yesterday morning. Following the clues given, complete the sentence under each picture.

1. Ayer Pepito _____ a las seis.

2. _____ de la cama inmediatamente.

3. Entró al baño a _____ _____ .

4. _____

5. Salió del baño y _____ _____ .

6. _____

7. Después de vestirse _____ y
fue a desayunar.

8. Después del desayuno _____ .

9. _____ «Adiós» a su mamá y _____ de la casa.

Buscapalabras Hidden in the puzzle are the names of 11 sports and 5 pieces of equipment needed for sports. Circle the words from left to right, right to left, up or down, or diagonally.

A	B	U	K	A	R	A	T	E	Í
L	E	T	A	B	U	E	N	U	L
O	Ñ	L	N	É	F	R	Q	O	U
B	A	O	A	I	V	S	L	O	C
T	T	B	T	S	E	L	O	M	H
E	E	T	A	B	S	B	B	S	A
U	U	Ú	C	O	A	P	I	I	L
Q	Q	F	I	L	S	N	L	L	I
S	A	L	Ó	B	E	B	O	C	B
Á	R	N	N	T	P	L	V	I	R
B	O	X	E	O	C	S	A	C	E

These people used to do different things during the summer. Complete the sentence under each picture, using the imperfect of the appropriate verb.

1. Rosa _____ .

2. Juanita y Julia _____ .

3. El Sr. Gómez _____ .

4. Tú _____ .

5. Uds. _____ .

6. Jorge _____ .

7. Nosotros _____ .

8. Yo _____ .

Actividad D

¿Es Ud. un buen testigo? You are walking down the street when a thief races out of a store and gets into a waiting car, which then speeds away. You have seen the whole incident and are asked to describe what you saw. Examine the following picture very carefully. Then cover the picture and try to answer the following questions.

1. ¿Qué hora era?

_____

2. ¿Cómo era el carro?

_____

3. ¿Cuál era el número de la placa?

_____

4. ¿Tenía el ladrón la cara cubierta?

_____

5. ¿Tenía barba o bigote?

_____

6. ¿Llevaba sombrero?

_____

7. ¿Cuántas personas había en el carro?

_____

8. ¿Qué llevaba el ladrón en las manos?

_____

9. ¿Qué vio el hombre con el periódico?

_____

10. ¿Cuántas personas había en la calle? ¿Dónde estaban?

_____

Crucigrama

		¹B				²		³					
		A			⁴								
		L		⁵									
⁶		O											
		N		⁷									
⁸		C	⁹										
¹⁰		E											
		S											
		T											
		O					¹¹			¹²			
		¹³											
						¹⁴							
						¹⁵							

HORIZONTALES		VERTICALES
1. baseball bat	**10.** martial arts	**1.** basketball (sport)
2. volleyball (sport)	**11.** ball (baseball, tennis)	**3.** wrestling
5. swimming	**13.** helmet	**4.** skating
6. ski; skiing	**14.** ball (basketball, football)	**8.** skates
7. gymnastics	**15.** basket	**9.** sword
		12. tennis

Actividad F

Las seis diferencias

Pablo arrived late to school today. Ms. Fernandez wants to know why. Write a short story in Spanish about the situation you see in the pictures in which Pablo explains the reasons why he was late and how his teacher responds:

Perdón, señora Fernández, pero mi reloj despertador no funcionó y me levanté tarde.

_____

_____

_____

_____

_____

_____

Tercera Parte

11

En la tienda de ropa

Direct-Object Pronouns

1  **Vocabulario**

vestidor

la cliente

la blusa

la sudadera

el maniquí

la bata de baño

el abrigo

la falda

la dependiente

las medias

la bufanda

los zapatos

los guantes

las zapatillas

la camisa de dormir

los calcetines

el cinturón

el bolso la cartera

la gorra

la gabardina/ el impermeable

la pijama

la bata de casa

la camisa

el suéter

el chaleco

la camiseta

el paraguas

el saco de sport

la chaqueta

los zapatos de tenis

Actividad A

You need to buy some clothes and you go shopping with a friend. What would you buy in this store? Work with a partner. One student says: **¿Te gusta esto? ¿Quieres ese saco? ¿Qué (más) necesitas?**

EXAMPLE: **¿Quieres** *esta bufanda?*

Sí, necesito *una bufanda* **para el invierno.**

1. _____   5. _____

2. _____   6. _____

3. _____   7. _____

4. _____   8. _____

Actividad B

You are writing a story and have four characters in mind. Here are their descriptions. What clothes would you have them wear? Use the new words and those you already know. Here are some more helpful expressions.

de manga corta	*short-sleeved*	**el cuello**	*collar*
de manga larga	*long-sleeved*	**(ultra)moderno**	*(ultra)modern*
sin mangas	*sleeveless*	**estrecho**	*narrow*

el algodón *cotton*	**el botón** *button*
la lana *wool*	**de tres botones** *three-buttoned*
ancho *wide*	**el raso** *satin*
la tela *fabric, material*	**la seda** *silk*
a rayas *striped*	**de piel** *leather*
a cuadros *check, plaid*	**de goma** *rubber*

Some people are coming down from college. Read each of the descriptions that follow and select the correct person.

Tomás: Un joven de 20 años. Toma clases en la universidad. Tiene ideas muy modernas y originales. Quiere ser actor.

Mario: Un hombre de 30 años. Es un abogado serio, inteligente y práctico. Quiere ganar mucho dinero.

Dolores: Una chica de 21 años. Es refinada y elegante. Quiere ser modelo y le gusta la música moderna.

Sarita: Una chica de 19 años. De día, trabaja de secretaria y, de noche, toma cursos en la universidad. Quiere ser científica. Es alegre, simpática y estudiosa.

Tomás lleva _____

_____

Mario lleva _____

_____

Dolores lleva _____

_____

Sarita lleva _____

_____

Un vestido de fiesta

Liliana recibió el regalo de Navidad de sus padres— ¡doscientos dólares! ¿Qué va a hacer con tanto dinero? Pues hay una fiesta de año nuevo en casa de Blanquita. Sí, con el dinero que tiene puede comprar un vestido magnífico. Va a ser la chica más elegante de la fiesta. Necesita un vestido especial, y sabe exactamente en qué tienda **lo** puede comprar— la boutique francesa «Chez Fifí». Cuando entra en la tienda, una vendedora **la** saluda:

VENDEDORA: Buenas tardes, señorita. ¿En qué puedo servirle?

LILIANA: Necesito un vestido de fiesta de talla siete para un baile de año nuevo.

VENDEDORA: ¿Qué le parece este vestido de raso rojo?

LILIANA: No me gusta. Me parece muy ordinario.

VENDEDORA: Esta combinación de blusa blanca de encaje y minifalda negra es muy popular ahora. Sólo vale cien dólares.

LILIANA: No está mal. Pero yo prefiero algo más original, más sofisticado.

VENDEDORA: Ajá. Entiendo perfectamente. Aquí tiene un vestido de seda azul que es precisamente para Ud. Es único. No hay otro igual.

LILIANA: Oh, me encanta. ¿Puedo probar**lo**?

VENDEDORA: Sí, claro. Sígame, señorita. (Liliana se **lo** prueba. Está encantada.)

VENDEDORA: El vestido le va muy bien. Es además muy «chic», muy de moda.

LILIANA: **Lo** compro. ¿Cuánto cuesta?

VENDEDORA: Para Ud., solamente 250 dólares.

LILIANA: Pero tengo sólo doscientos dólares. ¡Qué lástima! Entonces compro la blusa con minifalda.

La noche de la fiesta, Liliana entra en casa de Blanquita y ve a sus tres amigas, Conchita, Lolita y Panchita. Las tres tienen la cara triste y están vestidas exactamente igual— ¡con un vestido de seda azul!

LILIANA: ¿Qué pasó, chicas? ¿Por qué tan tristes? ¿Cómo es que llevan el mismo vestido?

CONCHITA: ¿No te gusta mi vestido muy «chic»?

LOLITA: Sí, es único. No hay otro igual en el mundo.

PANCHITA: Si veo a la vendedora de Chez Fifí **la** mato.

me encanta
  I love it
probar *to try on*

ir bien *to fit*
de moda
  fashionable,
  in-style

matar *to kill*

Actividad C

Answer the following questions about the story.

1. ¿Cuánto dinero recibió Liliana?

   _____

2. ¿Qué tipo de fiesta hay en casa de Blanquita?

   _____

3. ¿Qué quiere comprar Liliana?

   _____

4. ¿En qué tienda piensa encontrar el vestido que busca?

   _____

5. ¿Por qué no le gusta a Liliana el vestido rojo?

   _____

6. Según la vendedora, ¿cómo es el vestido de seda azul?

   _____

7. ¿Por qué no compra Liliana el vestido azul?

   _____

8. ¿Qué ropa compra Liliana para la fiesta?

   _____

9. ¿Cómo se llaman las tres amigas de Liliana?

   _____

10. ¿Por qué están tristes?

    _____

2   Examine the following paragraph.

I have a Spanish book. I find my Spanish book very useful. I read my Spanish book, study my Spanish book, and refer to my Spanish book before taking a test.

Pretty repetitious! How about his version:

I have a Spanish book. I find it very useful. I read it, study it, and refer to it before taking a test.

Much better, isn't it? What have we done? We have substituted an object pronoun (*it*) instead of repeating the same noun (*Spanish book*). We can do the same thing in Spanish. Look at these sentences from the story.

> **Ella necesita un vestido especial y sabe dónde *lo* puede comprar.**
>
> *She needs a special dress, and she knows where she can buy it.*

> **Cuando la chica entra en la tienda, una vendedora *la* saluda.**
>
> *When the girl enters the store, a saleswoman greets her.*

Which noun in the first sentence is replaced by **lo**? _____ . What

is the gender of **el vestido**? _____ . Which noun in the second

sentence is replaced by **la**? _____ . What is the gender of **la chica**?

_____ .

Lo and **la** are direct-object pronouns; **lo** replaces a masculine singular noun, and **la** replaces a feminine singular noun. **Lo** and **la** have the plural forms **los** and **las**. **Lo, la, los,** and **las** may refer to people or things.

Look at these other examples.

> **¿Compras el impermeable? Sí, *lo* compro.**
>
> *Are you buying the raincoat? Yes, I'm buying it.*

> **¿Ves a la vendedora? No, no *la* veo.**
>
> *Do you see the saleswoman? No, I don't see her.*

> **¿Recibiste los regalos? Sí, *los* recibí.**
>
> *Did you receive the books? Yes, I received them.*

> **¿Venden batas aquí? No, no *las* venden.**
>
> *Do they sell robes here? No, they don't sell them.*

Where do **lo, la,** and **las** stand in relation to the verb? _____ . Contrary to English, the Spanish object pronoun comes directly before the verb.

Substitute a direct-object pronoun for the word in italic type.

EXAMPLE: **Necesito** *el libro*.   *Lo* **necesito.**

1. El doctor examina *los ojos*.

   _____

2. Ellos traen *un vaso*.

   _____

3. No veo *la pizarra*.

   _____

4. No escribimos *las cartas*.

   _____

5. El maestro explica *la lección*.

   _____

6. ¿Compras *los periódicos*?

   _____

7. La señora no vende *frutas*.

   _____

8. Tenemos *el abrigo* aquí.

   _____

You are going on a trip and your mother wants to know what you are taking with you. Answer her questions.

EXAMPLE: **¿Llevas** *la camisa* **de seda?**   **Sí,** *la* **llevo.**

1. ¿Llevas los pantalones negros?

   _____

2. ¿Llevas el impermeable?

_____

3. ¿Llevas la bufanda azul?

_____

4. ¿Llevas las botas de piel?

_____

5. ¿Llevas ese sombrero viejo?

_____

6. ¿Llevas la bata de casa?

_____

7. ¿Llevas las pantuflas?

_____

8. ¿Llevas los suéteres nuevos?

_____

You are giving a party and your best friend wants to know who is going and what foods you will serve. Answer his questions.

EXAMPLE: **¿Invitaste a Juan?**   **Sí,** _lo_ **invité.**

1. ¿Invitaste a Rosa?

_____

2. ¿Invitaste a los hermanos Gómez?

_____

3. ¿Invitaste a Julia y a María?

_____

4. ¿Compraste los helados de chocolate?

_____

5. ¿Preparaste sándwiches de queso?

_____

6. ¿Hizo tu mamá la torta?

_____

7. ¿Tienes bastantes sodas?

_____

8. ¿Compraste el pastel?

_____

Carmen has just met Andrés at a party. They discover that they have a lot in common. Work with a partner.

EXAMPLE: CARMEN:—**Yo hago las tareas por la noche.**

ANDRÉS:—**Yo también** _las_ **hago por la noche.**

CARMEN: Yo tomo el autobús para ir a la escuela.

ANDRÉS: _____

CARMEN: Yo tengo amigos mexicanos.

ANDRÉS: _____

CARMEN: Yo estudio matemáticas.

ANDRÉS: _____

CARMEN: Yo toco el piano muy bien.

ANDRÉS: _____

CARMEN: Yo escucho música clásica todos los días.

ANDRÉS: _____

How can you tell your best friend in Spanish that you saw him?
How do you ask him if he saw you? Look at this short dialog.

TÚ:	**Ayer *te* vi por la calle con tus padres.**
TU AMIGO:	**¿Sí? ¿*Nos* viste? ¿Por qué no *nos* saludaste?**
TÚ:	**Uds. estaban muy lejos. ¿No *me* viste tú?**
TU AMIGO:	**No, no *te* vi.**

Here's a complete table of the Spanish direct-object pronouns.

me	*me*
te	*you* (familiar)
lo	*you* (formal), *him, it* (masculine)
la	*you* (formal), *her, it* (feminine)
nos	*us*
los	*them, you* (masculine plural)
las	*them, you* (feminine plural)

Express the following in Spanish:

EXAMPLE: (*called me*) **Mi mamá me llamó hace una hora.**

1. Nuestros abuelos siempre _____ _____ al cine. (*take us*)

2. Tus amigos _____ _____ muchas veces. (*visit you*)

3. Usted _____ _____ esta mañana. (*saw her*)

4. Yo _____ _____ a la fiesta. (*invited them* [feminine])

5. ¿ _____ _____ Uds. en el juego de béisbol? (*saw us*)

6. ¿ _____ _____ tus padres? (*understand you*)

7. Mis padres no _____ _____ (*understand me*)

 We saw that the direct-object pronouns come before the verb. There are some situations, however, in which they take a different position. Look at these examples:

Compra el libro. Cómpra*lo*.	*Buy the book. Buy it.*
Abre la ventana. Ábre*la*.	*Open the window. Open it.*
Escriba Ud. las cartas. Escríba*las*.	*Write the letters. Write them.*
Visita a tus abuelos. Visíta*los*.	*Visit you grandparents. Visit them.*

Are these commands affirmative or negative? _____ . Where is the

direct-object pronoun in these commands? _____ .

RULE: In affirmative (but NOT negative) commands, the direct-object pronoun follows the verb and is attached to it. In negative commands (informal and formal) the direct-object pronoun goes <u>before</u> the verb.

> FORMAL: **No lo compre Ud.**
>
> INFORMAL: **No lo compres.**

NOTE: When attaching a pronoun to an affirmative command, an accent mark is placed on the stressed vowel to keep the original stress. Why is this necessary?

First, let's review some rules of Spanish pronunciation:

- Words ending in a vowel, **n**, or **s** are stressed on the next-to-last syllable (the one just before the end):

casa	**Car**men	**te**nis
clase	**ha**blan	hambur**gue**sa
como		

- When a word ends in a consonant (except **n** or **s**), the stress is on the last syllable:

a**zul**	hospi**tal**	profe**sor**
ten**er**	cami**nar**	liber**tad**

- Any word not following the above rules must have a written accent mark over the vowel of the syllable being stressed:

fútbol	te**lé**fono	cora**zón**	lec**ción**
lágrima	**mú**sica	**Bár**bara	Fran**cés**

Now let's look at some affirmative commands:

compra   **a**bre   es**cri**ba

The stress is on the next-to-the-last syllable. Now add a pronoun:

cómpralo   **á**brela   es**crí**balas

According to the rules of Spanish pronunciation, the stress should fall on the next-to-the last syllable of these words, but to keep the original stress, we must add an accent mark.

compralo: **có**mpralo   abrela: **á**brela   escribalas: es**crí**bales

Repeat the following commands, replacing the noun by a direct-object pronoun.

1. Aprende la lección.

_____

2. Estudia los verbos.

_____

3. No cierres la puerta.

_____

4. Compra las revistas.

_____

5. Llama a Juan.

_____

6. No despiertes a tu hermana.

_____

7. Escucha al profesor.

_____

8. Lee esos capítulos.

_____

9. Haz las tareas.

_____

10. No prepares la comida.

_____

5 Now look at these sentences:

I	II	MEANING
Quiero *verte* **hoy.**	**Te** *quiero* **ver hoy.**	*I want to see you today.*
Pedro va a *llamarme.*	**Pedro** *me va* **a llamar.**	*Peter is going to call me.*
Él viene a *visitarnos.*	**Él** *nos viene* **a visitar.**	*He is coming to visit us.*
Voy a *comprarlos.*	**Los voy** **a comprar.**	*I'm going to buy them.*

How many verbs are in each Spanish sentence? _____ . Which form

does the second verb have? _____ . Where is the direct-object pronoun

in column I? _____ . Is it attached to the infinitive? _____ .

Where is the direct-object pronoun in column II? _____ .

RULE: When a direct-object pronoun is used with an infinitive, it may follow
and is attached to the infinitive, or it may precede the conjugated form of
the other verb.

Actividad **J**

Work with a partner. You are told to do some things and you answer that you will
do them:

EXAMPLES: lavar los platos
        MADRE: **Lava los platos.**
        UD.: **Voy a lavarlos.**

1. hacer las tareas

MAESTRA: _____

UD.: _____

2. lavar el carro

PADRE: _____

UD.: _____

3. leer el artículo

PROFESOR: _____

UD.: _____

4. comer las legumbres

HERMANA: _____

UD.: _____

5. abrir la ventana

ESTUDIANTE: _____

UD.: _____

6. llamar al doctor

POLICÍA: _____

UD.: _____

7. comprar los zapatos

HERMANO: _____

UD.: _____

8. servir la comida

MAMÁ: _____

UD.: _____

9. escribir las cartas

PADRES: _____

UDS.: _____

10. traer el dinero

COMERCIANTE: _____

UD.: _____

Actividad K

Work with a partner. You're talking on the phone with a friend. Answer the questions, using a direct-object pronoun in each sentence.

EXAMPLES: **¿Escuchaste las noticias hoy?**
Sí, *las* escuché.

1. ¿Viste el vídeo nuevo que salió?

_____

2. ¿Leíste el periódico esta mañana?

_____

3. ¿Viste a Gloria y a Clara en el concierto?

_____

4. ¿Quieres visitar a Raúl?

_____

5. ¿Terminaste la tarea de biología?

_____

6. ¿Miraste el partido de béisbol en la televisión?

_____

7. ¿Vas a comprar las entradas para el cine?

_____

8. ¿Conociste a la nueva profesora?

_____

Preguntas Personales

1. ¿Cómo te vistes para ir a una fiesta elegante?

   _____

2. ¿Cómo te vistes para ir a la escuela?

   _____

3. ¿Qué ropa recibiste en tu último cumpleaños?

   _____

4. ¿Cuándo compras ropa nueva?

   _____

5. ¿Qué compraste la última vez que fuiste de compras?

   _____

DIÁLOGO

You go into a department store to buy some presents.

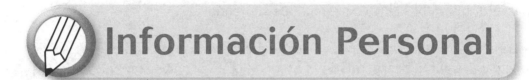

Your parents just gave you $500 to buy clothes. What are some things you would buy, in what colors, material, and so on: **Voy a comprar** . . .

1. _____

   _____

2. _____

   _____

3. _____

   _____

4. _____

   _____

5. _____

   _____

6. _____

   _____

Cápsula cultural

La ropa, los colores y la suerte

Es obvio que la ropa es esencial en nuestra sociedad de hoy. Una nota interesante son las prendas que se usan para ciertas fechas o festividades. Es importante la prenda y también el color de la prenda.

Por ejemplo, en la mayoría de los países hispanoamericanos existe una tradición curiosa para atraer la prosperidad y el amor en la Víspera de Año Nuevo. Hay que ponerse una prenda interior de cierto color. En Puerto Rico, las mujeres se ponen ropa interior amarilla para la buena suerte. Lo mismo pasa en Colombia, aunque en ese país hay que ponerse la prenda revés. En México los colores son el amarillo y el rojo: amarillo para la prosperidad y rojo para el amor. En España, la ropa interior es rosada. Además, estas prendas tienen que ser nuevas.

Otra costumbre que encontramos en algunas regiones de España es que las novias tienen que llevar algo viejo y algo prestado el día de su casamiento. Una costumbre bonita entre los mexicanos ocurre al principio de la primavera: la gente se viste de blanco, indicando así el fin de una temporada y el comienzo de otra, y van a las pirámides de Teotihuacán.

Discusión

1. ¿Cuáles son algunas costumbres curiosas de algunos países hispanoamericanos?

2. ¿Qué quiere la gente generalmente para Año Nuevo?

3. ¿Qué tradición de las novias hispanas es similar a la de las novias americanas?

4. ¿Qué hacen los mexicanos al principio de la primavera? ¿Por qué?

5. Describe algunas costumbres curiosas en los Estados Unidos.

VOCABULARIO

la prenda *article of clothing*
lo mismo *the same*
aunque *although*
al revés *inside out*

la novia *bride*
el casamiento *wedding, marriage*
vestirse *to get dressed*

12

Vivimos en la ciudad

Indirect-Object Pronouns

1 Vocabulary

el rascacielos — el letrero — el aeropuerto — el supermercado — la carretera — el edificio — la iglesia — el semáforo — la calle — la estación de bomberos — el banco — la avenida — la acera — el taxi — la farola — la patrulla (de policía) — la señal de tráfico — el camión — la moto — el subterráneo / el metro — la parada de autobús — los pasajeros — el conductor — el peatón — el/la policía — la cabina telefónica

Your five-year-old nephew is visiting you from the country. You take a ride on the bus with him pointing out different things found in the city.

EXAMPLE: **Mira** *el supermercado.*

1. _____

2. _____

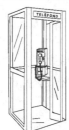

3. _____

4. _____

5. _____

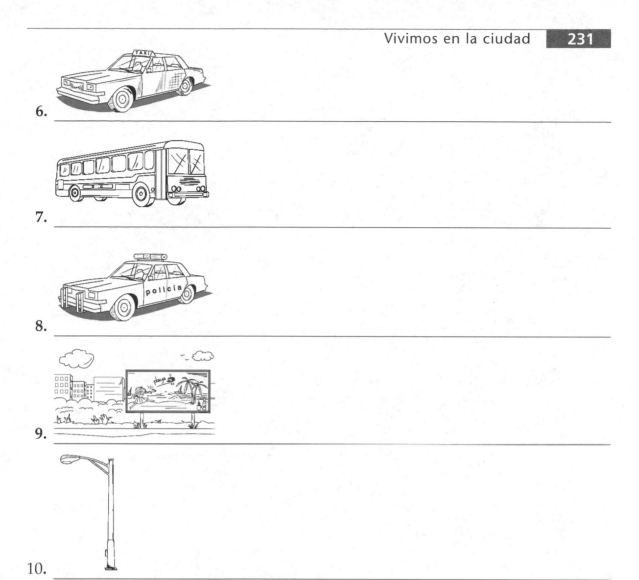

6. _____

7. _____

8. _____

9. _____

10. _____

Actividad B

Where are they going? Work with a partner. One student asks the questions; the other one answers, telling where each person is going.

EXAMPLE: **¿Adónde va el enfermo?**   _Va al doctor._

1. _____

2. _____

3. _____

4. _____

5. _____

6. _____

7. _____

8. _____

9. _____

Pepita aprende a manejar

You have already learned the direct-object pronouns. Pay attention now to other pronouns you will find in this story.

Los padres de Pepita **le** van a dar un carro deportivo rojo para su cumpleaños. Antes de comprarlo, el papá decidió dar**le** unas clases de manejar a Pepita. Ella tiene hoy su primera clase y está muy nerviosa porque su padre **le** habla contínuamente.

manejar _to drive_

Primero, **le** muestra todas las diferentes partes del automóvil y **le** dice: —«Recuerda, hija, maneja siempre muy despacio». Es importante. Pepita lo hace bastante bien. Sin embargo, su papá **le** grita: «Presta atención a las señales de tránsito. Maneja con cuidado. Tienes una parada en esa esquina. Mira los otros carros. Ten cuidado. Presta atención a los peatones, especialmente a los niños.» Y **les** grita a los otros choferes: «¡Cuidado! Mi hija está aprendiendo a manejar».

Al final de la clase Pepita está completamente exhausta y más nerviosa que antes. Está muy contenta de ser pasajera otra vez. Su padre está contentísimo porque Pepita no tuvo un accidente. **Le** dice: «Gracias a Dios que no mataste a nadie, pero antes de compra**rte** el carro, tengo que da**rte** muchas clases más. Tienes mucho que aprender.»

De repente, oyen la sirena de un carro de policía que estaba en la esquina. Un policía sale del carro y **les** dice: «Señor, ¿no vio Ud. la luz roja? Lo siento, pero tengo que poner**le** una multa. Me parece que Ud. necesita algunas clases de manejar. ¿No es verdad, señorita?»

multa *fine, ticket*

Conteste con frases completas:

1. ¿Qué regalo va a recibir Pepita?

_____

2. ¿Qué decidió su papá antes de comprarlo?

_____

3. ¿Cómo está Pepita antes de la clase? ¿Por qué?

_____

4. ¿Qué le muestra su padre?

_____

5. ¿Cómo maneja Pepita?

_____

6. ¿A quiénes debe prestar atención Pepita?

_____

7. ¿Qué les grita el padre a los otros choferes?

_____

8. ¿Cómo está Pepita al final de la clase?

_____

9. ¿Qué dice el policía al papá de Pepita?

_____

10. ¿Qué hace el policía?

_____

Actividad C

There's been an accident at the corner of _____ and _____ . There were two witnesses. Unfortunately, they described the scene differently. Can you spot the six discrepancies?

Las seis diferencias

 Look at the following sentences:

Él dio un regalo *a su mamá.* { *He gave her mother a present.*
                                     He gave a present to her mother.

Ella dio un regalo *a sus amigos.* { *She gave her friends a present.*
                                         She gave a present to her friends.

What is the subject in both Spanish sentences? _____ The verb?

_____ The direct object? _____ . What are **a su madre** and

a sus amigos? _____ . They are indirect objects. An indirect object

indicates *to whom* or *for whom* the action is done.

Now look at these sentences:

Ella *le dio* un regalo. { *She gave her a present.*
                               She gave a present to her.

Ella *les dio* un regalo. { *She gave them a present.*
                                She gave a present to them.

Which word has replaced **a su mamá** in the first sentence? _____ .

Which word has replaced **a sus amigos** in the second sentence? _____ .

Le and **les** are indirect-object pronouns. They stand before the verb and may refer
to either masculine or feminine nouns. Here are some more examples:

Le doy un reloj *a mi hermano.* { *I give my brother a watch.*
                                       I give a watch to my brother.

Le doy un reloj. { *I give him a watch.*
                       I give a watch to him.

Le presto un disco *a Ud.* { *I lend you a record.*
                                  I lend a record to you.

Le presto un disco. { *I lend you a record.*
                          I lend a record to you.

Él *les* presta libros *a Uds.*   *He lends you books.*
Él *les* presta libros.   *He lends books to you.*

Les doy un regalo *a mis hermanas.*   *I give a present to my sisters.*
Les doy un regalo.   *I give them a present.*

NOTE: Indirect-object pronouns stand before the verb. In everyday Spanish
indirect-object pronouns are normally used, even when the indirect-object
noun is expressed.

Les **digo la verdad** *a mis padres.*   *I tell the truth to my parents.*

Le **sirvo el café** *a Juan.*   *I serve coffee to Juan.*

Here's a table of the indirect-object pronouns:

me	*(to, for) me*
te	*(to, for) you*
le	*(to, for) you* (formal), *him, her*
nos	*(to, for) us*
les	*(to, for) you* (plural), *them*

Substitute an indirect-object pronoun for the expression in parentheses. Work with a partner.

EXAMPLE: Compañero: Presto dinero (*a mi hermano*)
Ud.:   ***Le*** **presto dinero.**

1. La maestra enseña la lección   (*a los alumnos*)

_____

2. El Sr. Pérez da flores   (*a su esposa*)

_____

3. El policía pone una multa   (*al chofer*)

_____

4. José hace una pregunta   (*a las muchachas*)

_____

5. Muestro mi carro nuevo   (*a mis amigos*)

_____

6. Mi papá compró un regalo   (*a mi mamá*)

_____

7. El abuelo cuenta historias   (*a los niños*)

_____

8. Mi hermano presta su bicicleta   (*a su amigo*)

_____

9. La vendedora vendió un vestido   (*a Mercedes*)

_____

10. Ud. da trabajo   (*a los jóvenes*)

_____

 Where do the direct-object pronouns stand in affirmative commands?

Cómpra*lo*.   *Buy it.*

Escríba*los*.   *Write them*

Where do they stand in sentences with an infinitive?

Voy a comprar*lo*. ⎫
_Lo_ voy a comprar. ⎭   *I'm going to buy it.*

The same rules apply to the indirect-object pronouns:

Escriba una carta a sus padres.   **_Escríbales_ una carta.**
Write you parents a letter.   *Write them a letter.*

Trae la comida a tu hermanito.   **_Tráele_ la comida.**
Bring the food to your brother.   *Bring him the food.*

Quiero _preguntarle_ algo. ⎫
Le quiero preguntar algo. ⎭   *I want to ask him (her, you) something.*

You are on a trip with your parents and your mother is trying to decide what presents to buy and what postcards to send. You are helping her.

EXAMPLE: ¿Mando esta tarjeta a Pablo?   **Sí, mánda*le* esta tarjeta.**

1. ¿Regalo esa bufanda? (*a mi hermana*)

2. ¿Mando esa tarjeta?   (*a tus abuelos*)

_____

3. ¿Compro esos discos?   (*a mis amigos*)

_____

4. ¿Escribo esas tarjetas?   (*a los Gómez*)

_____

5. ¿Mando aquella tarjeta?   (*a José*)

_____

6. ¿Compro este juguete?   (*a tu hermanito*)

_____

Actividad **F**

Your brother always wants to do what you do:

EXAMPLE: Tú dices: Quiero dar flores a mamá.
            Él dice: **Yo también quiero darle flores.**

1. Necesito hablar.   (*a mis padres*)

_____

2. Quiero escribir una carta.   (*al editor*)

_____

3. Debo servir refrescos.   (*a mis amigos*)

_____

4. Voy a prestar mi bicicleta.   (*a Juan*)

_____

5. Quiero dar unos discos.   (*a Juan y a Tomás*)

_____

6. Voy a hacer una pregunta.   (*a la profesora*)

_____

Actividad G

Your mother is a wonderful cook and likes to prepare special dishes for each member of the family. Express in Spanish what she prepares for various family members.

EXAMPLE: arroz con pollo / mi papá
Le prepara **arroz con pollo a mi papá.**

1. carne con papas / mis hermanos

_____

2. flan / mi abuela

_____

3. pollo / mis tías

_____

4. pescado / mi hermana

_____

5. legumbres / mi abuelo

_____

4   Look at these sentences:

Mis padres *me* regalaron un carro deportivo.   *My parents gave me a sports car.*

¿Qué *te* dieron de regalo de cumpleaños?   *What did they give you as a birthday present?*

La profesora *nos* preparó una sorpresa.   *The teacher prepared a surprise for us.*

What object pronouns do you recognize in these sentences? _____ , _____ , and _____ . In Spanish, **me, te,** and **nos** are both direct and indirect-object pronouns.

Actividad H

A friend asks you these questions. What are your answers? Work with a partner.

1. ¿Cuándo me darás el dinero?

_____

2. ¿Qué tareas les dieron hoy?

_____

3. ¿Me ayudas con el trabajo?

_____

4. ¿Puedes explicarme la lección?

_____

5. ¿Quién te compró esa bicicleta?

_____

6. ¿Qué te dieron tus padres?

_____

7. ¿Quién les dio la noticia?

_____

8. ¿Qué te preguntó el policía?

_____

Actividad I

You are writing a letter to a friend. Complete it with the appropriate indirect-object pronouns:

Querida Rosario:

Hoy fui de compras. A mi mamá _____ compré un suéter muy bonito
                                                1.
y a mis hermanos _____ compré juguetes. No _____ escribí
                              2.   3.
antes porque estuve muy ocupada. Ayer _____ mandé tarjetas a todos
                                                  4.

los chicos de la clase. A José, por supuesto, _____ escribí una larga
                                              5.
carta. El viaje _____ gustó mucho; el guía _____ prometió a
                 6.   7.
nosotros una excursión para mañana. Bueno, ya _____ conté muchas
                                                    8.
cosas. ¡Escribe _____ pronto!
                    9.

Actividad J

You are telling your friend Pablo what happened last night at a restaurant. Express the following in Spanish:

1. The waiter brought us the menu.

   _____

2. My mother told him: "Bring me a sandwich."

   _____

3. The waiter answered her: "I'm sorry, but at this hour I cannot serve you (plural) sandwiches."

   _____

4. "What can you serve us?" my mother asked him.

   _____

5. We didn't like anything.

   _____

6. We went out and my mother said to my father: "I told you (informal) that this restaurant is bad."

   _____

Preguntas Personales

1. ¿Qué instituciones te pueden ayudar en caso de emergencias?

   _____

2. ¿Adónde vas si tienes una enfermedad seria?

_____

3. ¿Cómo viajas de una parte a otra en tu ciudad?

_____

4. ¿Por qué es preferible ir de compras en un supermercado?

_____

5. ¿Cuáles son las ventajas y desventajas de los rascacielos?

_____

Información Personal

Tell how you get about town, how do you get to school, what means of transportation do you use when going out, etc.

_____

_____

_____

_____

_____

_____

_____

_____

_____

Composición

Talk about the city you live in. What are some of the advantages and disadvantages of living there. Take a ride through you neighborhood and describe what you see in the streets.

DIÁLOGO

Rosalinda is riding in a taxi.

Cápsula cultural

La ciudad más grande del mundo hispano

Cuando llegó a México, el conquistador Hernán Cortés descubrió la bella ciudad azteca de Tenochtitlán. La ciudad estaba construida sobre pequeñas islas en medio de un lago enorme—el Lago Texcoco. El lago, rodeado de montañas, estaba al lado de dos volcanes cubiertos perpetuamente de nieve—Ixtaccíhuatl y Popocatépetl. La ciudad con sus 300,000 (trescientos mil) habitantes tenía un sistema avanzado de puentes, grandes avenidas, templos, mercados y edificios públicos comparables a cualquier ciudad europea de ese tiempo.

Había canales por toda la ciudad y los acueductos llevaban agua fresca a la ciudad desde manantiales de una colina cercana. Carreteras con puentes levadizos conectaban Tenochtitlán a la tierra que la rodeaba.

Hoy día la ciudad de México D.F. (Distrito Federal), construida sobre las ruinas de la ciudad azteca de Tenochtitlán, es la capital más antigua del continente americano y la concentración urbana más grande del mundo hispano. Esta ciudad enorme de edificios modernos y de rascacielos tiene una población de más de 20,000,000 (veinte millones) de habitantes y todavía está creciendo rápidamente mientras que miles de mexicanos llegan a la capital en busca de trabajo. En la Ciudad de México, hay más de 18,000 taxis y aproximadamente dos y medio millones más de vehículos de toda clase.

Discusión

1. Describa la ciudad azteca de Tenochtitlán en los tiempos de Cortés.

2. ¿Dónde estaba la ciudad? ¿Para qué servían las carreteras y puentes?

3. ¿Cuál es la capital de México hoy? ¿Qué significan las letras D.F.?

4. Describa la capital hoy. ¿Qué cree que son sus mayores problemas?

Para investigar

¿Cuáles son las cinco ciudades más grandes del mundo hispano? Descríbalas.

VOCABULARIO

rodeado *surrounded*

el manantial *(water) spring*

la colina *hill*

el puente levadizo *drawbridge*

el rascacielos *skyscraper*

crecer *to grow*

en busca de *in search of*

13

En la farmacia

las vitaminas

el jabón

las aspirinas

la venda

el papel higiénico

la curita

el yodo

los pañuelos de papel

el algodón

el antibiótico

el desodorante

el cliente

las pastillas

el farmacéutico

la receta

el peine

el cepillo de dientes

el jarabe para la tos

el termómetro

la pasta de dientes

You have learned the names of certain things you can buy in a drugstore. Let's read a conversation between Isabel and a pharmacist. Isabel's little brother is sick and her mother has sent her to the drugstore to buy some things.

FARMACÉUTICO: ¿En qué puedo servirle?

ISABEL: Mi hermanito está enfermo y mi mamá dice que necesita varias medicinas y un termómetro.

FARMACÉUTICO: ¿Tiene fiebre su hermanito?

ISABEL: Creo que sí. Pero no tenemos termómetro para tomársela.

FARMACÉUTICO: ¿Qué más necesita?

ISABEL: Mi hermanito también tose y estornuda mucho. Le duelen la cabeza y la garganta.

toser *to cough*
estornudar *to sneeze*
la gripe *flu*
el catarro *cold*

FARMACÉUTICO: Seguramente tiene gripe o un catarro muy fuerte. Déle estas aspirinas cada cuatro horas. Aquí tiene también un jarabe para la tos y unas pastillas para la garganta.

ISABEL: Gracias. Como mi hermanito estornuda mucho, siempre tiene que sonarse las narices. Déme una caja de pañuelos de papel y un paquete de chicle, por favor.

sonarse las narices *to blow one's nose*
la caja *box*
chicle *chewing gum*

FARMACÉUTICO: Aquí está todo. Pero no comprendo por qué su mamá necesita chicle para su hermano.

ISABEL: El chicle no es para mi hermano. ¡Es para mí!

Actividad A

Your mother has sent you to the drugstore with a shopping list. Tell what you would like. **Necesito . . .**

1. _____   2. _____

3. _____

4. _____

5. _____

6. _____

7. _____

8. _____

Actividad B

Work with a partner. You are the pharmacist in the neighborhood drugstore. The people in the pictures below seem to be suffering from something. What do they need? (Some people may need more than one item!)

EXAMPLE: CLIENTE: No sé si tengo fiebre.
           FARMACÉUTICO: **Ud. necesita *un termómetro*.**

1. _____

_____

2. _____

_____

3. _____

4. _____

5. _____

6. _____

 Do you think that advertisements influence your life? Let's read a story about them.

Los anuncios comerciales

La influencia de los anuncios comerciales está en todas partes—en los periódicos, en las revistas, en la televisión, en los autobuses y en carteleras por las carreteras. Para bien o para mal, son una parte importante de nuestra cultura y de nuestra vida diaria. Ellos nos dicen qué debemos comer, beber, llevar y comprar para vivir bien. ¿Tiene Ud. dolor de cabeza? Sólo cierta marca de aspirina puede ayudarle. ¿Va Ud. a una cita importante? Entonces necesita cierto desodorante o jabón para "estar seguro". Muchos niños aprenden las melodías y la letra de los anuncios comerciales antes de aprender a leer y a escribir. Aquí tiene varios anuncios comunes. ¿Reconoce algunos?

la cartelera *billboard*
la carretera *highway*

la cita *appointment*

la letra *lyrics*

Oportunidad única

¿Lo miran a Ud., tratando de no reírse, cuando Ud. pasa con su carro viejo y feo? Ud. puede ser la envidia de sus amigos y conocidos. Por solo unos pocos dólares, Ud. puede manejar el carro que siempre deseaba. ¿No tiene dinero? No hay problema. ¿Tiene crédito malo? No importa. Vaya hoy mismo a nuestro lote de carros usados de último modelo y siéntese dentro del volante del automóvil de sus sueños.

¡Yo tenía miedo de sonreír!

Iba por el mundo con la boca cerrada. No quería mostrar mis dientes amarillos y manchados. Me sentía tímido y extraño. Luego descubrí la pasta de dientes "*Dentiblanc*" y con ella el secreto de los dientes blancos y limpios. "*Dentiblanc*" está basada en una fórmula secreta europea de doble acción, que deja los dientes brillantes y el aliento agradable. Compre un tubo hoy, y si no está completamente satisfecho, puede devolvérnoslo para recibir todo el dinero que pagó. Le enviamos de vuelta el dinero que pagó por él. "*Dentiblanc*" le permite sonreír con confianza otra vez!

manchado *stained*

dejar *to leave*
el aliento *breath*
devolver *to return*

Discusión

1. ¿Dónde hay anuncios comerciales?

_____

2. ¿Qué nos dicen los anuncios?

_____

3. ¿Qué aprenden muchos niños?

_____

4. ¿Cuánto dinero necesita para vivir bien?

_____

5. Describe tu anuncio de televisión favorito.

_____

6. En el anuncio, ¿por qué iba el hombre por el mundo con la boca cerrada?

_____

7. ¿Qué hace la fórmula secreta de la pasta de dientes?

_____

2   You have already learned the direct- and indirect-object pronouns. Here they are again summarized.

DIRECT-OBJECT PRONOUNS		INDIRECT-OBJECT PRONOUNS	
me	*me*	**me**	*(to) me*
te	*you* (familiar)	**te**	*(to) you*
lo	*you* (formal), *him, it* (masculine)	**le**	*(to) you* (formal) *him, her*
la	*you* (formal), *her, it* (feminine)	**nos**	*(to) us*
nos	*us*	**les**	*(to) you* (plural), *them*
los	*them, you* (masculine plural)		
las	*them, you* (feminine plural)		

There are many times when you need to use the above pronouns together. Look at the following sentences:

Ella *me* **da** *la pasta de dientes.*	*She gives me the toothpaste.*
Ella *me la* **da.**	*She gives it to me.*
Tu mamá *te* **compró** *el peine.*	*Your mother bought you the comb.*
Tu mamá *te lo* **compró.**	*Your mother bought it for you.*
Juan *nos* **prestó** *los discos.*	*Juan lent us the records.*
Juan *nos los* **prestó.**	*Juan lent them to us.*

When you use two object pronouns together in Spanish, where do they

stand in relation to the verb? _____ . Which pronoun comes first?

_____ . Which pronoun comes directly before the verb?

RULE: In Spanish, contrary to English, the indirect-object pronoun comes before the direct-object pronoun and both stand before the verb.

Your little sister is always asking questions. Answer them in complete phrases.

EXAMPLE: ¿Me prestas tu raqueta de tenis?   **Sí, *te la presto*.**

1. ¿Me compras un helado?   _____

2. ¿Me traes un vaso de agua?   _____

3. ¿Te enseña ella el español?   _____

4. ¿Te compró papá los zapatos?   _____

5. ¿Te vendieron las pastillas para la tos?   _____

6. ¿Me cuentas un cuento?   _____

7. ¿Me prestas tu abrigo?   _____

8. ¿Nos dijo mamá la verdad?   _____

9. ¿Me muestras esos libros?   _____

10. ¿Nos presta tu amigo la bicicleta?   _____

Now study the following examples.

Pablo *le dio* *el peine* **a María.**	*Pablo gave the comb to Mary.*
Pablo *se lo* **dio.**	*Pablo gave it to her.*
Yo *le compré* *unos pañuelos* **a papá.**	*I bought some handkerchiefs for dad.*
Yo *se los* **compré.**	*I bought them for him.*
Mario *les prestó* *las vendas* **a ellos.**	*Mario lent them the bandages.*
Mario *se las* **prestó.**	*Mario lent them to them.*
Yo *les digo la verdad* **a Uds.**	*I am telling you the truth.*
Yo *se la* **digo.**	*I am telling it to you.*

Look at the first two sets of examples. What happened to the indirect-object pronoun **(le)** when it was used together with the direct-object pronoun **lo** or **los**? _____ Now look at the last two sets of examples. What happened to the indirect-object pronoun les when it was used with the direct-object pronoun **lo** or **los**? _____

RULE: **Se** replaces **le** and **les** before direct-object pronouns **lo, la, los,** and **las**.

Yo le envié el dinero.	*I sent him (her) the money.*
Yo *se lo* **envié.**	*I sent it to him (her).*
Yo le envié la carta.	*I sent him (her) the letter.*
Yo *se la* **envié.**	*I sent it to him (her).*

As you can see, the pronoun **se** can have many meanings. Therefore, the indirect object is normally used together with **se**, either for clarification, emphasis, or reinforcement.

¿A quién le diste el periódico?	*To whom did you give the newspaper?*
Se lo di a mi papá.	*I gave it to my father.*

¿*Se* **lo diste a** *tu papá?*   *Did you give it to your father?*
Sí, *se* **lo di** *a él.*   *Yes, I gave it to him.*

Ella les mostró las fotos a sus amigos.   *She showed the pictures to her friends.*
Ella *se* **las mostró** *a ellos.*   *She showed them to them.*

Work with a partner. You and your friend are playing a game in which you describe what different people do. Confirm you friend's statements.

EXAMPLE: Un médico da medicinas a los pacientes. **Sí,** *se las* **da.**

1. Un cartero lleva las cartas a la gente.

   _____

2. Un ladrón roba las joyas a las personas.

   _____

3. Un mesero sirve la comida a los clientes.

   _____

4. Una vendedora vende ropa a mi hermana.

   _____

5. Una profesora enseña el español a la clase.

   _____

6. Un banco presta dinero a mi papá.

   _____

7. Una abuela lee historias a los niños.

   _____

8. Un consejero da consejos al alumno.

   _____

9. Un policía pone multas a los choferes.

   _____

10. Un turista escribe tarjetas a los amigos.

    _____

Actividad F

Work with a partner. You mother wants to know if you did certain things. Respond negatively:

EXAMPLE: ¿Escribiste la carta a tus abuelos?   **No, no** *se la* **escribí.**

1. ¿Contaste el cuento a tus amigos?

_____

2. ¿Explicaste tu problema al profesor?

_____

3. ¿Diste el dinero a Manuel?

_____

4. ¿Prestaste tus discos a tus amigos?

_____

5. ¿Serviste el café a tu papá?

_____

6. ¿Mandaste la tarjeta a tus tíos?

_____

7. ¿Escribiste la nota al director?

_____

8. ¿Diste las vitaminas a tu hermanita?

_____

Actividad G

Your teacher wants to know if you gave certain things to your classmates. Respond affirmatively:

EXAMPLE: el cuaderno / Rosa   **Sí,** *se lo* **di a Rosa.**

1. el libro / Manuel   _____

2. los ejercicios / Ud.   _____

3. el examen / Juan y Javier _____

4. los lápices / los alumnos _____

5. la regla / Mercedes _____

6. las plumas / todos _____

Where does the single-object pronoun stand in affirmative commands or in sentences with an infinitive?

_____

Where does the single-object pronoun stand in affirmative commands?

_____

The same rules apply to double-object pronouns:

Dígame la verdad.	*Tell me the truth.*
Dígamela.	*Tell it to me.*
Cuéntele un cuento a Juan.	*Tell a story to Juan.*
Cuénteselo.	*Tell it ot him.*
Quiero escribirle una tarjeta a Josefina.	*I want to write a postcard to Josefina.*
Quiero escribírsela. ⎫	
Se la **quiero escribir.** ⎭	*I want to write it to her.*

The double-object pronoun (first the indirect, then the direct) follows an affirmative command and may also follow an infinitive. When the double-object pronoun follows and is attached to a command or an infinitive, an accent mark is required on the stressed syllable.

Actividad H

Work with a partner. Your friend tells you what she wants to do. Encourage her to do it:

EXAMPLE: Quiero mandarle un regalo a Mercedes. **Mándaselo.**

1. Necesito comprarme un jarabe para la tos. _____

2. Voy a escribirle una carta al director.   _____

3. Quiero mostrarles esas fotos a mis amigos.   _____

4. Voy a leerte este artículo.   _____

5. Necesito darle el dinero a la maestra.   _____

6. Quiero hacerte varias preguntas.   _____

7. Voy a contarte mi problema.   _____

8. Quiero comprarme unos pañuelos de papel.   _____

Work with a partner. You are going shopping for holiday presents with a friend. Respond to your friend.

EXAMPLE: Voy a comprarle ese disco a José.   { **Sí, debes comprár***selo*.
 Sí, *se lo* **debes comprar.**

1. Voy a comprarle esa bufanda a mi mamá.

_____

2. Voy a comprarme ese radio.

_____

3. Voy a comprarles esos juguetes a mis hermanos.

_____

4. Voy a comprarte ese casete.

_____

5. Voy a comprarle aquel reloj a mi papá.

_____

6. Voy a comprarles esos dulces a mis amigos.

_____

7. Voy a comprarle esas pantuflas a mi abuela.

_____

8. Voy a comprar helado.

_____

Actividad J

Express in Spanish the following conversation between two friends.

1. I need a new bicycle.

_____

2. Why don't you buy it?

_____

3. I don't have enough money to buy it.

_____

4. Your parents can buy it for you.

_____

5. They say that I don't need it.

_____

6. They don't want to give me the money.

_____

7. My grandparents can buy it for me.

_____

8. If they buy it for you, can you lend it to me?

_____

Preguntas Personales

1. ¿Por qué algunos anuncios son más efectivos que otros?

_____

2. ¿Qué valor tienen los anuncios?

_____

3. ¿Por qué no compras todos los productos que ves en los anuncios de la televisión?

4. ¿Qué importancia tienen los antibióticos?

_____

5. ¿Qué compras en una farmacia cuando tienes gripe?

_____

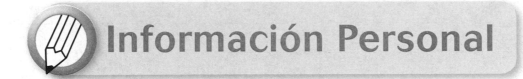

Información Personal

Write five sentences in Spanish about things you do for other people. Then rewrite the sentences using object pronouns:

EXAMPLE: Le sirvo el café a mi mamá.   _Se lo_ **sirvo.**

1. (a) _____

(b) _____

2. (a) _____

(b) _____

3. (a) _____

(b) _____

4. (a) _____

(b) _____

5. (a) _____

(b) _____

Composición

You are being interviewed for a job in an advertising agency. You are asked to compose a sample advertisement for any product you want (soda, toothpaste, deodorant, and the like) to see how imaginative you are:

_____

_____

_____

_____

_____

_____

_____

_____

_____

3 You have been learning about personal pronouns that are direct or indirect objects of the verb. Other personal pronouns are used after prepositions. You already know most of them. First, let's recall the most common prepositions in Spanish:

a	*to*	**en**	*in, on, at*
cerca de	*near*	**hacia**	*toward*
con	*with*	**hasta**	*as far as; up to; until*
contra	*against*	**lejos do**	*far from*
de	*of, from*	**para**	*for*
debajo de	*under, beneath*	**por**	*for*
delate de	*in front of*	**sin**	*without*
detrás de	*behind*	**sobre**	*on, over*

Now look at these sentences:

Juan vive *cerca de nosotros.*   *John lives near us.*

Voy a salir *sin ellos* **(ellas).**   *I am going to go out without them.*

La casa está *lejos de Ud.* **(Uds.).**   *The house is far from you.*

Tú vas de compras *con él* **(ella).**   *You go shopping with him (her).*

What do you notice about the pronouns that follow the prepositions? _____

_____

They are the same as the subject pronouns.

Replace the expression in bold type by an appropriate pronoun:

EXAMPLE:　Les llevo la comida **a Jorge y a Juan.**
　　　　　　Les llevo la comida *a ellos.*

1. Yo estudio con María.

_____

2. ¿Quieres trabajar para mi padre?

_____

3. Siempre hablan de Elisa y de Juana.

_____

4. No salgas sin tu hermana.

_____

5. Enrique se sienta detrás de Josefina.

_____

6. El gato está debajo de la cama.

_____

7. El avión vuela sobre los edificios.

_____

8. Mi hermana quiere vivir lejos de mis padres y yo.

_____

Did you notice that we did not use the pronouns **yo** and **tú**? That's because they are the only ones that change after a preposition:

　　　Este vestido es para *ti.*　　　*This dress is for you.*

　　　No puedes salir sin *mí.*　　　*You can't go out without me.*

Furthermore, when used with the preposition con, **mi** and **ti** form a new word:

　　　Venga Ud. *conmigo.*　　　　*Come with me.*

　　　El director quiere hablar *contigo.*　　*The principal wants to speak with you.*

Actividad L

You went shopping and your friend is trying to guess for whom you bought presents.

EXAMPLE: El suéter es para Luis, ¿verdad?   **Sí, es para *él*.**

1. La blusa es para Ana, ¿verdad?

_____

2. Los dulces son para tu hermano y para ti, ¿verdad?

_____

3. Esa camisa es para ti, ¿verdad?

_____

4. Los pantalones son para tu papá, ¿verdad?

_____

5. Los chocolates son para papá y para mí, ¿verdad?

_____

6. Este regalo es para tus padres, ¿verdad?

_____

Actividad M

You are in a contrary mood today. Your father is trying to convince you to go out and do something.

EXAMPLE: PADRE: **Los muchachos van a jugar al fútbol.**
            TÚ: **No quiero jugar *con ellos*.**

1. Elena va a ir al parque.   _____

2. Tu hermano va a jugar al tenis.   _____

3. Mamá y yo vamos a ir al cine.   _____

4. Yo voy a ir al supermercado.   _____

5. Gloria y María van a nadar. _____

6. Tus amigos van a jugar al béisbol. _____

Answer your little sister's questions, using prepositional pronouns:

1. ¿Vas a salir con Mónica el sábado por la noche?

_____

_____

2. ¿Puedo salir con Uds.?

_____

_____

3. ¿Quién se sienta delante de ti en la clase?

_____

_____

4. ¿Puedo ir contigo a la escuela?

_____

_____

5. ¿Quieres ir conmigo al cine?

_____

_____

6. ¿Puedes devolver este libro por mí?

_____

_____

7. ¿Compraste esa camiseta para ti?

_____

_____

8. ¿Vas a salir sin mí?

_____

_____

An announcer is interviewing you about a particular product:

Cápsula cultural

El curandero

El curandero es una figura común en los países de Hispanoamérica. Es una persona que se dedica a curar a los enfermos con remedios caseros, especialmente en los pueblos pequeños o en áreas remotas donde no hay hospitales o doctores. Básicamente hay tres tipos de curandero: el yerbero, que trata las enfermedades con plantas y productos naturales; la partera (casi siempre una mujer), que ayuda a las mujeres durante el parto; y el sobador, que se especializa en masajes.

Alguna gente cree que los curanderos tienen poderes sobrenaturales y por eso los consultan cuando creen ser víctimas de algún mal. El tratamiento prescrito por los curanderos consiste generalmente en rituales religiosos, remedios herbales y oraciones; pero quizás lo más importante es la fe del paciente.

Discusión

1. ¿Qué es un curandero?
2. ¿Por qué hay generalmente curanderos en áreas remotas?
3. ¿Cuántos tipos de curandero hay? ¿En qué se especializan?
4. ¿Tienen valor los remedios naturales? ¿Por qué?

Para investigar

Menciona algunos remedios caseros que utiliza la gente en el mundo hispano y en los Estados Unidos.

VOCABULARIO

curandero *healer*
casero *home (made)*
el yerbero *herbalist*
la partera *midwife*

el parto *birth*
el sobador *masseur*
prescrito *prescribed*
la fe *faith*

14

En la mueblería

Cardinal and Ordinal Numbers

1 Vocabulario

las cortinas

el espejo

el librero
el estante
para libros

la cómoda

la cama

la mesita
de noche

el florero

el sofá

$300

la mesita
de café

la alfombra

la butaca

el sillón

el juego de
comedor

la lámpara

el congelador

el escritorio

la nevera
el refrigerador
el microondas

la lavadora

la secadora

el lavaplatos

el horno

Does this kitchen look all right to you? There are seven items you don't normally find in a kitchen and seven that do.

En la cocina hay

_____

_____

_____

_____

_____

_____

En la cocina no hay

_____

_____

_____

_____

_____

_____

¡Qué precios!

Let's read a story about a couple who goes shopping for furniture. See if you can figure out how much money they spend.

ANITA: Ricardo, nunca podemos invitar a nadie al apartamento. Todos nuestros muebles son tan viejos . . . ¡Vamos a comprar muebles nuevos!

RICARDO: Está bien. Pero hoy día todo es muy caro. No quiero gastar una fortuna en cosas innecesarias.

ANITA: Para mí una casa bonita es una necesidad. Además, hay una venta especial de verano en «La Casa Elegante,» la mueblería más grande de la ciudad.

RICARDO: Bueno, vamos a ver qué tienen.

Un poco más tarde, llegan a la mueblería. En el primer piso están los muebles de dormitorio.

ANITA: Me encanta ese juego de dormitorio. Es muy moderno.   **juego** *set*

RICARDO: Pero mira el precio, quinientos cincuenta dólares.

ANITA: ¿Qué importa? Es un sueño. En el segundo piso hay muebles de sala. Vamos a comprar ese sofá blanco, las dos butacas y la mesita.

RICARDO: Ay, no, mujer. Cuestan un ojo de la cara—casi seiscientos dólares.   **costar un ojo de la cara** *to cost a fortune*

ANITA: Para eso tenemos dinero, mi amor, para gastarlo.

En el tercer piso están los muebles de comedor.

ANITA: ¡Qué bonito ese juego con las seis sillas!

RICARDO: Pero, el precio, el precio . . . No estás considerando el precio. Cuestan casi setecientos dólares.

ANITA: Amorcito, no seas tacaño.   **tacaño** *stingy*

Al final, Anita hace una lista de todos los muebles que quiere y se la muestra a un vendedor.

VENDEDOR: Bueno, señora. El precio de todo, con el impuesto del ocho por ciento y menos el descuento del veinticinco por ciento, es mil trescientos ochenta y nueve dólares.   **el impuesto** *tax*

RICARDO: ¡Casi mil cuatrocientos dólares! ¡No puedo gastar tanto dinero, no soy millonario! Con esos precios, prefiero vivir con mis muebles viejos.

VENDEDOR: Señor, es evidente que Ud. es inteligente y muy prudente. Espere, tengo la solución. Les propongo un trato especial a Uds., mis queridos amigos. Sólo tiene que pagarme   **el trato** *deal* quinientos dólares por ahora. El resto lo puede pagar a plazos, en pequeños pagos cada mes.

a plazos *in installments*

RICARDO: Eso parece mejor. Déme el contrato. Tú ves, Anita, es importante pensar antes de hacer una compra. Así se ahorra dinero.

ahorrar *to save*

Al salir de la tienda, Anita lee el contrato: quinientos dólares ahora, y después, setenta dólares al mes durante dieciocho meses.

ANITA: (sarcásticamente) Oh, sí, Ricardo. ¡Ahorraste mucho dinero!

Actividad B

Conteste en frases completas.

1. ¿Por qué quiere Anita comprar muebles nuevos?

   _____

2. ¿Dónde hay una venta especial?

   _____

3. ¿En qué piso están los muebles de dormitorio?

   _____

4. ¿Cuánto cuesta el juego de muebles que le gustó a Anita?

   _____

5. ¿Qué hay en el segundo piso?

   _____

6. ¿Qué quiere comprar Anita allá?

   _____

7. ¿Qué quiere Anita para el comedor?

_____

8. ¿Cuál es el precio de todo lo que compran?

_____

9. ¿Cuánto tiene que pagar Ricardo inmediatamente?

_____

10. ¿Cuánto paga Ricardo por los muebles con el trato especial del vendedor?

_____

 You have already learned the cardinal numbers from 0 to 100. Let's review them.

0	cero	13	trece	50	cincuenta
1	uno	14	catorce	54	cincuenta y cuatro
2	dos	15	quince	60	sesenta
3	tres	16	dieciséis	65	sesenta y cinco
4	cuatro	17	diecisiete	70	setenta
5	cinco	18	dieciocho	76	setenta y seis
6	seis	19	diecinueve	80	ochenta
7	siete	20	veinte	87	ochenta y siete
8	ocho	21	veintiuno	90	noventa
9	nueve	30	treinta	98	noventa y ocho
10	diez	32	treinta y dos	100	cien
11	once	40	cuarenta		
12	doce	43	cuarenta y tres		

Numbers over 100.

200	doscientos	600	seiscientos	1.000	mil
300	trescientos	700	setecientos	100.000	cien mil
400	cuatrocientos	800	ochocientos	200.000	doscientos mil
500	quinientos	900	novecientos	1.000.000	un millón (de)

NOTE: Periods are used instead of commas to separate numbers. Commas are used instead of periods to mark decimals.

Actividad C

You are a clerk in a large hotel. Several people come to check in. Tell them their room number and then write it in Spanish.

EXAMPLE: Sra. Ramírez / 118   **Sra. Ramírez, su cuarto es el** *ciento dieciocho.*

1. Doctor López / 213

_____

2. Srta. Gómez / 304

_____

3. Sr. y Sra. Pérez / 521

_____

4. Doctora Peláez / 417

_____

5. Srta. Casas / 745

_____

6. Sres. Ramos / 132

_____

7. Sra. Montes / 866

_____

8. Srta. Gallo / 901

_____

9. Sr. Torres / 658

_____

Match the numbers on the left with the numerals on the right.

1. ciento ochenta y cuatro _____

2. doscientos cincuenta y seis _____

3. cuatrocientos ochenta y nueve _____

4. ochocientos quince _____

5. quinientos veinte y tres _____

6. mil quinientos cincuenta _____

7. tres mil novecientos diez _____

8. diez mil setecientos treinta _____

9. ciento veinte mil _____

10. cien mil trescientos cuarenta _____

523
120.000
10.730
256
100.340
489
1.550
815
184
3.910

Write in Spanish the year in which the following things happened:

EXAMPLE: Cristóbal Colón llegó a América en 1492.
       mil cuatrocientos noventa y dos

1. La independencia de los Estados Unidos se declaró en 1776.

_____

2. Juan Ponce de León llegó a la Florida en 1512.

_____

3. Jorge Washington nació en 1732.

_____

4. La Guerra de Independencia Mexicana comenzó en 1810.

_____

5. La Organización de las Naciones Unidas se estableció en 1945.

_____

6. El nuevo milenio comenzó en el año 2001.

_____

 The numbers 200 to 900 agree in gender with the nouns they accompany.

trescient*as* mesitas   **ochocient*as* cincuenta alfombras**

trescient*os* escritorios   **ochocient*os* cincuenta floreros**

What happens to the number 100? Look at these examples:

cien **lámparas**

ciento veinte lámparas

cien espejos

ciento veinte espejos

cien **mil habitantes**

cien **millones de habitantes**

Ciento becomes **cien** before any noun, masculine or feminine, and before the numbers **mil** and **millones**.

Actividad F

Write in Spanish the numerals in parentheses.

1. (500) _____ casas.

2. (1,400) _____ alumnos.

3. (750) _____ personas.

4. (100,000) _____ soldados.

5. (365) _____ días.

6. (872) _____ páginas.

7. (680) _____ camas.

8. (250,000,000) _____ de norteamericanos.

4 Let's look again at the number **uno**.

| **Quiero comprar** _un_ **horno y** _una_ **butaca.** | _I want to buy one oven and one easy chair._ |

Uno becomes **un** before a masculine singular noun. It changes to **una** before a feminine singular noun. This also applies to compound numbers (**31, 41, 51**, etc.).

Veintiún has an accent mark.

Anoche leí _veintiún_ **capítulos y escribí cuarenta** _y una_ **páginas.**

Last night I read thirty-one chapters and wrote forty-one pages.

Actividad **G**

The teacher is making a list of materials needed for the class. Write the numbers in Spanish.

1. (21) _____ libros.

2. (51) _____ lápices.

3. (31) _____ reglas.

4. (61) _____ cuadernos.

5. (41) _____ plumas.

6. (71) _____ mesas.

Actividad **H**

You are the teller in the foreign-exchange division of a bank. Several people need different types of currency. Can you help them?

EXAMPLE: Sr. López / 1.120 dólares
El Sr. López necesita mil ciento veinte dólares.

1. Sra. Martínez / 350.100 pesos mexicanos _____

2. Srta. Gómez / 8.671 pesetas _____

3. Sr. Pérez / 989 dólares _____

4. Sr. Ramos / 25.500 pesos colombianos _____

5. Sra. Vélez / 10.431 colones _____

6. Doctor Villa / 5.500 quetzales _____

5 Do you remember the adjectives **primero** and **tercero**? They are ordinal numbers. Ordinal numbers are used to rank people or things and put them in a certain order. Ordinal numbers are adjectives and agree in number and gender with the noun they describe. **Primero** and **tercero** drop the **o** before a singular masculine noun.

1°	**primer(o)**	*first*
2°	**segundo**	*second*
3°	**tercer(o)**	*third*
4°	**cuarto**	*fourth*
5°	**quinto**	*fifth*
6°	**sexto**	*sixth*
7°	**séptimo**	*seventh*
8°	**octavo**	*eighth*
9°	**noveno**	*ninth*
10°	**décimo**	*tenth*

Enero es el *primer* mes del año. *January is the first month of the year.*

Carlos V (*Quinto*) fue un rey muy importante.* *Charles the Fifth was a very important king.*

Vivo en la Cuarta (4°)Avenida. *I live on 4th Avenue.*

Alfonso XIII (*Trece*) fue un rey español. *Alphonso the Thirteenth was a Spanish king.*

NOTE: In Spanish, a numbered street is expressed with a cardinal number.

Vamos al Festival de la Calle *Ocho*. *Let's go to the Eight Street Festival.*

Ordinal numbers used with royalty names are usually expressed with Roman numerals.

Felipe II (Segundo) fue muy famoso.   *Philip II was very famous.*

You are going shopping in a large department store. On which floor do you find the following things?

EXAMPLE: muebles / 4°   **Los muebles están en el *cuarto piso*.**

1. ropa de hombre / 8°   _____

2. ropa de mujer / 5°   _____

3. televisores / 9°   _____

4. cafetería / 2°   _____

5. zapatos / 3°   _____

6. toallas / 6°   _____

7. sombreros / 1°   _____

There were tryouts for the track team in your school. You are telling the order of arrival in the first race.

EXAMPLE: Rosa / 1°   **Rosa fue *la primera*.**

1. Jorge / 3°   _____

2. María / 5°   _____

3. Raúl / 2°   _____

4. Mercedes / 4°   _____

5. Josefina / 8°   _____

6. Mario / 9° _____

7. Elisa / 7° _____

8. Miguel / 6° _____

DIÁLOGO

You are in a furniture store. Tell the salesman what you want.

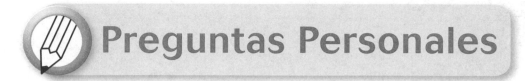

Preguntas Personales

1. ¿Qué muebles hay en la sala de tu casa? ¿En tu dormitorio?

_____

2. En el centro comercial, ¿cuáles son tus tiendas favoritas? ¿Por qué?

_____

3. ¿Cuánto tiempo pasas en el centro comercial? ¿Qué haces allí?

_____

4. ¿Prefieres comprar en el centro comercial o en el Internet? Menciona las ventajas y desventajas de cada método.

_____

5. Si ganas mil dólares, ¿qué cosas desearás comprar?

_____

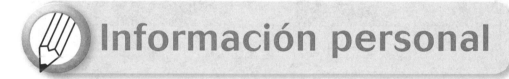

Información personal

1. Voy a terminar la escuela superior en al año _____ .
2. Tengo un televisor que costó _____ .
3. El carro que más me gusta cuesta _____ .
4. Estoy en el _____ año de español.
5. Yo nací en el año _____ .

Composición

Describe your room. (Tell what kind of furniture you have, when it was bought, how much you think it cost, whether you like it or not, what color the curtains, the rug, etc.)

 # Cápsula cultural

Casas sin muebles

Muchas veces cuando una familia va a mudarse a una casa o apartamento, la primera necesidad es ir a comprar muebles nuevos para poder amueblar el lugar.

Pero en la provincia de Esmeralda, al norte del Ecuador, vive una comunidad distinguida por su autosuficiencia. Es principalmente una comunidad de campesinos que han podido mantener sus costumbres sencillas, poco influenciadas por la modernidad. Lo que llama la atención de esta comunidad es que viven en casas construidas con una especie de bambú. Son construidas sobre unos palos y así tienen bastante altura para protegerlas de posibles inundaciones.

En el interior de estas casas, casi no hay muebles. Viven estrictamente con lo necesario. Por ejemplo, a la hora de la comida, la familia se sienta en círculo en el suelo y ponen la comida en el centro del círculo, en el piso.

Para dormir en vez de camas, duermen sobre petates de paja, que ellos fabrican. También, hacen sus propias sábanas y almohadas, bordadas con colores.

Esta comunidad representa un ejemplo de sencillez y vivienda ecológica para el resto del mundo.

¿Qué cree Ud.?

Discusión

1. ¿Dónde está situada la provincia de Esmeralda?

2. ¿Por qué se distingue la comunidad mencionada en la lectura?

3. Da algunos ejemplos de la autosuficiencia de los campesinos de Esmeralda.

4. ¿Son necesarios los muebles? ¿Por qué (no)?

5. Algunos científicos dicen que nuestras sociedades modernas consumen demasiado y destruyen el ambiente. ¿Qué debemos hacer?

VOCABULARIO

la autosuficiencia *self-sufficiency*
el palo *stilt*
la inundación *flood*
el petate *sleeping mat*

la paja *straw*
la sábana *bedsheet*
la almohada *pillow*
bordado *embroidered*

Repaso III

Lección 11

a. Direct-object pronouns

me	*me*		nos	*us*
te	*you* (informal)		los	*them, you* (masculine plural)
lo	*you* (formal), *him, it* (masculine)		las	*them, you* (feminine plural)
la	*you* (formal), *her, it* (feminine)			

b. Direct-object pronouns normally come directly before the verb.

Yo *te* vi ayer.   *I saw you yesterday.*

Él no *la* llamó.   *He didn't call her.*

There are two situations, however, in which direct-object pronouns take a different position:

1. In affirmative commands, direct-object pronouns follow the verb and are attached to it. An accent mark is required on the stressed syllable.

Lláma*me*.   *Call me.*
Acompáña*los*.   *Accompany them.*

2. When the direct-object pronoun is used with an infinitive, it may follow and is then attached to the infinitive, or it may precede the conjugated form of the other verb.

Quiero comprar*la*.   *I want to buy it.*
***La* quiero comprar.**   *I want to buy it.*

Lección 12

a. Indirect-object pronouns

me	(to, for) *me*	**nos**	(to, for) *us*
te	(to, for) *you*	**les**	(to, for) *you* (plural), *them*
le	(to, for) *you* (formal), *him, her*		

b. Indirect-object pronouns normally come before the verb.

Te escribo una carta.   *I write a letter to you.*

Like direct-object pronouns, indirect-object pronouns follow the verb and are attached to it in affirmative commands.

Cómprale el regalo.   *Buy him the present.*

When used with an infinitive, indirect-object pronouns may follow the infinitive and are then attached to it, or they may precede the conjugated form of the other verb.

Quiero comprarle un regalo.   *I want to buy him a present.*
Le quiero comprar un regalo.   *I want to buy him a present.*

c. In Spanish, the indirect-object pronoun is normally used even when the indirect-object noun is expressed:

Le escribí una carta a mi amigo.   *I wrote a letter to my friend.*

Lección 13

Double-object pronouns

a. When using two-object pronouns in Spanish, the indirect-object pronoun comes before the direct-object pronoun and both stand before the verb.

La profesora *nos lo* dio.   *The teacher gave it to us.*

b. **Se** replaces **le** and **les** before the direct-object pronouns **lo, la, los,** and **las.**

Yo *se* lo di *a ella*.   *I gave it to her.*

c. Double-object pronouns (first the indirect, then the direct) follow an affirmative command and may also follow an infinitive. When the double-object pronoun follows and is attached to a command or an infinitive, an accent mark is required on the stressed syllable:

Tráemelo.   *Bring it to me.*

Tengo que comprártela. *}*
Te la **tengo que comprar.** *}*   *I have to buy it for you.*

d. Common prepositions

a	*to*	**en**	*in, on, at*
cerca de	*near*	**hacia**	*toward*
con	*for*	**hasta**	*as far as, until, up to*
contra	*with*	**lejos de**	*far from*
de	*of, from*	**para**	*for*
debajo de	*under*	**por**	*for*
delante de	*in front of*	**sin**	*without*
detrás de	*behind*	**sobre**	*on, over*

e. Personal pronouns used after prepositions

mí	**nosotros**
ti	**Uds.**
Ud.	**Uds.**
él	**ellos**
ella	**ellos**

f. **Mí** and **ti** form a new word with the preposition **con: conmigo** and **contigo**.

Ella fue al cine *conmigo.*   *She went to the movies with me.*

Lección 14

a.

200	**doscientos**	600	**seiscientos**	1.000	**mil**
300	**trescientos**	700	**setecientos**	100.000	**cien mil**
400	**cuatrocientos**	800	**ochocientos**	200.000	**doscientos mil**
500	**quinientos**	900	**novecientos**	1.000.000	**un millón (de)**

The numbers 200 to 900 agree in gender with the nouns they accompany.

El libro tiene *trescientas* páginas.

b. **Ciento** becomes **cien** before any noun, masculine or feminine, and before the numbers **mil** and **millones**.

Anoche leí *cien* páginas del libro.

La biblioteca tiene *cien* mil libros.

c. **Uno** becomes **un** before a masculine singular noun. It changes to **una** before a feminine singular noun.

Enero tiene treinta y *un* días.

En la clase hay cuarenta y *una* sillas.

d. Ordinal numbers

$$1° \quad \text{primer(o)}$$
$$2° \quad \text{segund(o)}$$
$$3° \quad \text{tercer(o)}$$
$$4° \quad \text{cuart(o)}$$
$$5° \quad \text{quint(o)}$$
$$6° \quad \text{sext(o)}$$
$$7° \quad \text{séptim(o)}$$
$$8° \quad \text{octav(o)}$$
$$9° \quad \text{noven(o)}$$
$$10° \quad \text{décim(o)}$$

After ten, cardinal numbers are normally used.

Ordinal numbers are adjectives and agree in gender and number with the noun they describe.

Vivo en el *segundo* edificio de la *quinta* avenida.

e. **Primero** and **tercero** drop the final **o** before a singular masculine noun.

Terminé el *primer* capítulo.

Subí al *tercer* piso.

Los siete errores

En la tienda de ropa.

Unscramble the words. Then unscramble the letters to find out what Carmen bought in the clothing store.

ASTIECAM

TARCEAR

APZALLITAS

SOBAT ED AGOM

IMAPAJ

Carmen compró un

Actividad C

Your mother asks you to bring in one of the clothing articles hanging on the line. Pick it out from her description. Place an X in the correct circle.

1. Tiene mangas.
2. Tiene un bolsillo pequeño.
3. Tiene botones.
4. Tiene cuello.
5. La tela es a rayas.

Actividad D

Crucigrama.

HORIZONTALES

4. syrup
5. comb
7. vitamin
9. toothpaste
11. prescription
12. antibiotic

VERTICALES

1. pharmacist
2. deodorant
3. bandage
6. tablet
8. aspirin
10. cotton

Actividad

Picture Story   Can you read this story? Whenever you come to a picture, read it as if it were a Spanish word.

Hoy sale Carlos de viaje para España. Ayer puso todas sus ,

 y  sobre la para decidir qué llevaba. Como no sabe si va a

, decidió llevar también su y sus . Lleva también dos

, sus y una . Del sacó el , un , un

, un tubo de , un y un y los puso sobre la

. Su mamá le dijo: "Lleva también ,  y unas . Y no

olvides llevar una y un para ponerte si vas a una

o a un ." Ahora su

lo llama y los dos salen en un . El viaje

al no es largo. Carlos tiene tiempo de comprar varias y un

. Muy pronto anuncian que el vuelo (flight) número 614 sale en

15 minutos. En el van más de 300 pasajeros. Carlos está muy .

Cuarta Parte

La superstición

Verbs With Spelling Changes

 **Vocabulario**

el cementerio

el duende

la bruja

la escoba / la poción

el brujo

los signos del zodíaco

la astrología

la varita mágica

el esqueleto

la fantasía

el hada

la calabaza

el sueño

la pesadilla

Work with a partner. One person reads the statement in Column A and asks the question **¿Qué es?** The other person answers, using the phrases in Column B.

A	B

A

1. Estudio de la influencia de las estrellas. _____
2. Según la superstición, el día que trae mala suerte. _____
3. La consecuencia de romper un espejo. _____
4. Persona que crea ilusiones. _____
5. Vuela en una escoba. _____
6. Un mal sueño. _____
7. Una creación de la imaginación. _____
8. Animal que vuela por la noche. _____

B

a. la bruja
b. la pesadilla
c. la fantasía
d. la mala suerte
e. el viernes trece
f. el mago
g. la astrología
h. el murciélago

Describe what's happening in the following pictures.

1. _____ 2. _____

3. _____   4. _____

5. _____   6. _____

7. _____   8. _____

Las supersticiones

Are you superstitious? Read this story about superstitions and see if you recognize any of them. Pay attention to the spelling of the verbs in boldface.

Acérquese, por favor. Quiero preguntarle algo. ¿Es Ud. una persona supersticiosa? ¡Claro que no! La idea es ridícula. Ud. es inteligente, moderno, lógico y no cree en cosas como la mala suerte. La superstición es para los viejos y los ignorantes.

Y sin embargo . . . dígame, ¿qué hacen algunas personas cuando un gato negro pasa por delante de ellas, cuando tienen que pasar por debajo de una escalera, cuando rompen un espejo o cuando alguien abre un paraguas dentro de su casa? ¿Tocan madera? ¿Cruzan los dedos?

acercarse *to come near*
¡Claro que no! *of course not*

el paraguas *umbrella*

¿Qué piensa Ud. cuando ve que es viernes trece? (¿Sabe Ud. que en los aviones no hay asientos con el número trece y que en muchos edificios no hay pisos con ese número?)

Como ve, el mundo está lleno de supersticiones. Muchos científicos afirman que la superstición se basa en la ignorancia y en el miedo. No obstante, muchas veces la superstición tiene influencia en nuestra vida diaria. Muchas de estas supersticiones son universales. Otras se ven en ciertas culturas solamente. Entre los hispanos supersti ciosos, por ejemplo, es mala suerte casarse o viajar los martes, especialmente si es el día 13.

no obstante *nevertheless*

Al contrario, si tienen un sueño con toros es porque van a ganar la lotería. Y si ven a tres curas juntos, van a recibir un regalo. Además, algunos creen que hay objetos que traen buena suerte: una pata de conejo, un trébol de cuatro hojas o una estatua de un elefante blanco. Y si no quiere visitas aburridas en la casa, **coloque** una escoba detrás de la puerta: la visita se irá pronto.

el cura *priest*

la pata de conejo *rabbit foot*
trébol *clover*
colocar *to place*

¿Está confundido ahora? Entonces, **siga** todas las supersticiones y **aprenda** así a evitar la mala suerte. **Toque** madera, **cruce** los dedos, no **llegue** de viaje el día trece. El problema es que muchas veces las supersticiones tienen significados **contrarios** en diferentes lugares del mundo. La vida es complicada, ¿verdad?

Actividad **C**

Conteste con frases completas.

1. ¿Qué tipo de persona no cree en la mala suerte?

_____

2. ¿Quiénes creen en las supersticiones?

_____

3. ¿Por qué los supersticiosos no pasan por debajo de una escalera?

_____

4. ¿Qué no abre en su casa una persona supersticiosa?

   _____

5. ¿Qué hacen con los dedos muchos supersticiosos para tener buena suerte?

   _____

6. ¿Según algunos, qué número trae mala suerte?

   _____

7. ¿En qué está basada la superstición, según muchos científicos?

   _____

8. ¿En qué día no debe uno viajar o casarse, según algunos supersticiosos?

   _____

9. ¿Cuáles son algunos objetos que traen buena suerte?

   _____

10. ¿Es posible creer en todas las supersticiones? ¿Por qué no?

   _____

2   Note the following sentences.

Toque **madera.**	*Knock on wood.*
No *llegue* **de un viaje el trece.**	*Don't arrive from a trip on the thirteenth.*
Cruce **los dedos.**	*Cross your fingers.*

What are the infinitives of these verbs?

toque _____

llegue _____

cruce _____

What happened to the **c** in **tocar**?   _____

What happened to the **g** in **llegar**?   _____

What happened to the **z** in **cruzar**?   _____

The **c** changed to **qu**, and **g** changed to **gu**, and the **z** changed to **c**.

RULE: Verbs ending in **–car**, **-gar**, and **–zar** change their spelling in the first person (**yo**) of the preterite and in the formal commands in order to maintain the original sound of the infinitive.

$$\left.\begin{array}{l} \text{c to } \textbf{qu} \\ \text{g to } \textbf{gu} \\ \text{z to } \textbf{c} \end{array}\right\} \text{ before } \textbf{e}$$

Here are more examples:

explicar:	**Yo** *expliqué* **la lección.**	*I explained the lesson.*
	Explíquela **Ud. ahora.**	*Explain it now.*
jugar:	**Yo ya** *jugué* **con ese juego.**	*I already played with that game.*
	Jueguen **Uds. con él.**	*Play with it.*
almorzar:	**Ya** *almorcé*. **Almuerce Ud. sin mí.**	*Thanks, I had lunch. Have lunch without me.*

Note that some verbs with spelling changes also have stem changes: **jugar (ue)**, **almorzar (ue)**, **comenzar (ie)**, **empezar (ie)**, and others.

What did you do yesterday?

EXAMPLES: pescar en el lago   *Pesqué* **en el lago.**

1. buscar un libro en la biblioteca   _____

2. sacar una buena nota en el examen   _____

3. tocar la guitarra   _____

4. explicar las tareas a mi hermanito   _____

5. acercarse a la escuela por la tarde   _____

Actividad E

Give the following commands.

EXAMPLES: empezar a trabajar ya   (Uds.)   *Empiecen* **a trabajar ya.**

1. almorzar en la cafetería   (Uds.)   _____

2. cruzar la calle con cuidado   (Uds.)   _____

3. comenzar a hacer las tareas   (Ud.)   _____

4. pagar la cuenta del gas   (Ud.)   _____

5. no jugar en la sala   (Uds.)   _____

6. llegar temprano a la casa   (Uds.)   _____

Actividad F

Answer the following questions.

1. ¿A qué hora almorzaste ayer?

_____

2. ¿Con quién jugaste el sábado pasado?

_____

3. ¿Qué nota sacaste en el último examen de español?

_____

4. ¿A qué hora comenzaste a ver televisión anoche?

_____

5. ¿Cruzaste muchas calles para llegar a la escuela?

_____

6. ¿A qué hora llegaste a casa ayer por la tarde?

_____

7. ¿Tocaste a la puerta?

_____

8. ¿Buscaste palabras en el diccionario para la tarea de español?

_____

3 Other verbs undergo different spelling changes to maintain the original sound of the infinitive. Look at these examples.

recoger: Yo _recojo_ **los juguetes.**   _I pick up the toys._
          Recoja **Ud. su ropa.**   _Pick up your clothes._

dirigir: Yo _dirijo_ **la obra de teatro.**   _I direct the play._
          Dirija **Ud. el coro.**   _Direct the choir._

What happened to the **g** in **recoger** an **dirigir**? _____

The **g** changed to **j** in the first person (**yo**) singular of the present tense and in the formal commands.

RULE: Verbs ending in **-ger** or **-gir** change the **g** to **j** before the vowels **a** and **o** to keep the original sound of the infinitive. Some **-ger** and **-gir** verbs also have stem changes: **corregir (i)** _to correct_ (**yo corrijo**) and **elegir (i)** _to elect_ (**yo elijo**).

Actividad **G**

Give the following commands.

EXAMPLES: recoger los platos sucios   (Ud.)
              Recoja los platos sucios.

1. corregir los errores en la composición   (Uds.) _____

2. proteger a los animales   (Uds.) _____

3. escoger una película cómica   (Ud.) _____

4. coger la pelota   (Ud.) _____

5. elegir al presidente de la clase   (Uds.)   _____

6. dirigir el coro en la clase de música   (Ud.)   _____

   Finally, verbs ending in **-guir** undergo a spelling change in the first person (**yo**) singular of the present tense and in the formal commands.

extin*guir*:   **Yo siempre** *extingo* **el fuego.**   *I always put out the fire.*
        Extinga **el fuego.**   *Put out the fire.*

In these sentences, **gu** changes to **g** before **o** and **a** to maintain the original sound of the infinitive. Note that some verbs with spelling changes also have stem changes: **seguir (i)** *to follow*, **perseguir (i)** *to pursue*, and **conseguir (i)** *to obtain, get.*

Sigan **a ese señor.**   *Follow that man.*

Answer the following questions.

1. ¿Escoges a tus maestros en la escuela?

_____

2. ¿Sigues algún curso de arte?

_____

3. ¿Recoges los platos sucios después de la comida?

_____

4. ¿Consigues siempre entradas para los conciertos que quieres ver?

_____

5. ¿Proteges a los animales?

_____

6. ¿Diriges algún proyecto en la escuela?

_____

Here are some statements you heard from some political candidates. Express them in Spanish.

1. I follow the advice of the people.

   _____

2. I knocked on every door.

   _____

3. I embraced (**abrazar**) a hundred babies.

   _____

4. I do not protect criminals.

   _____

5. I arrived in this city twenty years ago.

   _____

6. I always choose the correct solutions.

   _____

7. I correct my mistakes.

   _____

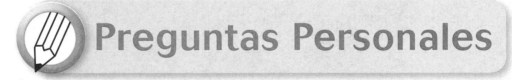

1. ¿En cuáles supersticiones cree mucha gente?

   _____

2. En tu opinión, ¿cuál es la superstición más ridícula?

   _____

3. ¿Tuviste mala suerte el año pasado? ¿Qué pasó?

   _____

4. ¿Tienes algún objeto de buena suerte?

_____

5. ¿Cuál es tu cuento de hadas favorito?

_____

Información Personal

You are a successful person. Using the following expressions, show the steps to your success.

escoger una carrera	**elegir una compañía**
seguir mis estudios	**conseguir un empleo**
comenzar a trabajar	**jugar en un equipo**
sacar buenas notas	

EXAMPLES: _Saqué_ **buenas notas en la escuela.**

_____

_____

_____

_____

_____

_____

_____

_____

_____

_____

DIÁLOGO

Your friend Francisco (a very superstitious person) is always a nervous wreck when he walks down the street. Anita is trying to calm him down.

Cápsula cultural

El dios malo: Juracán

Cada año, tormentas violentas con vientos de más de 100 millas por hora se forman en los océanos de las regiones tropicales.

Estos vientos destructivos pueden cubrir un área de miles de millas cuadradas, trayendo nubes que producen lluvias torrenciales y olas tremendas. Estas olas pueden inundar la tierra, ahogar a miles de personas y causar billones de dólares en daños.

Los vientos son tan fuertes que derrumban árboles y edificios y aún levantan automóviles. Estas tormentas, llamadas huracanes, son las más fuertes que existen en la tierra.

¿Pero, de dónde viene su nombre? Antes de la llegada de los españoles al Nuevo Mundo, una tribu de indios, los taínos, vivían en muchas de las islas del Mar Caribe. Fue esta gente quien dio a Puerto Rico su nombre original: Borinquen. Los taínos eran una gente apacible y trabajadora. Nos dieron muchas palabras indias que forman parte de la lengua española y de ahí pasaron al inglés, por ejemplo: la hamaca, el tabaco, la canoa y el maíz.

Como todos los pueblos antiguos y modernos, los taínos tenían sus supersticiones y creencias. Crearon una mitología para explicar la naturaleza y su mundo. Inventaron cuentos de sus dioses y sus poderes. Había muchos cuentos del dios malo, Juracán, que causaba tormentas terribles cuando estaba enojado. No es difícil ver por qué los taínos llamaron "huracán" a esas tormentas terribles que destruían su tierra.

Discusión

1. Describa lo que pasa durante un huracán.

2. ¿Quiénes eran los taínos? ¿Cómo eran?

3. Mencione algunas palabras taínas que son ahora parte de nuestra lengua.

4. ¿Quién era Juracán y que hacía?

5. ¿Cómo explicaban los eventos naturales los pueblos antiguos, como los romanos y los griegos?

VOCABULARIO

la tormenta *storm*
cuadrado *square*
la ola *wave*
inundar *to flood*
ahogar *to drown*
el daño *damage*
derrumbar *to knock down*

fue *it was*
apacible *peaceful*
la creencia *belief*
el poder *power*

Las maravillas del reino animal

Comparing People and Things

 **Vocabulario**

la ballena

el tiburón

la ardilla

la jirafa

la araña

el cocodrilo

la tortuga

la hormiga

el leopardo / la pantera

el oso

el canguro

la serpiente/la culebra

el ciervo

el pavo

la liebre

Did you ever play **"¿Quién soy?"**? This time we are going to play it with animals. See if you can guess the animal by what it says.

1. Soy un reptil, camino despacio y vivo por mucho tiempo.

   Soy ——————————————— .

2. Soy un pájaro que no puede volar. Vivo en las tierras frías del Antártico.

   Soy ——————————————— .

3. No tengo patas. Me muevo silenciosamente.

   Soy ——————————————— .

4. Vivo en el río. Soy feroz y la gente me tiene mucho miedo.

   Soy ——————————————— .

5. Salto en vez de correr y vengo de Australia.

   Soy ——————————————— .

6. Vivo en los árboles. Soy pequeña y tengo una cola larga y bonita.

   Soy ——————————————— .

7. Soy muy inteligente y vivo en el mar, pero no soy un pez.

   Soy ——————————————— .

8. Tengo ocho patas y atrapo insectos en mis telarañas.

   Soy ——————————————— .

9. Salto rápidamente y tengo orejas muy largas.

   Soy ——————————————— .

10. Soy muy grande y peludo. Duermo todo el invierno en una cueva.

    Soy ——————————————— .

¡Es increíble!

Let's read a story about some world records.

En todo el mundo a la gente le gusta discutir sobre cuál es la cosa más grande, la más pequeña, la más fría, la más caliente, la más alta, la más vieja, etc. Hacen preguntas como: ¿quién es el hombre más pesado del mundo?, ¿quién es el más rápido?, ¿quién bateó el «jonrón» más largo?, ¿cuál es el animal más grande?

Puede encontrar las respuestas a todas estas preguntas, y a miles más, en un solo libro, «El libro Guinness de récords ». La compañía Guinness produce cerveza y es la compañía más grande de Irlanda. Cuando publicó su libro por primera vez, no tenía la menor idea del éxito que iba a tener. El libro está publicado hoy día en 23 idiomas y hasta ahora ha vendido más de 30 millones de copias.

la cerveza *beer*

Aquí tenemos algunos récordes mundiales interesantes: la persona más alta del mundo, un hombre que medía 8 pies, 11 pulgadas; la persona más pequeña, una mujer que medía 23 pulgadas; la persona más pesada, un hombre que pesaba 1,069 libras; la persona más vieja, un japonés que murió a la edad de 120 años; el animal más grande y más pesado, una ballena azul que medía 110 pies y pesaba 195 toneladas; el animal más alto, una jirafa que medía 20 pies; el animal más veloz, el leopardo cazador, que puede correr de 96 a 101 kilómetros por hora (60–63 millas por hora); el animal terrestre más grande, un elefante africano que medía 13 pies de alto y pesaba 26,328 libras; el perro más pequeño, un chihuahüense que pesaba 10 onzas; la serpiente más larga y más pesada, una anaconda que medía 27 pies, 9 pulgadas; el reptil más grande y más pesado, un cocodrilo que medía 27 pies y pesaba 1,100 libras; el pez marino más grande, un tiburón que medía 60 pies, 9 pulgadas y pesaba 90,000 libras; el árbol más alto, una secoya gigante de California que medía 366 pies; el árbol más viejo, un pino de los Estados Unidos que tenía 4,900 años.

la pulgada *inch*

la libra *pound*
pesado *heavy*
la tonelada *ton*

el leopardo cazador *cheetah*

chihuahüense *from Chihuahua, Mexico*

la secoya *sequoia*

¿Le pareció interesante la información? ¿Sabe la respuesta a las siguientes preguntas? Algunas parecen ridículas, pero sin embargo están en el libro oficial de records mundiales. ¿Sabe Ud. cuál es . . .

(a) la pizza más grande del mundo?

(b) el mayor peso levantado por un ser humano?

(c) la perla más grande?

(d) la iglesia más grande?

(e) el «jonrón» más largo?

Las respuestas

(a) una que medía 80 pies y
pesaba 18,664 libras

(b) 6,270 libras

(c) una que pesó 14 libras,
una onza

(d) San Pedro en Roma, con
un área de 18,110 yardas
cuadradas

(e) 618 pies de distancia

Actividad B

Conteste con frases completas.

1. ¿Qué le gusta discutir a la gente?

_____

2. ¿Cuáles son algunas preguntas que hace la gente?

_____

3. ¿Dónde se encuentran las respuestas a esas preguntas?

_____

4. ¿En qué país está la compañía?

_____

5. ¿En cuántas lenguas está publicado el libro?

_____

6. ¿Cuánto medía el hombre más alto del mundo, según el libro?

_____

7. ¿De qué nacionalidad era el hombre más viejo?

_____

8. ¿De qué país viene el perro más pequeño?

_____

9. ¿Cuál es el animal más grande y más pesado del mundo?

_____

10. ¿Dónde está el árbol más alto del mundo?

_____

 In order to arrive at the facts you read in the story, people had to make comparisons. Let's look at some examples:

El elefante medía trece pies de alto.	_The elephant was 13 feet tall._
La jirafa medía veintitrés pies de alto.	_The giraffe was 23 feet tall._
La jirafa era _más alta que_ el elefante.	_The giraffe was taller than the elephant._
El elefante era _menos alto que_ la jirafa.	_The elephant was less tall than the giraffe._

In Spanish, to form a comparison stating that one thing (or person) is MORE than another, use **más** + adjective + **que**. To form a comparison stating that one thing (or person) is LESS than another, use **menos** + adjective + **que**. Remember that the adjective has to agree in gender and number with the noun it refers to:

María **es más estudiosa que Juan.**	_María is more studious than Juan._
Juan **es menos estudioso que María.**	_Juan is less studious than María._

Compare the animals illustrated using **más** and the clues given.

EXAMPLE: pequeño   **El gato es *más pequeño que* el cochino.**

1. alto

2. grande

3. rápidos

4. inteligente

5. feroces

6. bonito

7. pequeño

Actividad D

Give your opinion of the following things.

EXAMPLE: las películas románticas / las películas de horror (*emocionante*)
Las películas románticas son *más emocionantes que* las películas de horror.

1. el tenis / el béisbol   (*popular*)

_____

2. el fútbol / el fútbol americano   (*violento*)

_____

3. la comida en un picnic / la comida en un restaurante   (*sabroso*)

_____

4. la playa / la piscina   (*divertido*)

_____

5. la clase de español / la clase de matemáticas   (*difícil*)

_____

Using **más** or **menos**, compare the following things.

EXAMPLE: **novela policíaca / novela histórica** (*interesante*)
           La novela policíaca *es menos interesante que* **la novela histórica.**
           La novela policíaca *es más interesante que* **la novela histórica.**

1. Cristóbal Colón / Francisco Núñez de Coronado   (*famoso*)

_____

2. el dinero / la salud   (*importante*)

_____

3. los trenes / los aviones   (*rápidos*)

_____

4. la televisión / el cine   (*necesario*)

_____

5. los automóviles / las bicicletas   (*útiles*)

_____

 Now look at the following type of comparison.

Las serpientes son *tan largas* **como** *Snakes are as long as crocodiles.*
los cocodrilos.

Yo soy *tan alto(a)* **como tú.** *I am as tall as you.*

To form a *comparison of equality* in Spanish, use **tan** + adjective + **como**.

Compare the following, using **tan … como …**

EXAMPLE: Juan/Elisa   (*amable*)   **Juan** *es tan amable como* **Elisa.**

1. el profesor / el director   (*serio*)   _____

2. las frutas / las legumbres   (*bueno*)   _____

3. el policía / el bombero   (*valiente*)   _____

4. el perro / el gato   (*inteligente*)   _____

5. yo / tú   (*sincero*)   _____

 What happens if you want to express a superlative — that is, say that something or somebody is the greatest or the most intelligent? Look at the following examples.

Pablo es *el más alto de la clase.* *Pablo is the tallest in the class.*

Rosa *es la menos tímida de la clase.* *Rosa is the least timid in the class.*

Andrés y Mario son *los más pequeños* *Andrés and Mario are the*
del grupo. *smallest in the group.*

Elisa y Luisa son *las menos serias* *Elisa and Luisa are the least serious*
del grupo. *in the group.*

RULE: In Spanish, the superlative is expressed as follows:

definite article **(el, la, los, las)** + **más** / **menos** + adjective + **de**
(the + most / least + adjective + in)

Using the following adjectives, state who in your family is the most or the least:

EXAMPLE: estricto
Mi papá es *el más estricto de* **la familia.**
Mi mamá es *la menos estricta de* **la familia.**

1. alegre   _____

_____

2. serio   _____

_____

3. ambicioso   _____

_____

4. amable   _____

_____

5. divertido   _____

_____

6. generoso _____

_____

Actividad **H**

In your opinion, which are *the most* and *the least* in each category?

EXAMPLE: animal/rápido
            El leopardo es *el más rápido.*
            La tortuga es *la menos rápida.*

1. deporte/interesante

_____

_____

2. animal/inteligente

_____

_____

3. programa de televisión/aburrido

_____

_____

4. película/divertida

_____

_____

5. actor/guapo

_____

_____

6. automóvil/elegante

_____

_____

There are four adjectives with irregular comparative forms.

bueno *good*	**mejor** *better, best*	**Pablo es *mejor que* Jorge.** **Él es *el mejor alumno de* la clase.**
malo *bad*	**peor** *worse, worst*	**Ellos son *peores que* sus amigos.** **Ellos son *los peores de la* escuela.**
grande *big*	**mayor** *older, oldest* **más grande** *bigger, biggest*	**Francisco es *mayor que* yo, pero yo soy *más grande que* él.** **Él es *el mayor* y yo soy el *más grande de los* hermanos.**
pequeño *small*	**menor** *younger, youngest* **más pequeño** *smaller, smallest*	**María es mi hermana *menor* y es *la más pequeña de* la familia.**

Mayor and **menor** refer to age, **más grande** and **más pequeño** refer to physical size.

In your opinion, which was or is the best and the worst of these things?

EXAMPLE: novela de ciencia ficción
La mejor novela de ciencia ficción es «**El planeta desconocido**».
La peor novela de ciencia ficción es «**Noche de horror**».

1. película del año

_____

_____

2. actor de televisión

_____

_____

3. equipo de fútbol profesional

_____

_____

4. automóvil deportivo

_____

_____

5. grupo de rock

_____

_____

Write a description of your family (real or imaginary). Mention who is smaller, bigger, older, taller, smarter, etc.

EXAMPLE: **Tengo un hermano. Se llama Raúl. Raúl** _es más estudioso_ **que yo, pero yo soy** _más inteligente._

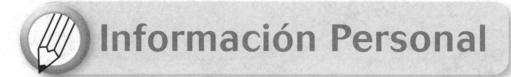

1. La mejor película qué vi el año pasado fue _____ .

2. El programa de televisión que más me gustó es _____ .

3. La experiencia más interesante que tuve fue _____ .

4. La clase que más me gustó fue _____ porque _____ .

5. Yo soy el / la mejor _____ de mi familia (de mi clase, de mi escuela).

DIÁLOGO

Your sister Carmencita is a very curious child. She's forever asking you difficult questions. Give your answers:

Composición

You are a camp counselor and have gone to the zoo with a group of small children. Write some of the questions the children ask you about the animals. For example, they want to know whether the leopard is as strong as the tiger; whether the crocodile is as dangerous as the shark; which is the longest snake in the zoo; which is the smallest animal in the zoo, and so on:

_____

_____

_____

_____

_____

Cápsula cultural

Los animales de la selva

El Amazonas es la selva más grande de nuestro planeta y ocupa un área de más de 2,5 millones de millas cuadradas e incluye grandes partes de nueve países sudamericanos. El Río Amazonas, el más grande de la tierra, tiene su origen en un pequeño arroyo en las alturas de los Andes. Este «río mar» corre 4.000 (cuatro mil) millas por Perú y Brasil hasta el Océano Atlántico. Más que un río, el Amazonas es una red de ríos, arroyos, lagos, islas y pantanos que se unen con la selva tropical para crear el ecosistema más grande que ha producido la naturaleza. La diversidad y abundancia de plantas y animales no tienen igual en ninguna otra parte de la tierra. Hay más especies de peces en el Río Amazonas que en el océano. En este ecosistema hay más pájaros (8.600 especies), más plantas (25.000 especies identificadas), más árboles, más mariposas — en efecto, más de casi todos los organismos.

Vamos a mencionar algunos de los animales hallados en esta selva:

el caimán: un reptil relacionado al cocodrilo y que crece hasta 15 pies de largo.

la piraña: un pez conocido por su ferocidad. Un grupo de pirañas puede comerse un animal grande en pocos minutos.

el jaguar: el gato salvaje más grande del hemisferio occidental.

la capibara: el roedor más grande del mundo. Mide 4 pies y pesa más de 100 libras.

la anaconda: una culebra gigante que puede crecer hasta 32 pies de largo.

Desafortunadamente, mucho de este mundo está desapareciendo como resultado de la deforestación causada por operaciones de minería, explotación forestal y el desmonte de la tierra para hacer sitio para la gente que huye de las áreas sobrepobladas. Si no se para esta destrucción, la tierra se hará un desierto y la vida que depende de ella se extinguirá.

Discusión

1. ¿Por qué se llama al Río Amazonas el «río mar»? Descríbalo.
2. ¿Por qué es única la selva del Amazonas?
3. Menciona algunas causas de la destrucción de la selva. ¿Cuáles son las consecuencias de esta destrucción?
4. ¿Cómo te afecta personalmente esta destrucción? ¿Qué podemos hacer para pararla?

Para investigar

Busca fotos de los animales del Amazonas en el Internet y compártelas con la clase.

VOCABULARIO

e *and*
el arroyo *brook*
el río mar *river sea*
correr *flow*
la red *web*
el pantano *marsh*

en efecto *in fact*
el roedor *rodent*
el desmonte *clearing*
hacer sitio *to make room*
pararse *to stop*

¿Cuál será tu profesión?

Future Tense of Regular Verbs

la programadora de computadoras

el electricista

la veterinaria

la peluquera

la aeromoza/ la azafata

la fotógrafa

el carnicero

la gerente

el zapatero

la empleada del banco

el piloto

el entrenador personal

el panadero

la reportera

*In this **Vocabulario**, we illustrate sometimes male, sometimes female professionals. Most of the professions, however, have both male and female practitioners.

Who does the following? Complete the sentences with the appropriate noun.

1. _____ corta el pelo a la gente.

2. _____ vende carne.

3. _____ prepara y vende el pan.

4. _____ trata a los animales cuando están enfermos.

5. _____ arregla computadoras.

6. _____ vende estampillas en el correo.

7. _____ saca fotos artísticas.

8. _____ escribe programas para las computadoras.

9. _____ entrena a la gente.

10. _____ maneja el avión.

11. _____ escribe en los periódicos.

12. _____ trabaja en el banco.

13. _____ combate los fuegos.

14. _____ ayuda a los pasajeros en el avión.

15. _____ supervisa un grupo de personas en una compañía.

16. _____ conecta los cables para la electricidad.

El horóscopo

Todo el mundo quiere saber qué **pasará** en el futuro? Los astrólogos dicen que nuestra personalidad y nuestro futuro están influenciados por las estrellas. Todos nacimos bajo uno de los doce signos del zodíaco, y hay personas que no toman ninguna decisión importante sin consultar su horóscopo. ¿Qué **traerá** el día de mañana? ¿Qué sorpresas **revelarán** las estrellas? Diviértase leyendo el siguiente horóscopo.

Acuario   21 de enero al 18 de febrero

Ud. es una persona generosa, romántica y poética. Muy pronto **recibirá** una noticia de gran importancia para su felicidad. **Realizará** su sueño de hacer un viaje largo.

 Piscis   19 de febrero al 20 de marzo

Ud. es una persona sensitiva, idealista y sentimental. En los próximos meses **conocerá** a alguien que **será** muy importante en su vida.

 Aries   21 de marzo al 20 de abril

Ud. es una persona valiente y decidida. Siempre **conseguirá** las cosas que quiere. Le **llegarán** noticias de un amigo querido.

 Tauro   21 de abril al 21 de mayo

Ud. tiene mucho sentido común. Es una persona práctica y realista. Este año le **sonreirá** la fortuna. **Recibirá** un dinero que no esperaba.

 Géminis   22 de mayo al 21 de junio

Ud. es impaciente e impulsivo(a). Los próximos meses **estará** muy ocupado(a) con actividades sociales. **Ganará** la admiración de una persona importante para Ud.

 Cáncer   22 de junio al 22 de julio

Ud. tiene un gran sentido común, es simpático(a) y le gusta ayudar a los demás. Pronto **resolverá** muchos de sus problemas. El próximo año **será** muy interesante.

Leo 23 de julio al 23 de agosto

Ud. es una persona segura de sí misma, con cualidades de líder. En las próximas semanas **establecerá** contactos importantes con personas que le **ayudarán** en el futuro.

Virgo 24 de agosto al 23 de septiembre

Ud. es perfeccionista. Antes de hacer algo, estudia todos los detalles y lo piensa bien. Los resultados de un examen que Ud. **tomará serán** brillantes.

Libra 24 de septiembre al 23 de octubre

Ud. es una persona tranquila, que busca la armonía en las cosas. **Ganará** mucho dinero este año, pero tenga cuidado porque, si no, lo **gastará** pronto.

Escorpión 24 de octubre al 22 de noviembre

A Ud. le gusta trabajar y es una persona determinada que no acepta el fracaso. Ud. **tratará** de cambiar su vida este año, pero los cambios no le **traerán** satisfacción.

Sagitario 23 de noviembre al 20 de diciembre

Ud. es una persona alegre, sincera y honesta, pero necesita tener más confianza misma. Los nuevos proyectos que **comenzará** pronto le **darán** prestigio.

Capricornio 21 de diciembre al 20 de enero

Ud. es independiente y ambicioso(a), pero también melancólico(a) y pesimista. Sus problemas de dinero no **durarán** mucho. Este año Ud. **empezará** un proyecto ambicioso.

durar *to last*

Answer the following questions with complete sentences.

1. ¿Qué dicen los astrólogos?

_____

2. ¿Qué hacen muchas personas antes de tomar una decisión importante?

_____

3. ¿Qué tipo de persona es un Leo?

_____

4. ¿Qué problema tiene un Sagitario?

_____

5. Según el horóscopo, ¿qué recibirá pronto un Acuario?

_____

6. ¿Qué tipo de persona es un Cáncer?

_____

7. ¿Bajo qué signo nacieron las personas sensitivas, idealistas y sentimentales?

_____

8. ¿Bajo qué signo naciste?

_____

Up to now, we have been talking in the present and the past tenses. How do we describe actions and events that will happen in the future? The horoscope in the story told you some things that will happen in the future. Let's look at some examples:

Ud. *realizará* su sueño.	*You will fulfill your dream.*
¿Qué *traerá* el día de mañana?	*What will tomorrow bring?*
Ud. *recibirá* una noticia importante.	*You will receive important news.*

Which are the infinitives of the three verbs used in these sentences?

_____ , _____ , and _____ . What ending was added to all three infinitives? _____ . It's easy to form the future tense in Spanish. There is only one set of endings for all verbs: **-ar, -er, ir**. You simply add the following endings to the infinitive: **-é, -ás, -á, -emos, -án.**

SUBJECT	INFINITIVE		
	hablar	**comer**	**vivir**
yo	hablaré	comeré	viviré
tú	hablarás	comerás	vivirás
Ud., él, ella	hablará	comerá	vivirá
nosotros, -as	hablaremos	comeremos	viviremos
Uds., ellos, ellas	hablarán	comerán	vivirán

Now try to supply the forms of the future tense for these verbs:

	estar	ser	abrir
yo	_____	_____	_____
tú	_____	_____	_____
Ud., él, ella	_____	_____	_____
nosotros, -as	_____	_____	_____
Uds., ellos, ellas	_____	_____	_____

Note that all endings, except for **nosotros**, have an accent.

Actividad C

You are going to spend your vacation at the beach. What will you do there?

EXAMPLE: tomar el sol   **Yo *tomaré* el sol.**

1. nadar en el mar _____
2. correr por la playa _____
3. construir castillos de arena _____
4. comer en restaurantes _____
5. recoger conchas _____

Actividad D

Here's a list of things your mother will do tomorrow.

EXAMPLE: comprar carne en la carnicería   **Ella *comprará* carne en la carnicería.**

1. ir con el gato al veterinario

_____

2. hablar con el fotógrafo

_____

3. leer el artículo de la periodista española

_____

4. dar instrucciones al electricista

_____

Actividad E

You are going to spend tomorrow afternoon at a friend's house. What will the two of you do there?

EXAMPLE: mirar la televisión   *Miraremos* **la televisión**

1. estudiar para el examen   _____

2. terminar las tareas   _____

3. escribir la composición   _____

4. leer el periódico   _____

5. escuchar unos discos   _____

Actividad F

Your school is going to have a party. How will everyone help?

EXAMPLE: la profesora / mandar las invitaciones
La profesora *mandará* las invitaciones.

1. los muchachos / traer los discos

_____

2. las muchachas / escoger la música

_____

3. tú / servir el ponche

_____

4. Uds. / ayudar a decorar

_____

5. el director / tocar la guitarra

_____

6. las madres / preparar los sándwiches

_____

7. tú / comprar los platos de papel

_____

8. yo / abrir la puerta

_____

9. Ud. / recoger la basura (*garbage*)

_____

10. todos nosotros / cantar y bailar

_____

Next week you are going to the flea market with some friends. Write what each of you will be doing, using the suggestions:

yo	estar allí temprano
Uds.	pasar el día allí
tú y yo	comprar muchas cosas
Carlos y Ana	vender los juguetes viejos
tú	comer hamburguesas
Roberto	gastar mucho dinero
todos nosotros	escoger libros de uso

EXAMPLE: **Tú y yo** *pasaremos* **el día allí.**

1. _____
2. _____
3. _____
4. _____
5. _____
6. _____

 You know that the future tense is used in Spanish to describe future actions or events. But look at these sentences.

¿Qué hora *será*?	*I wonder what time it is. (What time can it be?)*
No sé. *Serán* las seis.	*I don't know. It's probably six o'clock.*
¿Dónde *estará* tu mamá?	*I wonder where your mother is. (Where can your mother be?)*
No sé. *Estará* en la cocina.	*I don't know. I guess she's in the kitchen.*

In Spanish, the future tense is sometimes used to express wonder or probability in the present. It is then equivalent to English *I wonder, I guess, probably.*

Actividad **H**

Two exchange students will be flying in from Madrid to join your class. Everyone is wondering about them. Express their questions.

EXAMPLE: **ser simpáticos**   *¿Serán simpáticos?*

1. hablar sólo en español
2. ser atléticos
3. ayudarnos con los estudios
4. traer cosas de España
5. ir a nuestras fiestas

Preguntas Personales

1. ¿Qué tipo de persona eres?

_____

2. ¿En qué profesión piensas trabajar en el futuro? ¿Por qué?

_____

3. ¿Bajo que signo del zodíaco naciste? ¿Tiene alguna relación con tu personalidad?

_____

4. ¿Conoces a otras personas con tu personalidad? ¿Nacieron bajo el mismo signo?

_____

5. ¿Qué tipo de persona consulta su horóscopo antes de tomar una decisión importante?

_____

You are talking with your brother, wondering about the future.

Composición

Mis planes para el fin de semana. Tell what you will do this weekend. Here are some suggested verbs.

comenzar	comer	ir	ver
comprar	hablar	jugar	visitar

1. _____

2. _____

3. _____

4. _____

5. _____

Cápsula cultural

Desayunando con los pingüinos

Aproximadamente a 1.000 millas del sur de Buenos Aries, en la región de la Patagonia argentina, se sitúa la Bahía Bustamante, una estancia de ovejas que se extiende sobre 210.000 acres. Esta propiedad incluye parte de la costa atlántica, praderas, campos, desiertos y cañones donde una variedad de fauna y flora vive y prospera sin la intervención de humanos. El gobierno argentino convirtió la región de la costa y las islas en un parque nacional, pero la tierra es propiedad privada.

En pocos sitios del mundo existe tanta diversidad de especies que conviven con tanta proximidad. Animales domesticados como ovejas, perros, gatos y caballos recorren la propiedad libremente junto con animales salvajes tales como avestruces, zorros, armadillos y guanacos.

En las playas y en el océano se observan ballenas, delfines, leones marinos, orcas, pulpos y cientos de especies de pájaros que no existen en ningún otro lugar en el mundo.

A pesar de que Bahía Bustamante no es una isla como Galápagos, su estado aislado permite a los animales vivir en su hábitat durante generaciones. Las especies de la región son más similares a las de Nueva Zelanda y Australia que a otras especies en Sudamérica.

Solo admiten aproximadamente 400 visitantes al año mientras que Galápagos recibe más de 100.000. Así, los pocos visitantes afortunados pueden sentarse a comer un bocadillo mientras observan cientos de pingüinos sumergiéndose en el mar, nadando en busca de peces, y jugando con sus amigos.

Discusión

1. ¿Qué es la Bahía Bustamante?

2. ¿Cuáles animales se encuentran en esa area?

3. Menciona algunas causas de la destrucción de la selva. ¿Cuáles son las consecuencias de esta destrucción?

4. ¿Cómo te afecta personalmente esta destrucción? ¿Qué podemos hacer para pararla?

Para investigar

Compara la Bahía Bustamante con la Bahía Fosforescente de Vieques, Puerto Rico.

VOCABULARIO

la pradera *prairie*　　　　**el delfín** *dolphin*
el avestruz *ostrich*　　　**el león marino** *sea lion*
la ballena *whale*

18

La exploración del espacio

Future Tense of Irregular Verbs

1 **Vocabulario**

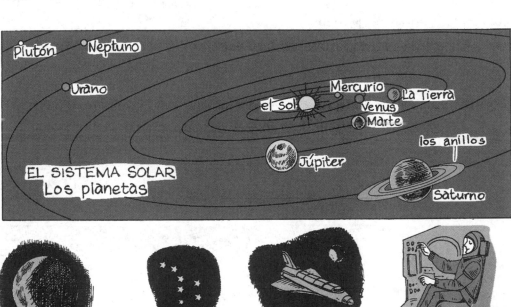

Plutón · Neptuno

Urano

el sol · Mercurio · La Tierra

Venus

Marte

los anillos

Júpiter

EL SISTEMA SOLAR
Los planetas

Saturno

la luna

las estrellas

la nave espacial/
la astronave

el astronauta/
el cosmonauta

el traje espacial

el cohete

la cápsula espacial

el satélite

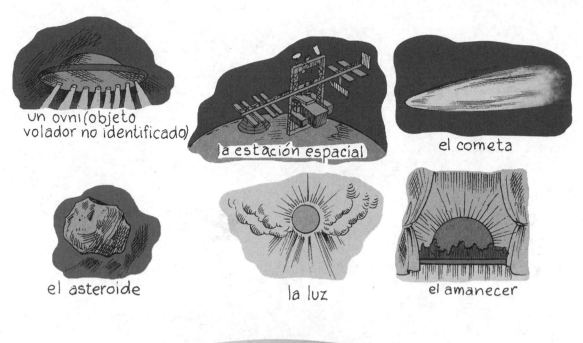

un ovni (objeto volador no identificado)

la estación espacial

el cometa

el asteroide

la luz

el amanecer

Picture story Can you read this story? Whenever you come to a picture, read it as if it were a Spanish word.

La  es un en el . Este sistema es parte de la Vía

Láctea, una de las galaxias del Universo. La viaja alrededor del , y

la alrededor de la Tierra.

La  que vemos durante el es la del . Por la

podemos ver la , las y otros cuerpos celestes. Uno de los

que podemos reconocer fácilmente es porque tiene .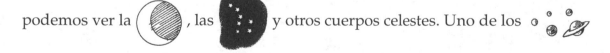

Humor espacial   Make up a funny caption for each situation.

Identify the five pictures and write the names horizontally in the spaces below. Each name has a different number of letters.

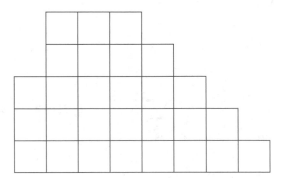

Una aventura en el espacio

Let's read a story about an adventure in space. Pay attention to the verbs in boldface.

CONTROL: ¿Listos para aterrizar en el planeta XGB-37 (equis, ge, b, treinta y siete)?
PILOTO: Estaremos listos en algunos minutos.
CONTROL: ¿Necesitarán nuestra ayuda?
PILOTO: No, no **tendremos** ningún problema. El conteo regresivo comenzará inmediatamente. 10, 9, 8, 7, 6, 5, 4, 3, 2, 1 . . . ¡Contacto!

el conteo regresivo
countdown

CONTROL: ¿Quiénes **pondrán** pie en el planeta?
PILOTO: Paco y Flaco, nuestros dos astronautas hispanos, serán los primeros. Ellos **saldrán** de la cápsula, observarán todo y nos **dirán** qué vieron. Por fin **sabremos** si hay vida en ese planeta o no.
CONTROL: Bueno, en un minuto Uds. estarán al otro lado del planeta y no **podremos** comunicarnos más.

Paco y Flaco aterrizan; salen de la cápsula y sólo ven unas plantas enormes por todas partes. De repente las plantas comienzan a moverse y rodean a los dos astronautas.

rodear *to surround*

PACO: ¡Ay, Flaco, esto no me gusta nada! ¿Qué crees que **harán** estas plantas?

Una de las plantas empieza a hablar.

PLANTA: ¿Por qué interrumpen la paz y la tranquilidad de nuestro mundo? ¿Uds. son seres terrestres, verdad? **¿Vendrán** otros detrás de Uds.?
FLACO: Sí, pero . . .
PLANTA: ¡Silencio! Conocemos muy bien las crueldades de su planeta. En la Tierra hacen ensaladas mixtas de nuestros hermanos. Preparan guacamole de nuestros primos, los aguacates. ¡Uds. son todos unos asesinos!
PACO: Claro que hacemos eso. Pero no somos asesinos. Los aguacates son solamente vegetales.
VEGETAL: ¡Solamente vegetales! Uds. pagarán ese insulto con la vida. ¡Morirán ahora mismo! Pronto, tráiganme la sal.

seres terrestres
earthlings

el aguacate
avocado

FLACO: Oh, no. Los vegetales nos van a comer. ¡Qué manera tan horrible de morir!

VEGETAL: Les **pondremos** también un poco de salsa.

PACO: No, no quiero morir así. ¡Auxilio! ¡Socorro! (Miguelito oye la voz de la mamá.)

MAMÁ: Miguelito, son las once. Apaga ya el televisor. Seguro que **tendrás** pesadillas a causa de esa basura de ciencia ficción.

¡Auxilio! ¡Socorro!
Help!

apagar *to turn off*
la basura *garbage*

Answer the following questions with complete sentences.

1. ¿Qué ven Paco y Flaco cuando aterrizan en el planeta desconocido?

   _____

2. ¿Cómo reciben las plantas a los astronautas? ¿Están contentas de verlos?

   _____

3. ¿Qué opinión tienen las plantas de los seres terrestres? ¿Por qué?

   _____

4. ¿Por qué necesitan sal y salsa las plantas?

   _____

5. ¿Qué piensa la mamá de Miguel de la ciencia ficción? ¿Y qué piensa Ud.?

   _____

Look at the pictures to solve the following puzzle. The boxed letters will answer the question:

¿Cómo se llama la galaxia donde está nuestro planeta?

__ uz

__ steroide

na __ e

T __ erra

s __ télite

So __

Lun __

__ onteo

10-9-8-7-6-5-4-3-2-1-0

es __ rella

coh __ te

astron __ uta

Solución:

2 Did you pay attention to the verbs in bold type in the story? They are all in the future tense. The y have regular endings, but their stem is not the infinitive.

No *podremos* comunicarnos.

We won't be able to communicate.

Por fin *sabremos* si hay vida en ese planeta o no.

Finally we will know if there is life on that planet or not.

What are the stems of **podrá** and **sabremos**? _____ and _____ .

What are the infinitives of these verbs? _____ and _____ . Can you figure out what happened to the infinitive to become **podr-** and **sabr-.**

Poder and **saber** drop the **e** of the infinitive and then add the endings of the future tense. **Querer** also belongs in this category.

Complete the verb tables below.

	poder	querer	saber
yo	podré	querré	sabré
tú	_____	_____	_____
Ud., él, ella	_____	_____	_____
nosotros, -as	_____	_____	_____
Uds., ellos, ellas	_____	_____	_____

Actividad F

You have invited a friend from another city to visit you and she has called to ask you some questions. Work with a partner and answer them.

1. ¿Podrás ir al aeropuerto a recibirme?

_____

2. ¿Querrán tus padres ir contigo?

_____

3. ¿Sabrás cómo llegar al aeropuerto?

_____

4. ¿Sabrán Uds. en qué puerta esperarme?

_____

5. ¿Podré llamar por teléfono a mis padres desde tu casa?

_____

6. ¿Podremos salir el sábado por la noche?

_____

7. ¿Querrá tu hermano salir con nosotros?

_____

8. ¿Podrán tus padres prestarte el carro?

_____

 Look now at these sentences from the story on page 335:

Les _pondremos_ también salsa.	_We will also put salsa on them._
No _tendremos_ ningún problema.	_We won't have any problem._
Ellos _saldrán_ de la cápsula.	_They will leave the capsule._
¿_Vendrán_ otros detrás de Uds.?	_Will others come behind you?_

Can you figure out how the stems of these verbs were formed?

INFINITIVE	STEM OF FUTURE TENSE
poner	pondr-
tener	tendr-
salir	saldr-
venir	vendr-

The **e** of **poner** and **tener** and the **i** of **salir** and **venir** change to **d**. Complete the following tables:

	poner	tener	salir	venir
yo	pondré	tendré	saldré	vendré
tú	_____	_____	_____	_____
Ud., él, ella	_____	_____	_____	_____
nosotros, -as	_____	_____	_____	_____
Uds., ellos, ellas	_____	_____	_____	_____

Actividad G

You are writing a letter to some friends who will come to visit you. Complete the letter with the appropriate form of the future tense:

Queridos amigos:

Yo _____ de la escuela temprano y _____ ir a la estación
     (salir)   (poder)

a recibirlos. Sé que Paula y Mario _____ ir conmigo. Como Uds. son
                                           (querer)

cuatro, yo _____ que hacer dos viajes a la estación. Mientras yo hago
                   (tener)

un viaje, los demás _____ esperarme en un café. Según me dicen, Uds.
                          (poder)

_____ en el tren de las cuatro.
   (venir)

Actividad H

You are going camping with some friends. Tell what each person will do, using the following suggestions.

yo	salir a las seis
mis amigos y yo	ponerse ropa cómoda
Ud.	querer ser el (la) guía
Roberto y Rosa	poder nadar en el lago
tú	tener que levantarse temprano
Mario	venir a visitarnos
Uds.	saber cómo llegar al campamento

EXAMPLE: **Usted *vendrá* a visitarnos.**

1. _____

2. _____

3. _____

4. _____

5. _____

6. _____

4 There are two more verbs with irregular future tense forms, **decir** and **hacer**:

Ellos nos *dirán* qué vieron.   *They will tell us what they saw.*

¿Qué *harán* estas plantas?   *What will these plants do?*

The stem of the future tense of **decir** is _____ . The stem of the future tense of **hacer** is _____ . Complete the following tables.

yo	dir _____	har _____
tú	_____	_____
Ud., él, ella	_____	_____
nosotros, -as	_____	_____
Uds., ellos, ellas	_____	_____

Actividad 1

Using the suggested expressions, write when the following people will do certain things.

más tarde	el año que viene	el próximo verano
los fines de semana	pasado mañana	mañana
de hoy en quince	de hoy en ocho	el mes que viene

EXAMPLE: mis padres / ir a Europa
Mis padres *irán* a Europa *el próximo verano*.

1. Enrique / tener que trabajar

_____

2. nosotros / venir a comer

_____

3. tú / hacer las tareas

_____

4. Uds. / querer salir

_____

5. Marta y Rosa / hacer una torta

_____

6. yo / salir de vacaciones

_____

7. Ud. / poder viajar

_____

8. tú y yo / saber hablar español

_____

Actividad **J**

Your father wants to know your plans for next weekend. Answer his questions. Work with a partner.

1. ¿Saldrás con tus amigos el sábado?

_____

2. ¿A qué hora te encontrarás con ellos?

_____

3. ¿Te dirán ellos adónde quieren ir?

_____

4. ¿Sabrás qué autobús coger?

_____

5. ¿Querrá tu hermano ir contigo?

_____

6. ¿Tendrás suficiente dinero?

_____

7. ¿Qué ropa te pondrás?

_____

8. ¿Qué harán Uds. el domingo?

_____

9. ¿Podrás lavar el carro?

_____

10. ¿Me dirás si piensas regresar muy tarde a casa?

_____

Preguntas Personales

1. ¿Cuántos años tendrás en el año 2025?

_____

2. ¿Por qué es importante explorar el espacio?

_____

3. ¿Qué crees que podrás hacer en el futuro?

_____

4. ¿Qué cualidades debe tener un astronauta? ¿Las tiene Ud.?

_____

5. ¿En qué nuevas formas nos comunicaremos en el futuro?

_____

DIÁLOGO

You are looking at a TV science-fiction movie with a friend. Complete the dialogue.

Información Personal

What will you do when you graduate from high school?

Después de graduarme, yo _____

_____

_____

_____

_____

_____

_____

_____

Composición

What will your life be like when you are 25 years old? Write about where you think you will live, what type of job you will have, how much money you will earn, whether you will be married or not, what kinds of clothes you will be wearing, and what kind of music will be in style, etc.

_____

_____

_____

_____

_____

_____

_____

_____

Cápsula cultural

La gente en el espacio

Uno de los sueños más grandes de la humanidad ha sido el de viajar y explorar el espacio. Nuestra tierra es un planeta que gira en órbita alrededor de una estrella — el sol. El sol es una de más de 100 billones de estrellas en nuestra galaxia, o grupo de estrellas – la Vía Láctea. La Vía Láctea es una de más de 100 billones de galaxias en el universo conocido. Así, se puede ver que no somos muy grande y que aún con nuestros telescopios más potentes nuestra habilidad de ver muy lejos es limitada.

En 1962, un astronauta norteamericano hizo órbita alrededor de la tierra. En 1969, Neil Amstrong fue el primer hombre que pisó la superficie de la luna.

El sueño de explorar el espacio ha sido compartido por todos, incluyendo a los hispanohablantes. El primer astronauta de habla española en ir al espacio fue el costarricense Franklin Chang Díaz, el segundo fue el español Miguel López Alegría y el español Pedro Duque fue el tercero.

Es interesante que la Universidad de Puerto Rico tiene el porcentaje más alto de ingenieros contratados por la Administración de Aeronáutica del Espacio del Espacio (NASA). El programa de estudio que ofrece la Universidad de Puerto Rico en materia de ingeniería es conocido y reconocido a nivel mundial, de manera que mucha gente fuera de Puerto Rico va a estudiar allí. La universidad está a la vanguardia en el campo de la ingeniería y su aplicación en la exploración del espacio.

En el observatorio de Arecibo, Puerto Rico, está el radiotelescopio más grande y más sensitivo del mundo. Está disponible para todos los científicos que desear hacer estudios en astronomía y ciencia atmosférica.

Discusión

1. ¿Cómo es nuestro planeta en relación al universo total?

2. ¿Qué es la Vía Láctea?

3. ¿De qué nacionalidad fue? ¿Y el primer hombre que puso pie en la luna?

4. ¿Cómo figura la Universidad de Puerto Rico en el campo de la exploración del espacio?

5. ¿Tienesentidogastarnuestrosrecursosenlaexploracióndelespacioenvezdeusarlos aquí en la tierra? ¿Cuál es su opinión?

Para investigar

Investiga la vida de otros astronautas de origen hispano y comparte la información con la clase.

VOCABULARIO

girar *to revolve*
llegar a ser *to become*
pisar *to step on*

la superficie *surface*
compartido *shared*
el nivel *level*

Repaso IV

Lección 15

Some Spanish verbs change their spelling in certain forms to maintain the original sound of the infinitive.

a. Verbs ending in **-car, -gar,** and **-zar** change the **c** to **qu,** the **g** to **gu,** and the **z** to **c** before **e**:

tocar:	Yo to*qué* a la puerta.	Toque Ud. ahora.
pagar:	Yo no pa*gué* la cuenta.	Pá*g*uela Ud.
comenzar:	Yo ya comen*cé* a hacer las tareas.	Comience Ud. también.

b. Verbs ending in **-ger** or **-gir** change the **g** to **j** before **a** and **o**:

coger:	Yo co*j*o esta pelota.	Co*j*a Ud. la otra.
corregir:	Yo corri*j*o los ejercicios.	Corrí*j*anlos Uds. también.

c. Verbs ending in **-guir** change the **gu** to **g** before **a** and **o**:

seguir:	Yo sigo su ejemplo.	Síganlo Uds. también.

Lección 16

a. **más** + adjective + **que** are used to form a comparison stating that one thing or person is more than another:

Ese edificio es *más alto que* éste.

menos + adjective + **que** are used to form a comparison stating that one thing or person is less than another:

Esta tarea es *menos difícil que* la otra.

b. **tan** + adjective + **como** are used to form a comparison of equality:

Este diccionario es *tan bueno como* **ése.**

c. In Spanish, the superlative is expressed as follows:

definite article (**el, la, los, las**) + **más** / **menos** + adjective + **de**

María es *la alumna más seria de la* **clase.**

d. Four adjectives have irregular comparative forms:

bueno	*good*	**mejor**	*better, best*
malo	*bad*	**peor**	*worse, worst*
grande	*big*	**mayor**	*older, oldest*
pequeño	*small*	**menor**	*younger, youngest*

Más grande and **más pequeño** refer to size, **mayor** and **menor** refer to age.

Lección 17

a. The future of regular verbs is formed by adding the fututre endings to the infinitive:

yo		-é
tú	estudiar	-ás
Ud., él, ella	aprender	-á
nosotros, -as	escribir	-emos
Uds., ellos, ellas		-án

b. In Spanish, the future tense is sometimes used to express wonder, or probability in the present:

¿Quién *llamará* **a esta hora?**   *I wonder who's calling at this hour.*

Será **Carlos.**   *It's probably Carlos.*

Lección 18

a. **Poder, querer,** and **saber** drop the **e** of the infinitive before adding the regular endings of the future tense.

Yo *podré* **visitarte mañana.**   *I'll be able to visit you tomorrow.*

Ella *querrá* **ir conmigo.**   *She will want to go with me.*

Mañana *sabremos* **los resultados del examen.**   *Tomorrow we'll learn the test results.*

b. Poner, tener, salir, and **venir** change the **e** and the **i** of the infinitive to **d** before adding the regular endings of the future tense.

Tú *pondrás* los libros en la mesa.	*You'll put the books on the table.*
Él *tendrá* que estudiar hoy.	*He'll have to study today.*
Uds. *saldrán* mañana para Europa.	*You will leave for Europe tomorrow.*
Ellas *vendrán* temprano.	*They will come early.*

c. Decir and **hacer** have irregular stems in the future tense forms:

Ud. me *dirá* la verdad.	*You will tell me the truth.*
Ellos *harán* las tareas esta noche.	*They will do their homework tonight.*

Put yourself in Lupe's place. Say that you've done all the activities pictured. Use the suggested verbs that follow.

almorzar	llegar	cruzar
pagar	perseguir	recoger
explicar	jugar	sacar

1. Ayer _____ con Juan.

2. _____ muy buenas notas.

3. Fui a la pizarra y _____ .

4. _____ $30 por una falda.

5. Cuando _____ la calle, ayudé a un señor.

6. Anoche _____ .

7. _____

8. Ayer _____ a casa a las tres y media.

9. Y _____ a la una.

Actividad B

Look at the pictures and compare the objects in them with the clues given. The answer depends sometimes on your point of view.

1. rápido: _____ .

2. importante: _____.

3. pequeño: _____.

4. interesante: _____.

5. alto: _____.

6. nuevo: _____.

7. grande: _____.

8. divertido: _____.

Actividad C

¿Qué será? Everyone has plans for the future. Tell what these people will do.

1. (salir) Yo _____.

2. (venir) Ellos _____.

3. (decir) Usted _____.

4. (hacer) Nosotros _____.

5. (tener) María _____.

6. (querer ir) el niño _____.

7. (saber) Él no _____.

8. (poner) Pepito _____ .

8. (poder) Tú no _____ .

Word search   There are 16 words hidden in the puzzle. They are all related to travel, on earth and in space. Can you find them? The words may be read from left to right, right to left, up or down, or diagonally.

A	N	A	U	D	A	M	N	D	I	E
A	S	T	R	O	N	A	V	E	A	J
T	Q	C	R	U	S	T	T	S	E	A
U	N	Á	E	A	A	E	I	P	T	P
A	Ó	P	N	T	T	V	E	E	R	I
N	I	S	Í	A	É	L	R	G	O	U
O	V	U	T	F	L	R	R	A	P	Q
R	A	L	E	A	I	S	A	R	A	E
T	N	A	L	Z	T	Z	U	U	S	B
S	M	C	A	A	E	L	U	N	A	L
A	Q	R	M	O	T	O	L	I	P	P

Actividad E

Jumble   Unscramble the words. Then unscramble the letters above the numbers to find out what Juanita dreamed (or had a nightmare) about.

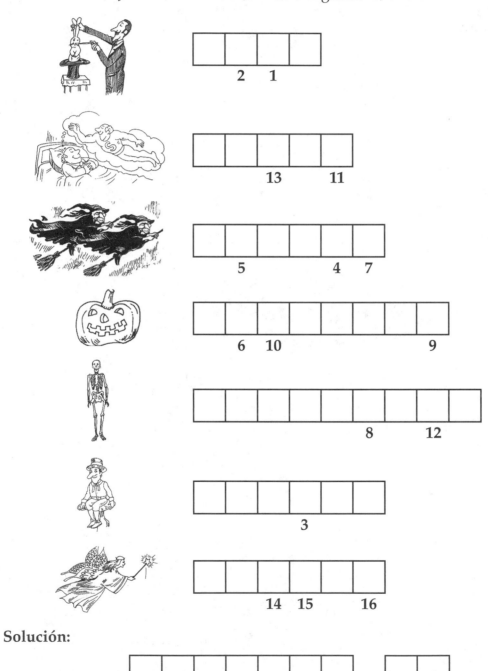

Solución:

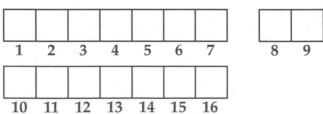

How many of these jobs do you remember? Fill in the Spanish words, then read down the boxed column to find the answer to this question: **¿Cuál es el trabajo de la señorita Gómez?**

1. __ __ __ __ __ __ __ __ __

2. __ __ __ __ __ __

3. __ __ __ __ __ __ __

4. __ __ __ __ __

5. __ __ __ __ __ __ __

6. __ __ __ __ __ __ __ __ __ __

7. __ __ __ __ __ __ __ __

8. __ __ __ __ __ __

9. __ __ __ __ __ __ __ __

10. __ __ __ __ __ __ __

11. __ __ __ __ __ __

12. __ __ __ __ __ __ __ __

Actividad G

You are one of a group of astronauts exploring a new planet. Describe your trip:

1. Aterrizamos en _____ .

2. La gente de ese planeta _____ .

3. Conocimos _____ .

4. Ellos _____ .

5. Para pasar el tiempo ellos _____ .

6. Cuando dejamos el planeta, los habitantes _____ .

It's the year 3000 and you, an inspector in the Earth's Department of Immigration, are interviewing newcomers from outer space. You have just received word to keep on the lookout for a particular creature that clones itself every 24 hours. You can see what a problem that would create. Spot this creature from the information given.

Le gustan los deportes.

No tiene aretes, pero sí una cadena larga.

Tiene antenas en vez de orejas.

Parece estar siempre contento.

Tiene tres ojos y lleva gafas.

Lleva botas.

Quinta Parte

19

La personalidad

The Conditional Tense

1 Vocabulario

Personality and Character Traits

timido

rebelde

generoso, bondadoso

cariñoso

tacaño

antipático

cortés

amable, sociable

terco

egoísta

optimista

travieso

pesimista

paciente

envidiosa

gracioso

celoso

considerado

mentiroso

trabajador

sincero

perezoso

curioso

aburrido

Actividad A

Here are some people you might know. Say something about their personality.

EXAMPLE: **El astronauta** *es inteligente.*

1. _____

2. _____

3. _____

4. _____

5. _____

6. _____

7. _____

8. _____

9. _____

10. _____

Do you recognize some of these personality types? Match the characteristics on the right with the descriptions on the left. Work with a partner.

EXAMPLE: Student 1:   **Nunca dice la verdad.**
                    Student 2:   **Es un** *mentiroso.*

1. No quiere gastar dinero.

_____

2. Tiene miedo. Casi no habla.

_____

3. Siempre espera las cosas malas.

_____

4. No está satisfecho. Quiere las cosas del otro.

_____

5. Es muy bueno con todo el mundo.

_____

6. Siempre dice lo que piensa.

_____

7. No le gusta trabajar. Prefiere dormir.

_____

8. Siempre hace cosas cómicas.

_____

9. Ayuda a sus amigos. Les presta dinero.

_____

10. Nunca cambia sus opiniones.

_____

a.   envidioso
b.   simpático
c.   perezoso
d.   gracioso
e.   generoso
f.   terco
g.   tímido, callado
h.   pesimista
i.   tacaño
j.   honesto, sincero

Un examen psicológico

¿Qué tipo de persona es Ud.? ¿Es simpático o antipático? ¿Tímido o agresivo? ¿Hace sus decisiones con confianza? Lea las siguientes situaciones e indique sus reacciones. Calcule los puntos que están al lado de sus respuestas. El total revelará su carácter.

1. Es sábado por la noche. Ud. quiere ir al cine. Sus amigos quieren ir a otro lugar que a Ud. no le interesa. ¿Qué haría?
   a. Iría al cine sin ellos.   ❏ 5
   b. Seguiría a mis amigos.   ❏ 1
   c. Propondría otra alternativa.   ❏ 3

2. Está en un restaurante. El mesero le da la cuenta y Ud. encuentra un error. ¿Qué haría?
   a. Le diría cortésmente al mesero que hay un error en la
       cuenta.   ❏ 4
   b. Pagaría la cuenta sin decir nada.   ❏ 1
   c. Le diría al mesero: «Ud. no sabe calcular».   ❏ 5

3. Una persona de importancia le cuenta una historia cómica que Ud. ya conoce. ¿Qué haría?
   a. Lo interrumpiría y le diría que Ud. ya conoce la historia. ❏ 5
   b. No diría nada. Escucharía toda la historia y reiría
       cortésmente.   ❏ 2
   c. Reiría histéricamente al final de la historia.   ❏ 1

4. Una amiga compra un vestido nuevo. A Ud. no le gusta. Su amiga le pide su opinión. Ud. le diría:
   a. Yo no saldría contigo con ese vestido horrible.   ❏ 5
   b. No sé. No soy experto(a) en esas cosas.   ❏ 3
   c. Me gusta mucho. Te va muy bien.   ❏ 1

5. Ud. tiene una cita con alguien a las dos. Él llega a las dos y media y no ofrece ninguna excusa. ¿Qué haría?
   a. Miraría su reloj y preguntaría: «¿Qué pasó?».   ❏ 4
   b. Saludaría sin mencionar que llegó tarde.   ❏ 1
   c. Se pondría furioso(a) por su actitud egoísta.   ❏ 5

6. Ud. está en una fiesta. Una persona muy aburrida lo atrapa en la cocina y no cesa de hablar. ¿Qué haría?
   a. Le diría: «Perdón, pero tengo que ir al baño».   ❏ 4
   b. Escucharía todo, pero pensaría en otra cosa.   ❏ 3
   c. Mostraría mucho interés en la conversación.   ❏ 2

7. Alguien le ofrece una posición en una oficina con buen
   sueldo y muchas oportunidades. Pero Ud. no tiene
   ninguna experiencia. ¿Qué haría?
   a. Aceptaría el trabajo sin decir nada.   ❏ 5
   b. Explicaría que no tiene la preparación necesaria.   ❏ 3
   c. No aceptaría la posición.   ❏ 1

8. Sus padres le dicen que no puede salir el fin de semana
   con sus amigos. ¿Qué haría?
   a. Saldría con ellos sin permiso.   ❏ 5
   b. Trataría de resolver el asunto con sus padres.   ❏ 4
   c. Aceptaría la decisión de sus padres.   ❏ 2

9. Un compañero de clase le pide prestados cinco
   dólares, que le pagaría mañana. Ud. sabe que él es un
   mentiroso. ¿Qué haría Ud.?
   a. Le prestaría un dólar y le diría: «No tengo más
      dinero conmigo».   ❏ 2
   b. Le prestaría los cinco dólares.   ❏ 1
   c. No le prestaría nada.   ❏ 5

10. Ud. hace una cita para ir a un juego de pelota por la
    noche. Pero al volver a casa se acuerda de que tiene un
    examen importante al día siguiente y tiene que estudiar.
    ¿Qué haría Ud.?
    a. Trataría de estudiar antes del juego.   ❏ 1
    b. Llamaría al amigo y le diría que no puede salir
       porque está enfermo.   ❏ 2
    c. Llamaría al amigo y le explicaría que no puede salir
       porque tiene que estudiar.   ❏ 4

Interpretación de los resultados

39–48 puntos: Tiene un carácter fuerte e independiente. Toma
sus decisiones con confianza. Es una persona
muy determinada, directa e impulsiva. Muchas
veces no es diplomático y puede ofender a la
gente. Ud. se considera honesto, pero la gente
puede creer que es arrogante o antipático.

27–38 puntos: Ud. es amable y simpático y generalmente
tiene buenas relaciones con todo el mundo.
Es paciente y sabe tratar a la gente. Tiene un
carácter bastante fuerte pero es diplomático
cuando es necesario.

amable *kind, nice*

12–26 puntos: Ud. es reservado y un poco tímido. Muchas
veces tiene miedo de decir la verdad. Nunca
ofende a nadie. Necesita ser más dinámico y
tener más confianza.

Conteste con frases completas.

1. ¿Qué tipo de examen es éste?

   _____

2. ¿Qué revela el examen?

   _____

3. ¿Qué hay al lado de cada respuesta?

   _____

4. ¿Qué es necesario hacer con los puntos al final?

   _____

5. ¿Qué carácter tiene una persona que recibe más de 39 puntos?

   _____

6. ¿Qué problemas puede tener esa persona?

   _____

7. ¿Cómo es una persona que recibe 30 puntos en el examen?

   _____

8. ¿Qué problemas puede tener una persona tímida?

   _____

9. ¿Qué necesita una persona tímida?

   _____

10. ¿Cuántos puntos recibió Ud.? ¿Refleja realmente su personalidad el examen?

    _____

Using an adjective of personality, describe the following people.

EXAMPLE: su cartero   **Mi cartero *es muy trabajador.***

1. su profesor(a) de español   _____

2. su mamá   _____

3. su papá   _____

4. su hermano(a)   _____

5. el director de la escuela   _____

6. el Presidente de los Estados Unidos   _____

7. un americano típico   _____

8. un alumno típico de su escuela   _____

9. su mejor amigo(a)   _____

10. Ud.   _____

Actividad E

One can often tell peoples' personality by their actions. Different people like to do different things. Here is a list of activities. Work with a partner and tell him (her) what you do or don't do. He (she) will then use an adjective to describe you.

EXAMPLE: **seguir las instrucciones**
                No sigo **las instrucciones de mis padres.**
                Ud. es *rebelde.*

1. dormir hasta mediodía

   _____

2. dar dinero a los pobres

   _____

3. considerarse la persona más importante

   _____

4. no decir nunca la verdad

   _____

5. no querer gastar dinero

   _____

6. investigar siempre las cosas

   _____

7. no querer cambiar sus ideas y sus opiniones

_____

8. decir siempre «por favor»

_____

9. demostrar mucho amor

_____

10. querer las cosas de otras personas

_____

 When you took the personality test, do you remember seeing the following sentences?

¿Qué _haría_ Ud.?	_What <u>would</u> you do?_
Iría **al cine.**	_I <u>would</u> to to the movies._
No _diría_ nada.	_I <u>would</u> not say anything._
Yo no _saldría_ contigo.	_I <u>would</u> not go out with you._

All of the verbs were in the _conditional tense_. The conditional tense expresses the idea of _would_ in English.

Me _gustaría_ ir.	_I would like to go._
Sería **muy triste.**	_It would be very sad._
Me dijo que _escribiría_.	_He told me he would write._

The conditional tense, like the future tense, has only one set of endings for all three conjugations: **-AR, -ER,** and **-IR** verbs. These endings **-ía, -ías, -ía, -íamos,** and **-ían** are attached to the whole infinitive of the verb.

	hablar _to speak_	responder _to answer_	recibir _to receive_
yo	hablaría	respondería	recibiría
tú	hablarías	responderías	recibirías
Ud., él, ella	hablaría	respondería	recibiría
nosotros, -as	hablaríamos	responderíamos	recibiríamos
Uds., ellos, ellas	hablarían	responderían	recibirían

NOTE: The endings **ía, ías, ía,** etc. are the same as the imperfect endings of **-ER** and **-IR** verbs.

Actividad F

Express what the following people would do.

EXAMPLE: (comprar)   **Lupe _compraría_ un regalo para sus padres.**

1. (hablar)   Los estudiantes _____ español con un cubano.

2. (vender)   Mi padre no _____ nuestra casa.

3. (vivir)   Yo _____ en México.

4. (llamar)   Nosotros _____ a la policía en una emergencia.

5. (comer)   Tú _____ bien en ese restaurante.

 There is a group of verbs that are irregular in the conditional. Just as in the future tense, they have regular endings, but their stem is not the infinitive. All irregular future verbs undergo the same changes they did in the future.

Irregular Verbs in the Future and Conditional Tenses

VERB	FUTURE TENSE (WILL)	CONDITIONAL TENSE (WOULD)
poder	podré, -as, -á, -emos, -án	podría, -ías, -ía, íamos, ían
querer	querré, -ás, -á, -emos, -án	querría, -ías, -ía, -íamos, -ían
saber	sabré, -ás, -á, -emos, -án	sabría, -ías, -ía, -íamos, -ían
poner	pondré, -ás, -á, -emos, -án	pondría, -ías, -ía, -íamos, -ían
salir	saldré, -ás, -á, -emos, -án	saldría, -ías, -ía, -íamos, -ían
tener	tendré, -ás, -á, -emos, -án	tendría, -ías, -ía, -íamos, -ían
venir	vendré, -ás, -á, -emos, -án	vendría, -ías, -ía, -íamos, -ían
decir	diré, -ás, -á, -emos, -án	diría, -ías, -ía, -íamos, -ían
hacer	haré, -ás, -á, -emos, -án	haría, -ías, -ía, -íamos, -ían

Actividad G

Express the following in the conditional tense.

1. (ir)   Paco dijo que _____ a la fiesta.

2. (querer)   ¿Qué _____ para tu cumpleaños?

3. (saber)   Ellos no _____ la diferencia.

4. (poner)   ¿Dónde _____ Ud. la lámpara?

5. (salir)   Yo _____ hoy.

6. (tener)   No sé cuando nosotros _____ el dinero.

7. (venir)   Ellos me dijeron que _____ mañana.

8. (poder)   Ella no _____ vivir sin su perro.

9. (decir)   ¿Te _____ tu amigo la verdad?

10. (hacer)   ¿Qué _____ Ud. en esa casa grande?

 To express the idea of *probably* or *I wonder if . . .* , Spanish uses the future and conditional tenses. The future is used to express probability in the present; the conditional to express probability in the past.

Mi mamá *estará* **en casa.**	*My mother is probably at home.*
Mi mamá *estaría* **en casa.**	*My mother was probably at home.*
¿Qué hora *será***?**	*I wonder what time it is.*
¿Qué hora *sería***?**	*I wonder what time it was.*
¿Adónde *irán***?**	*I wonder where they're going.*
¿Adónde *irían***?**	*I wonder where they went.*

Express the following using the future or conditional tenses.

1. I wonder if she's sick.   _____
                                                  (estar enferma)

2. He probably did the work.   _____
                                                  (hacer el trabajo)

3. They're probably coming tomorrow. _____
                                                  (venir mañana)

4. She probably took the train.   _____
                                                  (tomar el tren)

5. I wonder if we'll go to the beach. _____
                                                  (ir a la playa)

6. You (*tú*) will probably have the money. _____
                                                  (tener dinero)

7. They probably left for Spain.   _____
                                                  (salir para España)

8. I wonder if she's telling the truth.

_____

(decir la verdad)

9. I wonder if they know the difference.

_____

(saber la diferencia)

10. He was probably able to study.

_____

(poder estudiar)

Preguntas Personales

1. ¿Por qué son útiles los exámenes psicológicos?

_____

2. ¿Cuándo es necesario un examen psicológico?

_____

3. ¿En qué situaciones no dirías la verdad?

_____

4. Recibiste un telegrama. ¿Qué piensas si eres optimista (pesimista)?

_____

5. ¿Qué problemas tiene una persona antipática?

_____

Composición

You have been assigned to construct a personality test that will determine a person's ability to get along with others. Make up five questions for the test:

1. _____

2. _____

3. _____

4. _____

5. _____

DIÁLOGO

Complete the dialog between this student and his guidance counselor.

Cápsula cultural

Su personalidad y los signos del zodíaco

Cada día, todos los periódicos españoles y latinoamericanos publican una sección dedicada exclusivamente al horóscopo. Algunos lectores consideran esta columna más importante que las noticias diarias y comienzan su lectura con esta parte. Según ellos, todos nacimos bajo un signo del zodíaco y esos signos pueden revelar el carácter de cada persona.

La astrología esta basada en la creencia de que el movimiento y las posiciones de los planetas y las estrellas influyen las vidas de los individuos. El zodíaco está dividido en doce porciones o constelaciones, cada una con su propio signo.

¿Quiere descubrir su verdadera personalidad? (o por lo menos divertirse). Busque su signo en la tabla siguiente: (Y recuerde, dicen que las estrellas no mienten).

SIGNO	FECHA DE NACIMIENTO	CUALIDAD	DEFECTO
aries	21 marzo – 20 abril	valiente	impulsivo
tauro	21 abril – 21 mayo	paciente	obstinado
géminis	22 mayo – 21 junio	generoso	hablador
cáncer	22 junio – 22 julio	sensitivo	emocional
leo	23 julio – 23 agosto	simpático	intolerante
virgo	24 agosto – 23 septiembre	exacto	crítico
libra	24 septiembre – 23 octubre	fiel	indeciso
escorpión	24 octubre – 22 noviembre	vigoroso	extremista
sagitario	23 noviembre – 21 diciembre	sincero	impaciente
capricornio	22 diciembre – 20 enero	ambicioso	pesimista
acuario	21 enero – 18 febrero	independiente	desorganizado
piscis	19 febrero – 20 marzo	imaginativo	tímido

Discusión

1. ¿Por qué es importante para alguna gente la sección del horóscopo?

2. ¿En qué está basada la astrología?

3. ¿Cómo está dividido el zodíaco?

4. ¿Cómo es tu personalidad, según la tabla?

5. ¿Por qué alguna gente quiere creer en cosas fantásticas?

VOCABULARIO

el lector reader
según according to
la creencia belief

influir *to influence*
verdadera *true*
por lo menos *at least*

Hacemos un viaje

Past Participles; Present Perfect Tense

1 Vocabulario

el aeropuerto

despegar

EL VUELO 22

el horario

el vuelo		
211	7:35	3
17	8:02	5
22		7

el pasaporte

la visa

aterrizar

ÁREA DE CONTROL DE SEGURIDAD

personal de seguridad

el pasaje/boleto

la azafata

el pasajero

el equipaje

el piloto

LA ADUANA

el/la turista

la maleta (el baúl)

el maletero

Work with a partner. One tells what a person does; the other tells who that person is.

EXAMPLE: **ayudar a los pasajeros en el avión**
La *azafata ayuda* **a los pasajeros en el avión.**

1. llevar el equipaje de los pasajeros   _____

2. volar el avión   _____

3. examinar los documentos y el equipaje   _____

4. visitar países durante las vacaciones   _____

5. viajar en avión, autobús o tren   _____

Now describe various objects and name them.

EXAMPLE: **una lista de salidas y llegadas**
Un horario **es una lista de salidas y llegadas**

1. identificación oficial para entrar a un país

   _____

2. documento necesario para subir a un avión, un tren o un autobús

   _____

3. lugar donde se pone la ropa y otros artículos en un viaje

   _____

4. un medio de transporte en el mar

   _____

5. lugar adonde llegan y de donde salen los autobuses y los trenes.

   _____

Cruzando la frontera

Let's read a one-act play about a family's problems while traveling.
Pay attention to the verbs in bold type.

PERSONAJES: Mario Fuentes, un turista de unos 40 años
de edad
Matilde, su esposa, más o menos de la
misma edad
Minerva, la hija mayor, de 13 años
Maruja, la hija menor, de 8 años
ESCENA: En la frontera, la familia Fuentes espera su
turno para pasar la aduana. Han llegado en
carro y **han descargado** todo su equipaje.

MATILDE: ¿Mario, **has traído** todos los documentos que
vamos a necesitar?
MARIO: Creo que sí. **He traído** los pasaportes, las visas
y los certificados de salud y de vacunación.
MATILDE: Bien. **Hemos viajado** mucho hoy y estoy muy
cansada. No quiero problemas.
MARIO: No te preocupes, mi vida. Todo está en orden.
Allí viene el inspector.
ADUANERO: Buenas tardes, señores. ¿Tienen Uds. algo
que declarar?
MARIO: No señor, absolutamente nada.
ADUANERO: ¿**No han comprado** comida, cigarrillos,
licores, joyas u otros artículos de oro o de plata?
MARIO: No **hemos comprado** ni cigarrillos ni licor. Yo
no fumo ni bebo.
MATILDE: Bueno, **hemos traído** unas pocas cosas para
nuestro uso personal y regalos para unos pocos
amigos. Las únicas «joyas» que tenemos son nuestras
hijas.

la frontera border

preocuparse to
worry

ADUANERO: Veo nueve maletas. Parece que tienen muchos amigos. ¿Quiere Ud. abrir esa maleta verde, por favor?

MATILDE: (a Mario) No recuerdo ninguna maleta verde.

MARIO: (a Matilde) Ni yo tampoco.

ADUANERO: (abriendo la maleta) ¡Ajá! Uds. no fuman ni beben y **han comprado** sólo unas pocas cosas de uso personal. ¿Eh? ¿Cómo explican Uds. esto? Tres cartones de cigarrillos, tres botellas de coñac, dos de vino, dos relojes de oro . . .

MATILDE/MARIO: ¡Ay, Dios mío!

MINERVA: Pero, papá, esa maleta no es nuestra. Miren la etiqueta con el nombre y la dirección adentro: Héctor González.

MARUJA: Yo vi la maleta en el pasillo del hotel y la puse en el carro. Pensé que era nuestra.

MARIO: Señor, mi hija dice la verdad. Ud. puede verificarlo.

ADUANERO: Está bien. Uds. pueden cruzar la frontera. Nosotros se la devolveremos al señor González. Pero de ahora en adelante tengan cuidado con sus «joyas».

> **ni yo tampoco** *neither do I*

> **de ahora en adelante** *from now on*

Actividad C

Conteste las siguientes preguntas con frases completas.

1. ¿Qué espera la familia Fuentes?

   _____

2. ¿Quiénes son los miembros de la familia?

   _____

3. ¿Qué documentos ha traído el marido?

   _____

4. ¿Qué pregunta el aduanero?

   _____

5. ¿Qué artículos declara Mario?

_____

6. ¿Qué dice la mujer que tienen en las maletas?

_____

7. ¿Qué hay dentro de la maleta verde?

_____

8. ¿Quién puso la maleta en el carro? ¿Por qué?

_____

9. ¿Dónde encontró la chica la maleta?

_____

10. ¿Qué va a hacer el aduanero con la maleta?

_____

 Look at the following sentences.

El museo estaba _cerrado._	_The museum was closed._
El dinero está _escondido._	_The money is hidden._
Mi hermano está _aburrido._	_My brother is bored._

What are **cerrado, escondido,** and **aburrido** in these sentences? _____.
These adjectives are derived from the verbs **cerrar** (to close), **esconder** (to hide),
and **aburrir** (to bore), and they are called past participles. Can you figure out how
these past participles were formed? _____

RULE: To form the past participle remove the infinitive endings **-ar, -er, -ir** and
replace them with the corresponding endings **-ado, -ido,** and **-ido**.

You have been using many past participles as adjectives. Here are some that you
know. From which infinitives were they derived?

PAST PARTICIPLE		INFINITIVE
sentado	_seated_	_____
preocupado	_worried_	_____
vestido	_dressed_	_____
dormido	_asleep_	_____

Now let's try the opposite. Here are some infinitives you know. What are their past participles?

	INFINITIVE	PAST PARTICIPLE
apagar	to turn off	_____
encender	to turn on	_____
casar(se)	to marry, get married	_____
cansar(se)	to tire, get tired	_____
perder	to lose	_____

Remember that past participles used as adjectives agree in gender and number with the noun they accompany.

María y Juan **están** *sentados* **en la sala.**   *María and Juan are seated in the living room.*

Rosa **está** *sentada* **en el comedor.**   *Rosa is seated in the dining room.*

Actividad D

Complete the sentences, using the past participle of one of the following verbs.

descansar   dormir   apagar

aburrir   preocupar   encender

cansar

EXAMPLE: **Manuel durmió la siesta y ahora está** *descansado*.

1. Los muchachos corrieron diez millas y están _____ .

2. María no tiene nada que hacer y está _____ .

3. Mis padres oyeron malas noticias y están _____ .

4. Es muy tarde y el bebé está _____ .

5. Es de noche y las luces están _____ .

6. Es de mañana y la luz está _____ .

3 The past participle is used to form the present perfect tense. In Spanish, the present perfect consists of two words: the present tense form of the verb **haber** (*to have*) and a past participle. Let's start by learning the present tense of **haber**:

PRESENT TENSE	
yo	he
tú	has
Ud., él, ella	ha
nosotros, -as	hemos
Uds., ellos, ellas	han

NOTE: Do not confuse the verb **haber** with the verb **tener**. **Haber** is the only verb that can be used with a past participle to form the present perfect.

PRESENT PERFECT	
yo	he estudiado
tú	has estudiado
Ud., él, ella	ha estudiado
nosotros, -as	hemos estudiado
Uds., ellos, ellas	han estudiado

Note that the past participle does not change in the present perfect tense; it always ends in **o**. Look at these examples.

Esta semana *he ido* **dos veces al cine.**   *This week I have gone twice to the movies.*

¿Me *ha llamado* **alguien hoy?**   *Has anybody called me today?*

In Spanish, the present perfect is generally used to describe an action that happened in the past but is connected to the present.

Actividad E

You are having a picnic in the park. How has each of these people contributed?

EXAMPLE: **Ramón / comprar el pan**   **Ramón** *ha comprado* **el pan.**

1. Julio y Jaime / preparar la ensalada   _____

2. yo / encender el fuego   _____

3. Uds. / cocinar las hamburguesas   _____

4. Nora / buscar dónde comprar sodas   _____

5. tú / sacar fotos   _____

6. Ud. / decidir dónde hacer el picnic   _____

7. Mario y yo / lavar las frutas   _____

8. Rosa y Josefina / organizar los juegos   _____

Answer the following questions. Work with a partner.

1. ¿Qué has estudiado últimamente?

_____

2. ¿Adónde has ido recientemente?

_____

3. ¿Qué exámenes has tenido este semestre?

_____

4. ¿Qué has hecho para divertirse?

_____

5. ¿Qué artículo electrónico has comprado este año?

_____

 Now look at these examples:

¿Has hablado con Juan?	*Have you spoken with Juan?*
No, no *he hablado* con él.	*No, I haven't spoken with him.*

Where does **no** stand in the second Spanish sentence? _____ .

RULE: The two words forming the present perfect cannot be separated in Spanish; **no** stands before the conjugated form of **haber**.

What happens if you use an object pronoun?

¿Has *comido* **paella alguna vez?**	*Have you ever eaten paella?*
Sí, *la he* **comido.**	*Yes, I have eaten it.*
No, *no la he comido.*	*No, I haven't eaten it.*

RULE: The object pronoun comes before the conjugated form of **haber**. In negative sentences, **no** comes before the object pronoun.

Answer the following questions negatively. Work with a partner.

1. ¿Han terminado las clases?

_____

2. ¿Has estado en el Perú?

_____

3. ¿Has montado a caballo alguna vez?

_____

4. ¿Has visitado la Casa Blanca?

_____

5. ¿Ha llegado la profesora a clase?

_____

Answer these questions, using an object pronoun in your response. Work with a partner.

EXAMPLE: ¿Has escuchado las noticias?
               Sí, *las he escuchado.*

1. ¿Has buscado trabajo?   _____

2. ¿Ha preparado ella la comida?   _____

3. ¿Ha enseñado la profesora las lecciones? _____

4. ¿Han aprendido los alumnos español? _____

5. ¿Has escuchado muchos discos? _____

The past participles of **-ER** and **-IR** verbs with stems ending in a vowel have an accent mark.

STEM	ENDING	PAST PARTICIPLE	
ca	er	**caído**	*fallen*
cre	er	**creído**	*believed*
le	er	**leído**	*read*
o	ír	**oído**	*heard*
tra	er	**traído**	*brought*

A few verbs have irregular past participles, and you will have to memorize them.

INFINITIVE	PAST PARTICIPLE	
abrir	*abierto*	*open(ed)*
cubrir	*cubierto*	*covered*
decir	*dicho*	*said*
escribir	*escrito*	*written*
hacer	*hecho*	*done*
morir	*muerto*	*died*
poner	*puesto*	*put*
romper	*roto*	*broken*
ver	*visto*	*seen*
volver	*vuelto*	*returned*

Remember that compounds of the following verbs also have irregular past participles.

INFINITIVE	PAST PARTICIPLE	
describir	*descrito*	*described*
descubrir	*descubierto*	*discovered*
devolver	*devuelto*	*returned*

Actividad I

It's Sunday and you have slept till noon. Write what the other members of your family have done while you slept.

1. mi papá / leer el periódico   _____

2. mi mamá / poner la mesa   _____

3. mis hermanos / hacer las tareas   _____

4. mis hermanas / escribir cartas   _____

5. mi gato / descubrir un ratón   _____

6. mi perro / romper un florero   _____

7. mi tía / volver del supermercado   _____

8. tú / ver un programa de televisión   _____

Actividad J

What have these people done for your birthday party?

1. mi padre / traer los refrescos

_____

2. mis amigos / decir «¡Feliz cumpleaños!»

_____

3. mi mamá / hacer una torta

_____

4. mis hermanas / cubrir la torta con chocolate

_____

5. tú / escribir las invitaciones

_____

6. yo / abrir los regalos

_____

Actividad K

Describe what you and your friend Carlos have done before leaving for Spain. Use the following expressions.

sacar el pasaporte	pedir la visa
hacer las reservaciones	ir a la agencia de viajes
escribir a los hoteles	cambiar dólares por euros
leer las guías turísticas	oír casetes en español
ver al cónsul español	hacer las maletas
decir adiós a los amigos	devolver libros a la biblioteca

EXAMPLE: **Carlos y yo *hemos hecho* las reservaciones.**

1. _____
2. _____
3. _____
4. _____
5. _____
6. _____
7. _____
8. _____
9. _____
10. _____

Now look at these sentences.

¿Has hablado con Darío?	*Have you spoken with Dario?*
Sí, *acabo de hablar* con él.	*Yes, I have just spoken with him.*

¿Dónde está Consuelo?	*Where is Consuelo?*
Ella *acaba de salir*.	*She has just gone out.*

If you want to express in Spanish the idea that something has just taken place, use the following construction.

present tense of **acabar** + **de** + infinitive

El avión acaba de aterrizar.	*The plane has just landed.*
Acabo de levantarme.	*I have just gotten up.*
Acabamos de llegar.	*We have just arrived.*

Acabar is a regular -AR verb that by itself means *to finish*:

¿Cuándo vas a acabar las tareas?	*When are you going to finish your homework?*

You want to go out, but all your friends have called saying they are too tired from having done various physical activities.

EXAMPLE: Pedro / jugar al fútbol   **Pedro *acaba de jugar* al fútbol.**

1. Roberto y Raúl / correr cinco millas   _____

2. tú / limpiar tu cuarto   _____

3. Uds. / estudiar para un examen difícil _____

4. Rosario / trabajar en el jardín   _____

5. José / lavar el carro   _____

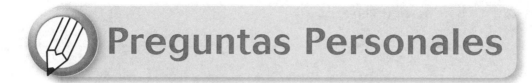

Preguntas Personales

1. ¿Has viajado a otro país? ¿Adónde?

   _____

2. ¿Qué documentos necesitas generalmente si vas salir de los Estados Unidos?

   _____

3. ¿Qué necesitas para viajar a Puerto Rico?

   _____

4. ¿Qué tienes que obtener para hacer un viaje a Europa?

   _____

5. ¿Prefieres viajar por autobús, por tren, por barco, o por avión?

   _____

6. ¿Cuáles son los medios de transporte más comunes? ¿Cuál prefieres? ¿Por qué?

   _____

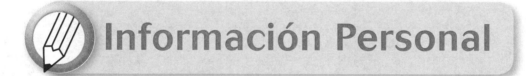

Información Personal

List some things you haven't done up to now but would like to do. You may use some of the suggested activities.

visitar	viajar
aprender	ir
comprar	hacer
ver	decir

EXAMPLE: **No** *he visto* **una ópera.**

_____

_____

_____

_____

_____

_____

Composición

The customs officials have been stopping all suspicious-looking luggage. They have asked you to fill out a form describing your recent activities before they allow you to cross the border. Tell where you have been, for how long, your reasons for going there, the nature of your work; list the merchandise you have purchased abroad and any other pertinent information that will convince the customs officials that you are an honest citizen.

_____

_____

_____

_____

_____

_____

_____

_____

You have come back from a trip to South America and the customs official is asking the usual questions. Complete the dialog.

Cápsula cultural

Un viaje por el Camino Real

El Camino Real es un sendero que cubre una distancia de 600 millas, desde San Diego a Sonoma. Fue establecido por frailes españoles, entre ellos el padre Junípero Serra, mientras exploraba y establecía comunidades en los nuevos territorios.

El Camino Real, actualmente *U.S. Highway 101*, comenzó como un sendero que conectaba las 21 misiones de los franciscanos. Cada misión estaba localizada a un día de viaje a caballo.

Una de las misiones más famosas es San Juan Capistrano, una hora al sur de Los Ángeles. Construida en 1776, esta «joya de las misiones» es el edificio más viejo de California. San Juan Capistrano es conocida por sus golondrinas. Cada 19 de marzo, miles de golondrinas vuelven de pasar el invierno en el sur para anidar en los arcos de la misión. Los pájaros no siempre llegan exactamente el 19 a causa de las condiciones del tiempo, pero siempre vuelven.

Junípero Serra murió en 1784, a la edad de 71 años. Su cuarto todavía esta allí, amueblado con un catre de madera, una sola frazada, una mesa, una silla, un cofre, un candelero y una calabaza para agua.

Su lema era: «siempre adelante, nunca atrás».

Discusión

1. ¿Qué sabemos de la exploración de California?

2. ¿Qué es El Camino Real? ¿Para qué servía al principio? ¿Cómo se llama ahora?

3. ¿Qué pasa todos los años en la misión de San Juan Capistrano?

4. ¿Quién fue Junípero Serra? Considerando el cuarto donde vivía Junípero, ¿qué tipo de persona era él?

5. ¿Cómo afectaron los exploradores españoles la historia de los Estados Unidos? ¿Qué efectos han tenido en nuestra historia y en nuestra lengua?

VOCABULARIO

el sendero *trail*

el fraile *friar*

entre *among*

actualmente *currently*

la golondrina *swallow*

anidar *to nest*

amueblado *furnished*

el catre *cot*

la frazada *blanket*

el cofre *chest, trunk*

la calabaza *gourd*

el lema *motto*

La ecología

Present Subjunctive

1 Vocabulario

Personality Character Traits

LA CONTAMINACIÓN AMBIENTAL

la contaminación del aire

la contaminación del agua

la deforestación

las emisiones de los autos

la extinción de las
especies de animales

la contaminación del mar

la contaminación de la tierra

SOLUCIONES

reciclamiento de productos de papel

reciclamiento de plásticos

reciclamiento de metales y aluminio

limpieza y mantenimiento del ambiente

reciclamiento de cristal

¡Planeta en peligro!

Cada año, **es probable que** la raza humana **destruya** un área de selva de casi la mitad del tamaño de Texas. El recurso natural más grande del mundo está quemándose literalmente; y más de 320 millas cuadradas de selva irremplazable son quemadas o cortadas cada día. Hace sólo veinte años, las selvas cubrían 14 por ciento del planeta. Hoy día, las selvas cubren menos del seis por ciento.

quemarse *to burn*

cubrir *to cover*

A este paso, **es posible que** esta parte importantísima del planeta **sea** totalmente destruida en unos cuarenta años. Con él se perderán tesoros todavía no descubiertos y recursos irremplazables obtenibles sólo dentro de estos ecosistemas únicos. **¿Duda que sean** importantes para nuestro mundo estos frágiles ecosistemas?

Considere estos datos:

datos *facts*

- Más de la mitad de las especies vivientes están allí. Dos acres y medio de la selva amazónica contienen 750 tipos de árboles— más variedades que en toda Norte América.

- En Perú hay una reserva forestal donde habitan más especies de pájaros que en todos los Estados Unidos.

- La selva amazónica produce veinte por ciento del oxígeno del mundo.

- El Río Amazonas contiene dos terceras partes del agua dulce del mundo.

  agua dulce *fresh water*

- Veinticinco por ciento de todos los productos farmacéuticos tienen su origen en plantas de la selva. Todavía se están descubriendo nuevas plantas y los científicos esperan nos den muchas de las medicinas del futuro.

A este paso, **es probable que** la contaminación del aire, de los ríos y del océano **continúe** por el mundo entero. Muchos temen que las emisiones de los coches y de las fábricas **sean** un riesgo a la zona ozono y que **causen** un aumento de la temperatura global.

Además, la población creciente contribuye a la erosión de nuestras costas y la contaminación de la tierra con químicos, plásticos y basura. ¿Crees que **haya** soluciones a estos problemas? Sabemos por ejemplo, que cada tonelada de papel reciclado salva diecisiete árboles de la destrucción. ¿Qué más podemos hacer para evitar la destrucción de nuestro planeta? ¿Tienes algunas sugerencias?

creciente *growing*

Actividad A

1. ¿Qué cantidad de la selva es destruida cada año? ¿Cada día?

   _____

   _____

2. Si el nivel de destrucción continúa así, ¿cuánto tiempo durará la selva?

   _____

   _____

3. Si la selva desaparece, ¿qué pasará a muchas especies de animales y plantas?

   _____

   _____

4. ¿Qué porcentaje del oxígeno del mundo se produce en la selva amazónica?

_____

_____

5. ¿Por qué son importantes las plantas de la selva?

_____

_____

6. Además de en la selva, ¿dónde más hay destrucción de nuestro ambiente?

_____

_____

7. ¿Cuáles son las causas de los diferentes tipos de contaminación?

_____

_____

8. ¿Qué problemas causa la sobrepoblación?

_____

_____

9. ¿Cuales son algunas cosas que debemos hacer para conservar nuestros recursos?

_____

_____

10. ¿Qué puedes hacer tú personalmente para proteger al planeta?

_____

_____

Actividad **B**

Work with a partner. One student poses a question dealing with an ecological problem. The other student answers with a possible solution.

EXAMPLE:　　Problema:　¿Qué podemos hacer para evitar la contaminación del aire?
　　　　　　Solución:　**Podemos usar más el transporte público y menos el automóvil.**

1. Problema: deforestación

   Solución: _____

2. Problema: extinción de especies animales y vegetales

   Solución: _____

3. Problema: acumulación de basura

   Solución: _____

4. Problema: emisiones de los automóviles

   Solución: _____

5. Problema: humo de las fábricas

   Solución: _____

6. Problema: derrames del petróleo

   Solución: _____

7. Problema: el nivel del ruido

   Solución: _____

8. Problema: erosión de la tierra

   Solución: _____

9. Problema: contaminación con químicos y plásticos

   Solución: _____

10. Problema: consumo excesivo de energía

    Solución: _____

2 When you read about our endangered planet, do you remember seeing the following statements?

Es probable **que la raza humana** *destruya* — *It's probable that the human race will destroy*

Es posible **que esta fuente** *sea* **destruida** — *It's possible that this source may be destroyed*

Los científicos *esperan* **que nos** *den* — *Scientists hope that we get*

Dejamos que **esta destrucción** *continúe* — *We allow this destruction to continue*

Temen que *sean* un riesgo a la zona de ozono   *They fear that they will be a risk to the ozone layer*

Destruya, sea, esperen, continúe are all verbs in the SUBJUNCTIVE. Up to now, we have been using verbs in the various tenses of the indicative mood.

Yo sé que ellos *están* aquí ahora.   *I know that they are here now.*

Es cierto que él *hablará*.   *It is true that he will speak.*

Ella dijo que Juan *vino* a casa.   *She said Juan came home.*

The indicative mood is based on knowledge or certainty. It is used to express what is actually happening, happened, or will happen.

There are times, however, when something is hoped for, feared, or desired. It is a possibility, but not an actual fact. At these times Spanish uses the SUBJUNCTIVE mood.

Yo espero que ellos *estén* aquí.   *I hope that they are here.*

Es dudoso que él *hable*.   *It's doubtful that he will speak.*

In the above examples the verbs **estén, hable**, and **venga** are all in the **subjunctive**. To learn this new concept, we must do **three** things:

• Learn how to form the subjunctive in Spanish.
• Learn when to use the subjunctive.
• Learn how to express the meaning of the subjunctive.

3   **Formation of the present subjunctive**

To form the present subjunctive drop the **-o** of the **yo**-form of the present indicative and add the "opposite" endings (**-AR** verbs add endings beginning with **-e**; **-ER** and **-IR** verbs add endings beginning with **-a**).

	hablar (hablo)	comer (como)	vivir (vivo)
yo	habl*e*	com*a*	viv*a*
tú	habl*es*	com*as*	viv*as*
Ud., él, ella	habl*e*	com*a*	viv*a*
nosotros, -as	habl*emos*	com*amos*	viv*amos*
Uds., ellos, ellas	habl*en*	com*an*	viv*an*

NOTES: **1.** The reason we use the **yo**-form minus the **-o** rather than the infinitive is that the **yo**-form is often irregular, and this irregularity is carried over into the subjunctive.

	poner (pongo)	poder (puedo)	salir (salgo)
yo	ponga	pueda	salga
tú	pongas	puedas	salgas
Ud., él, ella	ponga	pueda	salga
nosotros, -as	pongamos	podamos	salgamos
Uds., él, ella	pongan	puedan	salgan

2. Does all this sound familiar? It should, because these are the same rules we used to form the informal commands.

¡Venga (Ud.) ahora!	*Come now!*
¡Escriba (Ud.) la carta!	*Write the letter.*
¡Traigan (Uds.) el dinero!	*Bring the money.*
¡Hable (Ud.) despacio!	*Speak slowly.*

Actividad C

The following verbs are all in the present indicative. Change them to the present subjunctive.

EXAMPLE: ellos vienen **ellos** *vengan*

1. yo gano   yo _____

2. ellos salen   ellos _____

3. Pepe trabaja   Pepe _____

4. nosotros hacemos   nosotros _____

5. yo tengo   yo _____

6. ellos reciben   ellos _____

7. María piensa   María _____

8. ellos piden   ellos _____

9. yo conozco   yo _____

10. ellas ven   ellas _____

4 There are a few common verbs that are irregular because they do not follow the above rules.

d*ar*	dé, des, dé, demos, den
est*ar*	esté, estés, esté, estemos, estén
ir	vaya, vayas, vaya, vayamos, vayan
sab*er*	sepa, sepas, sepa, sepamos, sepan
s*er*	sea, seas, sea, seamos, sean

Actividad D

Give the proper form of the subjunctive, according to the subject.

1. yo _____   4. ellos _____
         (ser)   (estar)

2. él _____   5. tú _____
        (saber)   (ir)

3. nosotros _____
              (dar)

Actividad E

Complete the following sentences using the subjunctive, when necessary:

1. Es dudoso que ellos _____ a tiempo.
                        (regresar)

2. Es importante que nosotros _____ la tienda.
                               (abrir)

3. Es probable que Lupe _____ la comida.
                         (traer)

4. Es necesario que Uds. _____ temprano.
                          (venir)

5. Es imposible que ella _____ mañana.
   (ir)

6. Es importante que tú _____ bueno.
   (ser)

7. Es una lástima que ellos no me _____ la información.
   (dar)

8. Es evidente que Manuel no _____ en casa.
   (estar)

9. Es necesario que tú _____ la verdad.
   (saber)

10. Es mejor que Uds. _____ conmigo.
    (salir)

5 Compare the following sets of sentences.

Es importante *estudiar*.	*It's important to study.*
Es importante que Juan *estudie*.	*It's important that Juan study.*
Es mejor no *hablar*.	*It's better not to talk.*
Es mejor que Ud. no *hable*.	*It's better that you don't talk.*

NOTE: In order to use the subjunctive you must have **two** separate clauses with **two** definite subjects indicated. A general statement not referring to anyone in particular uses an infinitive.

As was stated in the introduction of the topic, the subjunctive is used when something is impossible, doubtful, uncertain, etc. Therefore, the subjunctive is used after expressions of emotions (fear, hope, anger, happiness), wishing or wanting, doubt, denial, uncertainty and the like.

RULE: The subjunctive is used **after** the following impersonal expressions:

es posible (imposible)   *it's possible (impossible)*

es probable   *it's probable*

es preciso (necesario)   *it's necessary*

es dudoso   *it's doubtful*

es importante   *it's important*

es una lástima   *it's a pity*

es mejor   *it's better*

NOTES: **1.** There are other expressions: **es ridículo** (it's ridiculous), **es necesario** (it's necessary), **es raro** (it's rare), etc., but the ones above are the most common.

2. The following impersonal expressions of certainty are followed by the indicative, not the subjunctive:

es seguro	*it is sure*	**es evidente**	*it is clear*
es cierto	*it is certain*	**es verdad**	*it is true*

Es *evidente que* **el alumno no** *sabe*   *It's evident that the student*
   la respuesta.   *doesn't know the answer.*

RULE: The subjunctive is used after certain verbs. The most common verbs requiring the subjunctive are:

querer, desear	*to want, to wish*	**temer**	*to fear*
pedir	*to ask*	**tener miedo de**	*to be afraid*
mandar	*to command*	**dudar**	*to doubt*
hacer	*to make*	**preferir**	*to prefer*
dejar	*to allow*	**permitir**	*to permit*
esperar	*to hope*	**prohibir**	*to forbid*
alegrarse	*to be glad*		

Dudamos que el carpintero termine   *We doubt that the carpenter will*
   el trabajo.   *finish the work.*

Yo prefiero que tú vayas solo.   *I prefer that you go alone.*

NOTE: As with the impersonal expressions there must be TWO clauses and TWO different subjects for the subjunctive to be used.

Él quiere hablar.   *He wants to speak.*

Él quiere que yo hable.   *He wants me to speak.*

In addition to the above verbs, negative and interrogative verbs of thinking and believing are followed by the subjunctive since there is doubt and uncertainty in the mind of the speaker.

    Creo que ella sale mañana.   *I think she's leaving tomorrow.*

But:

    No creo que ella salga mañana.   *I don't think she's leaving tomorrow.*

    ¿Cree Ud. que ella salga mañana?   *Do you think she's leaving tomorrow?*

Actividad F

Work with a partner. One student recites the indicative sentences. The partner, using the clues, changes the sentences to the subjunctive.

1. El médico viene hoy. Yo quiero que _____ .

2. Salgo mañana. Ella duda que _____ .

3. Aprendemos la lengua. Es importante que _____ .

4. El niño tiene un resfriado. Es una lástima que _____ .

5. Ellas traen la comida. El jefe manda que _____ .

6. Él es inteligente. ¿Crees que _____ ?

7. Ellos vuelven al país. El capitán prohíbe que _____ .

8. Ud. piensa en su hijo. Me alegro de que _____ .

9. El chico no estudia. Tengo miedo de que _____ .

10. Sabemos la lección. Es necesario que _____ .

There are many ways of translating the subjunctive into English. Here are some examples:

Él manda que ella *hable.*	*He orders her to speak.*
Pedimos que Ud. *estudie.*	*We ask you to study.* *We ask that you study.*
Es una lástima que tú *vayas.*	*It's a shame that you're going.* *It's a shame for you to go.*
Es importante que Ud. *sepa* **la verdad.**	*It's important for you to know the truth.* *It's important that you know the truth.*
Tengo miedo de que no *venga.*	*I'm afraid he's not coming.* *I'm afraid he won't come.*

As can be seen, no matter how the thought is interpreted and expressed in English, Spanish follows set patterns and set rules. If you follow them, you will always be correct.

Preguntas Personales

1. ¿Qué cosas reciclas para proteger el ambiente?

_____

2. ¿Cómo puedes ahorrar electricidad?

_____

3. ¿Qué harías para proteger el hábitat de los animales en peligro?

_____

4. ¿Menciona algunas cosas que haces para reducir la cantidad de agua que usas (cuando te bañas, cuando lavas el carro, etc.)?

_____

5. ¿Qué se puede hacer para conservar gasolina?

_____

Composición

You're writing an article for the local paper. Explain how citizens can do their part for a cleaner and healthier environment and show how each individual <u>does</u> make a difference.

_____

_____

_____

_____

_____

_____

_____

_____

_____

Complete el siguiente diálogo sobre la ecología.

Cápsula cultural

El ecoturismo

Los gobiernos de varios países hispanoamericanos están estimulando la conservación de sus recursos naturales por medio de un turismo sensitivo al ambiente. Están demostrando que pueden traer beneficios económicos a sus respectivos países y mejorar la calidad de la vida, a la vez que protegen su patrimonio ambiental.

Uno de estos países es Costa Rica. Mientras que muchos países explotan sus recursos naturales sin ningún control, Costa Rica está aumentando sus bosques y parques. Su sistema de parques nacionales, uno de los más comprensivos y extensos del mundo, protege una gran variedad de ecosistemas. Más de 10 por ciento del país ha sido declarado reserva forestal. Volcanes, selvas, playas y ríos están protegidos para siempre. Por esta razón, Costa Rica es conocida como "el santuario de los animales salvajes de las Américas".

En otros países de Suramérica, los viajeros tienen ahora la oportunidad de inspeccionar los animales salvajes en su estado natural. Un ranchero, dueño de la hacienda «Hato Piñero», ha prohibido la caza en su propiedad y la convirtió en un refugio de animales. Ahora los turistas pueden tener la experiencia maravillosa de ver jaguares, pumas, anacondas, halcones, ocelotes, monos, osos hormigueros, murciélagos, zorros y capibaras viviendo en su estado natural.

Discusión

1. ¿Qué es el ecoturismo?

2. ¿Qué ha hecho Costa Rica para conservar su ambiente?

3. ¿Qué es el «Hato Piñero»? ¿Qué tiene de especial?

4. ¿Cuáles son las ventajas del ecoturismo? ¿Cuáles son algunos de sus peligros?

Para investigar

Escribe una lista de otros lugares del mundo donde se practica el ecoturismo y compara la información con tus compañeros.

VOCABULARIO

el beneficio *benefit*
el patrimonio *heritage*
comprensivo *comprehensive*
la hacienda *farm, ranch*
la caza *hunting*

el mono *monkey*
el oso hormiguero *anteater*
el zorro *fox*
el murciélago *bat*

Repaso V

Lección 19

a. The conditional of regular verbs is formed by adding the conditional endings to the infinitive.

	estudia**r**	aprende**r**	escrib**ir**
yo	estudiar**ía**	aprender**ía**	escribir**ía**
tú	estudiar**ías**	aprender**ías**	escribir**ías**
Ud./él/ella	estudiar**ía**	aprender**ía**	escribir**ía**
nosotros, -as	estudiar**íamos**	aprender**íamos**	escribir**íamos**
Uds./ellos/ellas	estudiar**ían**	aprender**ían**	escribir**ían**

b. In Spanish, the conditional tense is sometimes used to express wonder or probability in the past.

¿Quién *llamaría* **a esta hora?**	*I wonder who was calling at that hour.*
Sería **Carlos.**	*It was probably Carlos.*

c. **Poder**, **querer**, and **saber** drop the **e** of the infinitive before adding the regular endings of the conditional tense.

Yo *podría* **visitarte.**	*I would be able to visit you.*
Ella *querría* **ir conmigo.**	*She would like to go with me.*
Sabríamos **los resultados del examen.**	*We would know the test results.*

d. **Poner, tener, salir,** and **venir** change the **e** and then the **i** of the infinitive to **d** before adding the regular endings of the conditional tense.

Tú *pondrías* **los libros en la mesa.**	*You would put the books on the table.*

Él *tendría* que estudiar.   *He would have to study.*

Uds. *saldrían* para Europa.   *You would leave for Europe.*

Ellas *vendrían* temprano.   *They would come early.*

e. **Decir** and **hacer** have irregular stems in the conditional tense forms.

Ud. me *diría* la verdad.   *You would tell me the truth.*

Ellos *harían* las tareas.   *They would to their homeworks.*

Lección 20

a. In Spanish, past participles are formed by dropping the **-ar, -er**, and **-ir** ending of the infinitive and adding **-ado, -ido**, and **-ido,** respectively.

sentar: *sentado*   *seated*

perder: *perdido*   *lost*

vestir: *vestido*   *dressed*

Many past participles can be used as adjectives, agreeing in gender and number with the noun they accompany.

Nosotros estamos *cansados.*   *We are tired.*

La niña está *vestida* de blanco.   *The girl is dressed in white.*

b. The past participle is used to form the present-perfect tense. The present perfect consists of the present-tense form of **haber** (to have) and a past participle.

	haber	PAST PARTICIPLE
yo	he	viajado
tú	has	viajado
Ud., él, ella	ha	viajado
nosotros, -as	hemos	viajado
Uds., ellos, ellas	han	viajado

In the present perfect tense, the past participle always ends in **o**.

c. The present perfect in Spanish describes an action that happened in the past but is connected to the present.

El correo *ha llegado*.   *The mail has arrived.*

d. In Spanish, contrary to English, the two words forming the present perfect cannot be separated.

Juan no me *ha llamado* todavía.   *Juan hasn't called me yet.*

e. The past participles of **-ER** and **-IR** verbs with stems ending in a vowel have an accent mark.

leer: *leído*

oír: *oído*

The following verbs have irregular past participles.

abrir:	*abierto*	*opened*		**morir:**	*muerto*	*dead*
cubrir:	*cubierto*	*covered*		**poner:**	*puesto*	*put*
decir:	*dicho*	*said*		**romper:**	*roto*	*broken*
escribir:	*escrito*	*written*		**ver:**	*visto*	*seen*
hacer:	*hecho*	*done, made*		**volver:**	*vuelto*	*returned*

f. In Spanish, the present tense of **acabar** + **de** + *infinitive* expresses the idea that something has just taken place.

Acabo de terminar **las tareas.**   *I have just finished my homework.*

Acabar is a regular **-AR** verb that by itself means to *finish*.

El electricista *acabó* el trabajo.   *The electrician finished the job.*

Lección 21

The subjunctive mood expresses a possibility rather than an actual fact.

The Subjunctive With Regular Verbs

The present subjunctive is formed by dropping the **o** of the **yo** ending of the present indicative and adding **-e, -es, -e, -emos,** and **-en** to **-AR** verbs and **-a, -as, -a, -amos,** and **-an** to **-ER** and **-IR** verbs.

	hablar	comer	vivir
yo	hable	coma	viva
tú	hables	comas	vivas
Ud., él, ella	hable	coma	viva
nosotros, -as	hablemos	comamos	vivamos
Uds., ellos, ellas	hablen	coman	vivan

The Subjunctive With Irregular Verbs

	dar	estar	ir	saber	ser
yo	dé	esté	vaya	sepa	sea
tú	des	estés	vayas	sepas	seas
Ud., él, ella	dé	esté	vaya	sepa	sea
nosotros, -as	demos	estemos	vayamos	sepamos	seamos
Uds., ellos, ellas	den	estén	vayan	sepan	sean

Uses of the Subjunctive

a. The subjunctive is used after the following impersonal expressions.

es posible (imposible) que   *it's possible (impossible) that*

es probable que   *it's probable that*

es preciso (necesario) que   *it's precise (necessary) that*

es dudoso que   *it's doubtful that*

es importante que   *it's important that*

es una lástima que   *it's a shame that*

es mejor que   *it's better that*

b. The subjunctive is used after the following verbs.

alegrarse   *to be happy*   **desear**   *to wish*

dejar   *to allot, let*   **dudar**   *to doubt*

esperar	*to hope*	permitir	*to allow*
hacer	*to make*	**preferir**	*to prefer*
mandar	*to order*	**prohibir**	*to prohibit*
no creer	*to not believe*	**querer**	*to want*
pedir	*to ask for*	**temer** **tener miedo de**	*to fear, to be afraid of*

NOTE: To use the subjunctive there must be **two** different clauses separated by
que and each clause has a different subject.

Yo dudo **que él** sepa.   *I doubt that he knows.*

Es importante **que nosotros** vayamos.   *It's important that we go.*

Tell all of the things you would do if you became rich.

EXAMPLE:

_____ **Yo** *compraría* un carro nuevo.
(comprar)

1. _____   **2.** _____
        (tener)   (ir)

3. _____
(hacer)

4. _____
(comer)

5. _____
(descansar)

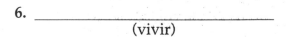

6. _____
(vivir)

7. _____
(ayudar)

8. _____
(salir con)

Actividad **B**

What have all these people done? Use a form of the verb **haber** + past participle.

1. El niño _____ el regalo.
(abrir)

2. Mi papá _____ el auto.
(cubrir)

3. Yo _____ una carta a mi amiga.
(escribir)

4. Nosotros _____ la tarea de español.
　　　　　　　(hacer)

5. Tú _____ los platos.
　　　　　(romper)

6. Yo no _____ la película.
　　　　　　(ver)

7. Mamá _____ la mesa.
　　　　　　(poner)

Actividad **C**

Complete the sentences with the correct form of the verb in parentheses.

1. Yo dudo que ellos _____ mañana.
　　　　　　　　　　(venir)

2. Temo que _____ hoy.
　　　　　　　(llover)

3. Yo prohibo que tú _____ con ese muchacho.
　　　　　　　　　(jugar)

4. Me alegro de que ellas _____ ahora.
　　　　　　　　　　(trabajar)

5. Es cierto que mis padres no _____ .
　　　　　　　　　　　(saber)

6. Ella prefiere que nosotros _____ más tarde.
　　　　　　　　　　　(ir)

7. El policía no cree que yo _____ verdad.
　　　　　　　　　　(decir)

8. Es una lástima que Uds. no _____ dinero.
　　　　　　　　　　(tener)

9. ¡Yo mando que tú _____ de esta casa!
　　　　　　　　　(salir)

10. Es preciso que nosotros _____ aquí.
　　　　　　　　　　(estar)

Complete the following Spanish crossword puzzle about personality traits.

HORIZONTALES

1. disagreeable, not nice
5. pessimist, pessimistic
6. envious
8. shy
10. funny
11. jealous
12. patient

VERTICALES

2. hard working
3. optimist
4. liar, lying
7. honest, sincere
9. egoist, egotistical

Work with a partner. Study the illustration and spot the things that are harming our environment. One student identifies the problem, the other gives the solutions.

_____   _____

_____   _____

_____   _____

_____   _____

_____   _____

_____   _____

_____   _____

_____   _____

_____   _____

Actividad F

Las siete diferencias

Work with a partner. Compare the following two scenes and find out 7 differences between them.

Actividad G

Picture Story

Nuestro  está en peligro. Estamos destruyendo los , los

y los .

Hay mucha contaminación:  y  producen y

contribuyen a la ácida y a la destrucción del ozono. Cortamos los y

las 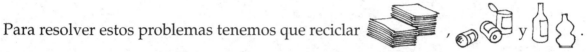 que se usan para producir medicinas. Además estamos contribuyendo

a la eliminación de varias especies de  .

Para resolver estos problemas tenemos que reciclar , y  .

Debemos utilizar la energía del 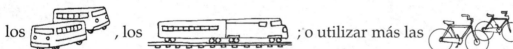 , el y el y reducir el

uso excesivo de la , la y el .

También debemos caminar y usar los medios de transportación pública, como

los , los ; o utilizar más las . Así

podremos salvar nuestro para las generaciones del futuro.

Appendix

Cosas de la lengua

 **«¡Zas! ¡Cataplúm!»**: Onomatopeia in Spanish

Sounds are universal. People the world over hear bells ringing, dogs barking, children crying, and so on. Each language, however, attempts to reproduce these sounds in its own individual way. The technical term for naming a sound with a word that is pronounced like the sound is *onomatopoeia*.

For example, if we see or listen to the English words "knock, knock," we recognize them as the sound of someone knocking at the door. In Spanish, however, the equivalent sound is **"pam, pam, pam"** or **"toc, toc."** "Cock a doodle doo" is immediately recognizable by English speakers as the crowing of a rooster. In Spanish, the same sound is represented by the words **"qui qui ri quí,"** which sounds "kee kee ree kee."

Here are some sounds made by other animals. Match the Spanish sounds with the English ones.

SPANISH	ENGLISH
pío, pío	bow wow
jau, jau	neigh
cuá, cuá	peep, peep
miau	meow
jiii	quack, quack

Here are some more everyday sounds. Match the Spanish and the English.

SPANISH	ENGLISH
bum	choo, choo
rataplán	whack
chuu, chuu, chuu	crash
cras	rat-a-tat
zas	boom

Finally, here are some sounds in Spanish with a description of the sounds on the right. Match the two columns.

SPANISH	ENGLISH
buaaa	person sneezing
din don	doorbell ringing
achiiis	engine revving up
room, room	bell chiming
glu, glu, glu	baby crying
riiin riiin	person out of breath
uf, uf	gurgling sound

 Compound Words (Word Building)

There are many words in Spanish that are combinations of other words in the language, forming compound words. If you know the meanings of the simple words, you can usually figure out the meaning of the more complex ones. Here are a few common examples:

abre (*open*) + **latas** (*cans*) = **abrelatas** (*can opener*)

ante (*before*) + **ojos** (*eyes*) = **anteojos** (*eyeglasses*)

saca (*take out*) + **puntas** (*points*) = **sacapuntas** (*pencil sharpener*)

para (*for*) + **aguas** (*water*) = **paraguas** (*umbrella*)

guarda (*keep*) + **ropa** (*clothing*) = **guardarropa** (*wardrobe*)

Now try these: they're a bit more difficult. Match the compound words with their English equivalents.

lava (*washes*) + **manos** (*hands*) = **lavamanos**   seesaw

monda (*cleans*) + **dientes** (*teeth*) = **mondadientes**   pastime

cuenta (*counts*) + **gotas** (*drops*) = **cuentagotas**   wash basin

pasa (*passes*) + **tiempo** (*time*) = **pasatiempo**   toothpick

sube (*goes up*) + **baja** (*goes down*) = **subibaja**   eyedropper

Finally, figure out the meanings of these words.

rompe (*breaks*) + **cabezas** (*heads*) = **rompecabezas**

rasca (*scratches*) + **cielo** (*sky*) = **rascacielo**

para (*for*) + **choques** (*crashes*) = **parachoques**

espanta (*frightens*) + **pájaros** (*birds*) = **espantapájaros**

3 «**Tiene un tornillo flojo**»: Idiomatic Expressions

In every language there are expressions called idioms, whose meanings make perfect sense to the native speaker, but not necessarily to the non native, especially if these expressions are translated word for word. In English, for example, we say things like, "it's raining cats and dogs," "he hit the ceiling," "that was the last straw," and so on. If we translated the words of these expressions into Spanish, they would make absolutely no sense to the Spanish speaker.

And yet, idioms are an essential part in speaking or understanding any language. What we must do then, is to find equivalent expressions in both Spanish and English. Here are some Spanish idioms (**modismos**) with their literal translations and their English equivalents.

Cuesta un ojo de la cara. (*It costs an eye of the face.*) It costs an arm and a leg. It costs a fortune.

Tiene el corazón hecho pedazos. (*He has his heart made pieces.*) His heart is broken.

Le toma el pelo. (*He's taking your hair.*) He's kidding you. He's pulling your leg.

Sólo hay cuatro gatos aquí. (*There are only four cats here.*) There's hardly anyone here. There's hardly a soul.

Here are some idioms with their English translations. Match them with their English equivalents.

1. **Es la gota que rebosa la copa.** (It's the drop that makes the glass overflow.)

2. **Es echar agua al mar.** (It's throwing water into the ocean.)

3. **No es cosa del otro mundo.** (It's not anything from another world.)

4. **Estoy entre dos aguas.** (I'm between two waters.)

5. **Son como dos gotas de agua.** (They're like two drops of water.)

   a. I'm undecided. I don't know what to do.
   b. It's nothing to write home about. It's nothing special.
   c. They're like two peas in a pod. They're very similar.
   d. It's pointless. It makes no sense.
   e. That's the straw that broke the camel's back.

 **«En boca cerrada no entran moscas»:** Spanish proverbs

One of the best ways to understand the language and culture of a people is through its common sayings. Each language has its own proverbs, little sayings of folk wisdom that develop over the years. In some cases, the way a proverb is expressed is unique to that particular culture. But in many cases, since proverbs are an outgrowth of experiences common to all cultures, these sayings, called **refranes** in Spanish, are almost identical from one language to another.

A **refrán** is a saying, often in the form of a rhyme, that is usually short and sweet, clever or funny, and contains useful knowledge that can be applied to reallife situations.

Here are a few common proverbs, together with a translation and their English equivalent.

SPANISH PROVERB	LITERAL TRANSLATION	EQUIVALENT ENGLISH PROVERB
Antes que te cases mira lo que haces.	Before you get married, look at what you're doing.	Look before you leap.
El consejo de mujer es poco y quien no lo toma es loco.	Advice from a woman is little and those who don't take it are crazy.	Always listen to what a woman tells you.

Al cabo de cien años todos seremos calvos.	In a 100 years, we'll all be bald.	Don't worry about life's small problems.
Si quieres vivir sano acuéstate y levántate temprano.	If you want to be healthy get up early and go to bed early.	Early to bed and early to rise makes a man healthy, wealthy, and wise.
Al mal tiempo buena cara.	To bad weather, good face.	Keep your chin up.

Now, here are some Spanish proverbs and their English translations. Match them with the appropriate English proverbs that follow.

1. Aunque la mona se vista de seda, mona se queda. (*Even though a monkey dresses in silk, it still is a monkey.*) _____

2. El gato escalfado del agua fría huye. (*The scalded cat runs away from cold water.*) _____

3. No hay que ahogarse en un vaso de agua. (*You shouldn't drown in a glass of water.*) _____

4. A lo hecho, pecho (*to what's done, chest*) _____

5. De tal palo, tal astilla (*from such a stick, such a splinter*) _____

    a.   Don't cry over spilled milk.
    b.   You can't make a silk purse out of a sow's ear.
    c.   A chip off the old block. Like father, like son.
    d.   Once bitten, twice shy.
    e.   Don't make a mountain out of a molehill.

 **Suffixes: Changing the meanings of words**

Some Spanish nouns may add endings that change the original meaning. They are called suffixes.

One common suffix is **-ito** or **-ita,** which indicates "little, small" or a feeling of affection. Thus, **mi casa** simply means *my house*. But **mi casita** is my "home, sweet, home." Similarly, **mi hermanito** is "my little brother." These endings can also be added to proper nouns: **Juan** becomes **Juanito, Ana** becomes **Anita, Jorge** becomes **Jorgito,** and so on.

Just as the ending **-ito/-ita** has an agreeable meaning, the ending **-illo/-illa** has a disagreeable one. **Un hombrecito** is a mature, well-mannered boy, "just like a grown-up." However **un hombrecillo** expresses contempt: a pipsqueak, a small insignificant man. Unlike **-ito** and **-illo,** the ending **-ón** enlarges a noun. **Un hombrón** is a hulk of a man.

Some endings are used so often that they become part of the word itself. The word with its ending then takes on a new meaning. Here are some examples:

el gatito (*kitten*), from **el gato**

el perrito (*puppy*), from **el perro**

el sillón (*armchair*), from **la silla**

la señorita (*miss*), from **la señora**

There are many suffixes in the Spanish language, such as

-ero/-era	**la carta** (*letter*)	**el cartero** (*postman, lettercarrier*)
-ura	**alto** (*tall*)	**altura** (*height*)
	largo (*long*)	**largura** (*length*)
-dad	**oscuro** (*dark*)	**oscuridad** (*darkness*)
	cruel (*cruel*)	**crueldad** (*cruelty*)
-ez/-eza	**rápido** (*fast*)	**rapidez** (*speed*)
	pobre (*poor*)	**pobreza** (*poverty*)

By learning the above suffixes, one can often figure out the meanings of many different words that belong to the same family.

la mesa (*table*)

la mesera   _____

el mesero   _____

la mesita   _____

enfermo (*sick*)

la enfermera   _____

la enfermedad   _____

la cocina (*kitchen*)

cocinar   _____

el cocinero   _____

la cocinera   _____

invitar (*to invite*)

el invitado   _____

la invitación   _____

escribir (*to write*)

el escritorio   _____

el escritor   _____

Spanish-English Vocabulary

The Spanish-English Vocabulary is intended to be complete for the contexts of this book.

Nouns are listed in the singular. Adjectives are listed in the masculine form. The following abbreviations are used:

m. = masculine   *sing.* = singular   *adj.* = adjective

f. = feminine   *pl.* = plural   *irr.* = irregular

m. & f. = masculine and feminine   *sing. & pl.* = singular and plural

Verbs with spelling changes, stem-changing verbs, and irregular verbs are identified by the type of change as follows: **poder (ue); tener** *(irr.)*.

A

a to, at
abajo below
abeja *f.* bee
abierto open
abogado(-a) lawyer; **abogado defensor** defense lawyer
abrigo *m.* coat
abrir to open
aburrido bored, boring
acabar to finish; **acabar de** to have just
aceite *m.* oil
acelerador *m.* accelerator, gas pedal
acera *f.* sidewalk
acercarse (qu) to approach, come near
acompañar to accompany, go with
acordarse de (ue) to remember
acostar (ue) to put to bed; **acostarse** to lie down, go to bed
activo active
acto *m.* act
actuar to act
acuerdo *m.* agreement; **estar de acuerdo** to agree; **de acuerdo** agreed; yes, of course

adelante forward; **de ahora en adelante** from now on
adelanto *m.* advance
además (de) besides
adentro inside
adivino(-a) fortune teller
adivinar to guess, foretell
¿adónde? where (to)?
aduana *f.* customs
aduanero(-a) customs official
aeromozo(-a) flight attendant
aeropuerto *m.* airport
afeitarse to shave
aficionado(-a) fan
afortunadamente fortunately, luckily
afuera outside; **comer afuera** to eat out
agresivo aggressive
agua *f.* **(el agua)** water
aguacate *m.* avocado
aguafiestas *m. & f.* partypooper, spoilsport
agüero *m.* omen
ahí there; **por ahí** that way, over there
ahora now; **ahora mismo** right now
aire acondicionado *m.* air conditioning

ahorrar to save
ajo *m.* garlic
alegre happy
alegremente happily
alemán(-ana) German
alfabeto *m.* alphabet
alfombra *f.* rug
algo something
algodón *m.* cotton
alguien somebody
alguno some, any
aliento *m.* breath
aliviar to relieve
alivio *m.* relief
allá there, over there
allí there
almacén *m.* store; warehouse; department store
almacenaje *m.* storage
almorzar (ue, c) to eat (have) lunch
almuerzo *m.* lunch
alrededor de around
alto tall, high
alunizar (c) to land on the moon
amable kind, nice
amanecer *m.* dawn
amarillento yellowish
amarillo yellow

ambicioso ambitious
amigo(-a) friend
amiguito(-a) little friend, pal
amor *m.* love; **amorcito** my love, my darling
ampliar to enlarge
amuleto *m.* charm
ancho wide
andar (*irr.*) to go about, walk
anillo *m.* ring
año *m.* year
anoche last night
anteayer the day before yesterday
antena *f.* antenna
antes (de) before
antiguo old, ancient
antipático unpleasant
anunciar to announce
anuncio *m.* announcement, sign; **anuncio clasificado** classified ad; **anuncio comercial** ad
apagar (gu) to turn off
aplauso *m.* applause, clapping
aprender to learn
aquel, aquella that
aquellos, aquellas those
aquí here; **por aquí** this way
araña *f.* spider
árbitro *m.* umpire
árbol *m.* tree
ardilla *f.* squirrel
arena *f.* sand
arete *m.* earring
armonía *f.* harmony
arrancar (qu) to start (auto)
arreglar to fix, repair
arrogante arrogant, haughty
arroz *m.* rice; **arroz con leche** rice pudding
artículo *m.* article; **artículo de fondo** editorial
ascensor *m.* elevator
asegurado insured
asegurar to insure; to assure
asesino(-a) murderer
así so, thus
asiento *m.* chair, seat; **tomar asiento** to take a seat, sit down
asistir to attend

asociación *f.* society
aspirina *f.* aspirin
astro *m.* star
astrología *f.* astrology
astronauta *m. & f.* astronaut
astronave *f.* spaceship
asunto *m.* matter, affair
atención *f.* attention; **prestar atención** to pay attention
atento attentive, polite
aterrizar (c) to land
atractivo attractive
atrapar to trap; to catch
atrás back, backwards
atropellar to run over
aún even
aunque even though
auto *m.*, **automóvil** *m.* car
auxilio *m.* help
avalúo *m.* appraisal
avanzar (c) to advance
avenida *f.* avenue
avión *m.* plane
ayer yesterday; **anteayer** the day before yesterday
ayuda *f.* help
ayudante *m. & f.* helper, assistant
ayudar to help
azafata *f.* flight attendant
azul blue

B

bailar to dance
baile *m.* dance
bajar to go (come) down
bajo short; under, underneath
balón *m.* large ball
baloncesto *m.* basketball
ballena *f.* whale
banco *m.* bank
banda *f.* band
bandera *f.* flag
bañar to bathe; **bañarse** to take a bath
baño *m.* bathroom; **traje de baño** *m.* bathing suit
barba *f.* beard
barbacoa *f.* barbecue
barco *m.* boat; **barco de vela** sailboat

barrio *m.* neighborhood
basado based
básquetbol *m.* basketball
bastante enough
basura *f.* garbage
bata *f.* robe, housecoat
bate *m.* bat
bateador(-ora) batter
batear to bat
batería *f.* battery
bautizo *m.* baptism
batir to beat, break a record
bebé *m. & f.* baby
béisbol *m.* baseball
beso *m.* kiss
biblioteca *f.* library
bien well; **está bien** it's all right; O.K.
bienvenido welcome
bigote *m.* mustache
blanco white
blando soft
blusa *f.* blouse
bobo silly, foolish
boca *f.* mouth
boda *f.* marriage, wedding
bola *f.* ball
bolera *f.* bowling alley
boleto *m.* ticket
bolo: jugar (ue, gu) a los bolos to bowl
bolsillo *m.* pocket
bolso *m.* purse
bombero(-a) firefighter
bondadoso generous
bonito pretty, good-looking
bota *f.* boot
botar to throw away
botella *f.* bottle
botón *m.* button
boxeo *m.* boxing
brazalete *m.* bracelet
brazo *m.* arm; **brazo gitano** sponge cake roll with fruit or cream filling
brillante shiny, brilliant
brillar to shine
brisa *f.* breeze
broche *m.* brooch, pin
bronceador *m.* tanning lotion
bruja *f.* witch

brujo *m.* wizard, sorcerer
buenaventura *f.* fortune, good luck; **decir** (*irr.*) **la buenaventura** to tell one's fortune
bueno good
bufanda *f.* scarf
buscar (qu) to look for
buscado looked for, searched
butaca *f.* armchair, easy chair
buzón *m.* mailbox

C

caballero *m.* gentleman
caballo *m.* horse; **montar a caballo** to go horseback riding
cabeza *f.* head
cabina telefónica *f.* phone booth
cada each, every
cadena *f.* chain
caer(se) (*irr.*) to fall (down)
café *m.* coffee; café
caída *f.* fall
caja *f.* box; **caja fuerte** safe
cajero(-a) cashier
calamar *m.* squid
calavera *f.* skull
caldo *m.* broth; **caldo gallego** soup with white beans, turnips, and potatoes
caliente hot
calle *f.* street
cama *f.* bed
camarón *m.* shrimp
cambiar to change, exchange
caminata *f.* hike, long walk; **dar** (*irr.*) **una caminata** to go hiking
caminar to walk
camión *m.* truck
camisa *f.* shirt; **camisa de dormir** nightgown
camiseta *f.* t-shirt
campamento *m.* camp
campeón(-ona) champion
campo *m.* country, field
canción *f.* song
canguro *m.* kangaroo
canjear to exchange

cansado tired
cantante *m. & f.* singer
cantar to sing
capital *f.* capital
capítulo *m.* chapter
capó *m.* hood
cápsula *f.* capsule
cara *f.* face
cárcel *f.* jail
carga *f.* freight
cariñoso caring
carne *f.* meat
carnicería *f.* butchershop
carnicero(-era) butcher
caro expensive
carrera *f.* race
carretera *f.* highway
carro *m.* car
carta *f.* letter
cartelera *f.* billboard
cartera *f.* purse
cartón *m.* carton, cardboard
casa *f.* house; **a casa** home; **en casa** at home
casado married
casarse to get married
casco *m.* helmet
casi almost
caso *m.* case
castillo *m.* castle
catarro *m.* cold
causa: a causa de because of
cavar to dig
celda *f.* cell
celoso jealous
cenar to have dinner
centro *m.* center, middle; downtown
cepillar(se) to brush
cepillo *m.* brush; **cepillo de dientes** toothbrush
cerca (de) near
cerrado closed
cerrar (ie) to close, shut
certificado *m.* certificate
cerveza *f.* beer
cesta *f.* basket
chaleco *m.* vest
chica *f.* girl
chico *m.* boy

chile *m.* red pepper; **chile con carne** spiced chopped meat with chili sauce
chiste *m.* joke
chocar (qu) to crash
chofer *m.* driver
chupar to suck; **chuparse el dedo** to suck one's finger
ciclismo *m.* cycling
ciclista *m. & f.* cyclist
cielo *m.* sky, heaven; **mi cielo** my love, sweetheart
ciencia *f.* science; **ciencia ficción** science fiction
científico(-a) scientist
ciento (one) hundred; **por ciento** percent
cierto certain, sure; **es cierto** it's true
ciervo *m.* deer
cigarrillo *m.* cigarette
cine *m.* movies
cintura *f.* waist; lower back
cinturón *m.* belt
cita *f.* date, appointment
ciudad *f.* city
ciudadano(-ana) citizen
claro light; clear; of course!; **claro que no** of course not; **claro que sí** of course!
clase *f.* class, kind
clave *f.* key (to code)
clima *m.* climate, weather
cobrar to charge
cocina *f.* kitchen
cocinar to cook
cocodrilo *m.* crocodile
coche *m.* car; carriage
codo *m.* elbow
coger (j) to grasp, grab, catch, take
cohete *m.* rocket
cola f. tail, line
colchón flotante de aire *m.* air mattress
colección *f.* collection
colocar (qu) to place, put
collar *m.* necklace
combatir to combat, fight
comedor m. dining room
comenzar (ie, c) to begin

comer to eat
cometa *m.* comet
cometer to commit
cómico funny, amusing, comical
comida *f.* food, meal
como as, like **¿cómo?** how?, what?
cómoda *f.* dresser
cómodo comfortable
comportamiento *m.* behavior
cómplice *m. & f.* accomplice
compra *f.* purchase; **de compras** shopping
comprador(-ora) buyer
comprar to buy
comprender to understand
comprensivo understanding
comprobar (ue) to check, verify
compromiso *m.* commitment; engagement
computadora *f.* computer
común common
comunidad *f.* community
con with
concierto *m.* concert; **sala de conciertos** *f.* concert hall
concursante *m. & f.* contestant
concurso *m.* contest
concha *f.* (sea)shell
conejo *m.* rabbit
confianza *f.* confidence, trust
congelador *m.* freezer
conjunto *m.* set
conmigo with me
conocer to know, be acquainted with
conocido(-ida) acquaintance
conseguir (i, g) to obtain
consejero(-era) counselor, adviser
consejo *m.* advice
considerar to consider
consistir (en) to consist of
consultorio *m.* doctor's office
contado: al/de contado cash down, for cash
contaminación contamination
contar (ue) to tell; to count
contento happy, satisfied

conteo count; **conteo regresivo** countdown
contestar to answer
contigo with you (fam.)
continuación *f.* continuation; **a continuación** next, as follows
continuo continuous
contra against
contrario opposite; **al contrario, por el contrario** on the contrary
contrato *m.* contract
convencer to convince
convertir (irr.) en to turn into
copa *f.* glass, goblet
coro *m.* choir
corregir (i, j) to correct
correo *m.* mail; post office
correr to run
cortar to cut
cortés courteous, polite
corto short
cortina *f.* curtain
cosa *f.* thing; **eso es otra cosa** that's something else
costar (ue) to cost; **costar un ojo de la cara** to cost a fortune
creencia *f.* belief
creer to believe
crema *f.* cream
criminal *m. & f.* criminal
cristal *m.* glass, crystal
crucero *m.* cruise, crossing; **hacer un crucero** to take a cruise
crueldad *f.* cruelty
cruzar (c) to cross
cuadro *m.* picture, painting; square; **a cuadros** plaid
cuadrado square
¿cuál? which (one)?, what?
cualidad *f.* quality, characteristic
cualquier any
¿cuándo? when?
¿cuánto? how much?; **¿cuántos?** how many?
cuarto *m.* room; *adj.* fourth
cubierta *m.* hood
cubierto covered

cubo *m.* pail
cubrir to cover
cuello *m.* neck; collar
cuenta *f.* bill; account
cuerpo *m.* body
cuidado *m.* care; **tener (irr.) cuidado** to be careful
cuidadoso careful
culebra *f.* snake
cumpleaños *m.* birthday
cura *m.* priest
curita *f.* bandage
curso *m.* course; session

D

dama *f.* lady
daño *m.* damage
dar (irr.) to give; **dar un paseo** to take a walk; **me da pena** it makes me sad
de of, from
debajo (de) underneath, under, below; **por debajo de** underneath
deber must
débil weak
decidir to decide
décimo tenth
decir (irr.) to say; **querer decir** to mean
declaración *f.* declaration, statement
declarar to declare; to testify
decorar to decorate
dedo *m.* finger
defectuoso defective
defender (ie) to defend
defensa *f.* defense; **defensa propia** self-defense
defensivo defensive; **a la defensiva** defensively
dejar to leave; to let, allow; **dejar de** to stop, give up
delante (de) in front (of)
delfín *m.* dolphin
delincuencia *f.* delinquency
demás: los demás the others, the rest
demasiado too much
demostrar (ue) to demonstrate

dentro de inside, in
dependiente *m. & f.* clerk
deporte *m.* sport
deportista *m. & f.* sportsman, sportswoman
deportivo sports (*adj.*)
derecho *m.* right (*law*)
derramar to spill
desarrollar(se) to develop
desarrollo *m.* development
desayuno *m.* breakfast
descansar to rest
descargar (gu) to unload
desconocido unknown; **lo desconocido** the unknown
describir to describe
descubrir to discover
desde since; from
desempacar to unpack
deseo *m.* desire, wish; **tener deseos de** to feel like
desesperado desperate
desierto empty, deserted
desodorante *m.* deodorant
desorden *m.* disorder
despacho *m.* office
despacio slowly
despedida *f.* farewell
despedir (i) to dismiss, fire
despegar (gu) to take off
despertar(se) (ie) to wake up
después later, afterwards; **después de** after
desvestirse (i) to undress
detalle *m.* detail
detrás (de) in back of, behind
devolver (ue) to return (an object)
día *m.* day; **al día siguiente** the following day; **del día** of the day; **hoy día** nowadays; **todos los días** every day
diamante *m.* diamond
diario *m.* newspaper, daily
diente *m.* tooth; **cepillo de dientes** toothbrush; **pasta de dientes** toothpaste
difícil difficult
dinámico dynamic
dinero *m.* money

dirección *m.* address
director(-ora) manager; principal
dirigir (j) to direct
disco compacto *m.* CD
discutir to discuss, argue
diseñar to design
distancia *f.* distance
divertido entertaining, enjoyable, amusing
divertir (ie) to amuse; **divertirse** to have fun (a good time)
divino divine, heavenly
dólar *m.* dollar
doler (ue) to hurt
dolor *m.* pain; **dolor de cabeza** headache
donde where; at (someone's place); **¿dónde?** where?
dormido asleep
dormir (ue) to sleep; **dormirse** to fall asleep
dormitorio *m.* bedroom
duda *f.* doubt
duende *m.* leprechaun, goblin
dueño(-a) owner
dulce *m.* sweet, candy; *adj.* sweet, gentle
durar to last

E

echar to throw, toss
edad *f.* age
edificio *m.* building
efectivo *m.* cash
egoísta selfish
ejemplo *m.* example; **por ejemplo** for example
ejercicio *m.* exercise
electricista *m. & f.* electrician
elegir (i, j) to elect
empanada *f.* meat pie
embarcar (qu) to sail away, embark
embargo: sin embargo however, nonetheless
empacar to pack
empezar (ie, c) to begin
empleado(-ada) employee

en in, on
enamorado in love
encabezamiento *m.* heading
encaje *m.* lace
encantador charming
encantar to enchant, charm; **me encanta** I love it
encender (ie) to light; to turn on
encontrar (ue) to find; **encontrarse** to find oneself; to meet (each other)
enchilada *f.* stuffed and rolled tortilla with chili sauce
endurecimiento *m.* hardening
enemigo(-a) *f.* enemy
enfermedad *f.* illness
enfermero(-a) nurse
enfermo sick
enojarse to get angry
enorme enormous, huge
ensalada *f.* salad; **ensalada mixta** mixed salad
ensayar to try
enseñar to teach
entender (ie) to understand
enterarse to find out
entero whole
entonces then
entrada *f.* entrance; ticket
entrar to enter, go in
entre among, between
entrenador(-ora) trainer
entrenar to train
entrevista *f.* interview
enviar to send; **enviar de regreso** to return, send back
envidia *f.* envy
envidioso envious
equipaje *m.* luggage
equipo *m.* set, equipment; team
equivalente equivalent
equivocado mistaken, wrong
equivocarse (qu) to make a mistake
error *m.* mistake, error
escalera *f.* stairs; ladder
escaparse to get away, run away

escenario *m.* stage
escoger (j) to choose
esconder to hide
escondido hidden
escritorio *m.* desk
escribir to write
escritor(-ora) writer
escuchar to listen to
escuela de automovilismo *f.* driving school
esa(-e, -o) that; **ésa, ése** that one; **en eso** just then
esas, esos those
escoba *f.* broom
esfuerzo *m.* effort
esgrima *f.* fencing
esmeralda *f.* emerald
espada *f.* sword
espalda *f.* back
espacial space
español Spanish
especial special; **en especial** especially
especialidad *f.* specialty
especializarse to specialize
especie *f.* species
espectáculo *m.* spectacle, show
espejo *m.* mirror; **espejo retrovisor** rear-view mirror
esperar to wait (for)
espíritu *m.* spirit
esposa *f.* wife
esqueleto *m.* skeleton
esquí *m.* ski; skiing
esquiar to ski
esquina *f.* corner
establecer to establish
estación *f.* station
estacionado parked
estacionamiento *m.* parking
estadio *m.* stadium
estado *m.* state; **Estados Unidos** United States
estampilla *f.* stamp
estante *m.* shelf; **estante para libros** bookshelf
estar (*irr.*) to be
esta(-e, -o) this; **ésta(-e)** this one

estas(-os) these; **éstas(-os)** these ones
estómago *m.* stomach, abdomen
estornudar to sneeze
estrecho narrow
estrella *f.* star
estricto strict, severe
estudiar to study
estudioso studious
estufa *f.* stove
estupendo great, marvelous
estupidez *f.* stupidity
estúpido stupid
eternidad *f.* eternity
etiqueta *f.* label, tag
evitar to avoid
exactamente exactly
examen *m.* exam, test
examinar to examine
exhibición *m.* exhibit
exhibirse to show oneself
existir to exist
éxito *m.* success; **tener** (*irr.*)
éxito to be successful
explicar (qu) to explain
extranjero foreign; **al extranjero** abroad
extraño strange

F

fabada *f.* thick bean soup with sausages
fácil easy
falda *f.* skirt
fama *f.* fame
familia *f.* family
fantasía *f.* fantasy
fantasma *m.* ghost
farmacéutico(-ica) pharmacist
farmacia *f.* pharmacy, drugstore
faro *m.* headlight
favor *m.* favor; **por favor** please
fecha *f.* date
felicitaciones congratulations
feo ugly
feroz fierce, savage

fiebre *f.* fever
fiesta *f.* party, celebration; **día de fiesta** *m.* holiday; **fiesta infantil** children's party
filmación *f.* filming
fin *m.* end; **por fin** finally
final *m.* end; **al final** in the end; **al final de** at the end of
financiamiento *m.* financing
firmar to sign
fiscal *m. & f.* prosecutor; district attorney
flaco skinny, thin
flan *m.* caramel custard
flor *f.* flower
florero *m.* vase
flota *f.* fleet
foca *f.* seal
foto *f.* picture; **sacar (qu) fotos** to take pictures
fotógrafo(-a) photographer
fracaso *m.* failure
francés(-esa) French
frase *f.* sentence
frecuentemente frequently, often
freno *m.* brake
frente *m.* front; **frente a** opposite, in front of
frijol *m.* bean
frío cold
frito fried
frontera *f.* border, frontier
fruta *f.* fruit
fuego *m.* fire
fuerte strong
fuerza *f.* strength
fugitivo *m.* fugitive
fumar to smoke
función *f.* show, performance
funcionar to work
fútbol *m.* soccer; **fútbol americano** football

G

gafas *f. pl.* glasses; **gafas de sol** sunglasses
ganador(-ora) winner
ganga *f.* bargain

ganar to win; to earn
garganta *f.* throat
gastar to spend
gato *m.* cat
gaviota *f.* seagull
gazpacho *m.* cold, fresh vegetable soup
general general; **por lo general** in general
generalmente generally
generoso generous
gente *f.* people
gerente *m. & f.* manager
giro postal postal money order
gitano(-a) Gypsy
globo *m.* balloon
golpe *m.* blow
goma *f.* rubber
gordo fat
gordura *f.* fat, fatness
gorra *f.* cap
grabar to record
gracias thanks; **dar** (*irr.*) **las gracias** to thank
gracioso funny
grado *m.* degree; stage
graduarse to graduate
grande large, big; great
gratuitamente free (of charge)
gripe *f.* flu
gritar to yell, scream, cry out
grito *m.* scream, cry
grupo *m.* group
guacamole *m.* avocado dip
guante *m.* glove
guapo handsome
guardafango *m.* fender
guardar to keep
guía *m. & f.* guide, *f.* guidebook
guiar to guide; to drive
gusano *m.* worm
gustar to like
gusto *m.* taste

H

haber (*inf.*) to have
había there was, there were
hábil skillful
habitación *f.* room

hábito *m.* habit
habla *f.* speech
hace ago; **hace poco** a little while ago
hacer (*irr.*) to do, make; **hacer calor** to be hot; **hacer caso de** to pay attention to; **hacer pedazos** to break into pieces; **hacer sol** to be sunny; **hacer un viaje** to take a trip; **hacerse** to become
hacia towards
hada *f.* (**el hada**) fairy
hasta until, up to; as far as
hay there is, there are; **hay que** it is necessary, one must
helado *m.* ice cream
herencia *f.* inheritance
hermana *f.* sister
hermano *m.* brother
hierba *f.* grass
hielo *m.* ice; **patinar en el hielo** to ice skate
hija *f.* daughter
hijo *m.* son; *pl.* sons, children
hipnotismo *m.* hypnotism
hipnotista *m. & f.* hypnotist
hogar *m.* home
hoja *f.* leaf
hombre *m.* man
hombro *m.* shoulder
honesto honest
horario *m.* schedule
hormiga *f.* ant
horno *m.* oven
hoy today; **hoy día** nowadays; **de hoy en ocho días** a week from today; **de hoy en quince días** two weeks from today
huella *f.* track, footprint; **huella digital** fingerprint
huevo *m.* egg

I

idear to devise, think of
idioma *m.* language
iglesia *f.* church
ignorancia *f.* ignorance
igual equal, the same, similar
ilimitado unlimited

impedir to impede, prevent
impermeable *m.* raincoat
importar to matter; **¿qué importa?** what difference does it make?
impuesto *m.* tax
impulsivo impulsive
incendio *m.* fire
inclinarse to bend over, bend down
increíble unbelievable
indicar (qu) to indicate, point out
individuo *m.* individual
inesperado unexpected
influencia *f.* influence
ingeniero(-era) engineer
inglés(-esa) English
ingrediente *m.* ingredient
iniciar to start, initiate
inseguridad *f.* insecurity
invierno *m.* winter
ir (*irr.*) to go; **irle bien (a una persona)** to go well; **irse** to go away, leave; **le va bien** it fits you well; **¡qué va!** no way!, nonsense!; **vamos a** let's
isla *f.* island
izquierdo left

J

jabón *m.* soap
jamás never, not ever
jarabe *m.* syrup; **jarabe para la tos** cough syrup
jardín *m.* garden
jirafa *f.* giraffe
jonrón *m.* homerun
joven *m. & f.* young man, young woman; *adj.* young
joya *f.* jewel
joyería *f.* jewelry store
juego *m.* game; set
juez *m. & f.* judge
jugador(-ora) player
jugar (ue, gu) to play
jugo *m.* juice
juguete *m.* toy
juntos together
jurar to swear

justamente precisely, exactly
justo just, fair
juvenil juvenile

L

lado *m.* side; **al lado** next to, beside; **al otro lado** on the other side; **de al lado** next
ladrar to bark
ladrillo *m.* brick
ladrón *m.* thief
lago *m.* lake
lámpara *f.* lamp
lana *f.* wool
largo long
lavadora *f.* washer
lavaplatos *m.* dishwasher
lavar to wash; **lavarse** to get washed, wash oneself
leche *f.* milk
legumbre *f.* vegetable
lejos far (away); **a lo lejos** in the distance
lengua *f.* tongue; language
lentamente slowly
leopardo *m.* leopard
letra *f.* letter; lyrics
letrero *m.* sign
levantar to lift, raise; **levantarse** to get up
libra *f.* pound
libre free
librero *m.* bookcase
libreta *f.* notebook
licor *m.* liquor
líder *m.* leader
liebre *f.* hare
liga *f.* league
ligero light
limpiar to clean
listo ready
llamada *f.* call
llamar to call; **llamarse** to be named, to be called
llanta *f.* tire
llegar (gu) to arrive
llevar to wear; to carry, take; **llevarse** to take away; **llevarse bien** to get along
llover (ue) to rain

local *m.* place, quarters
loción *f.* lotion
loco crazy
lucha *f.* fight; **lucha libre** wrestling
luego soon, then, later; **hasta luego** see you later
lugar *m.* place; **tener** (*irr.*) **lugar** to take place
lujoso luxurious
luna *f.* moon
luz *f.* light

M

madera *f.* wood
maestro(-a) teacher; master; **maestro de ceremonias** TV host, master of ceremonies
magia *f.* magic
magnífico magnificent, wonderful
mago *m.* magician
maíz *m.* corn
mal badly, poorly
maleducado ill-mannered, rude
maleta *f.* suitcase
maletero *m.* trunk
maletín *m.* briefcase; small bag
malo bad
manchado stained
manejar to drive
manera *f.* manner
manga *f.* sleeve
maniquí *m.* mannequin
mano *f.* hand
manta *f.* blanket
manzana *f.* apple
mañana tomorrow; **pasado mañana** the day after tomorrow
mapa *m.* map
máquina *f.* machine
mar *m.* ocean, sea
marca *f.* brand
marido *m.* husband
mariposa *f.* butterfly
mariscos *m. pl.* shellfish; **zarzuela de mariscos** *f.* shellfish stew

martes Tuesday
más more, most
matar to kill
matemáticas *f. pl.* mathematics
matrimonio *m.* married couple, husband and wife, marriage
mayonesa *f.* mayonnaise
mayor greater, greatest; older, oldest
medianoche *f.* midnight
medio half
medio *m.* means
medir (i) to measure
mejor better, best
mejorarse to get better
memoria *f.* memory; **aprender de memoria** to learn by heart; **saber** (*irr.*) **de memoria** to know by heart
mencionar to mention, name
menor least, slightest; younger, youngest
menos less
mensual monthly
mentir (ie) to lie
mentira *f.* lie
mentiroso(-a) liar
mes *m.* month; **al mes** per month
mesero *m.* waiter
mesita *f.* small table; **mesita de café** coffee table; **mesita de noche** night table
meter to place, to put in
método *m.* method
metro *m.* subway
mexicano Mexican
mi my
miedo *m.* fear; **tener** (*irr.*) **miedo** to be afraid
miembro *m. & f.* member
mientras while
mil a thousand
milla *f.* mile
millón *m.* a million
mirar to look at; **mirarse** to look at oneself
mismo same; **lo mismo** the same thing; **ahora mismo**

right now; **sí mismo** himself, herself; **ti mismo** yourself

moda *f.* fashion, style; **de moda** in fashion

mojado wet

moneda *f.* coin

monje *m.* monk

mono *m.* monkey

monopatín *m.* skateboard

montaña *f.* mountain

montar to mount; **montar a caballo** to ride a horse; **montar en bicicleta** to ride a bicycle

morder (ue) to bite

morir (ue) to die

mosca *f.* fly

mostrar (ue) to show

moto *f.* (from **motocicleta**) motorcycle

motor *m.* engine, motor

mover(se) (ue) to move

movimiento *m.* movement

mucho much, a lot; **muchos** many

mudanza *f.* moving

mueble *m.* piece of furniture; *pl.* furniture

mueblería *f.* furniture store

muerto *m.* dead man

mujer *f.* woman

multa *f.* ticket, fine; **poner** (*irr.*) **una multa** to issue a ticket

mundial world

murciélago *m.* bat (animal)

mundo *m.* world; **por todo el mundo** everywhere; **todo el mundo** everybody

muy very

N

nacer to be born

nada nothing

nadar to swim

nadie nobody

naranja *f.* orange

natación *f.* swimming

natilla *f.* soft custard

nave *f.* ship, vessel; **nave espacial** spaceship

navegar to sail

Navidad *f.* Christmas

necesitar to need

negro black; **de negro** in black

nervioso nervous

nevar (ie) to snow

nevera *f.* ice box, refrigerator

ni neither, nor

ninguno no, not any

niño(-a) child; **de niño** as a child

nivel *m.* level

noche *f.* night; **esta noche** tonight; **por la noche** at night

norteamericano North American

nota *f.* note; grade

noticia *f.* news item; **noticias** news

novela *f.* novel; **novela policíaca** detective story

noveno ninth

novia *f.* bride

nube *f.* cloud

nuestro our

nuevo new

número *m.* number

nunca never, not ever

O

obedecer to obey

objeto *m.* object

obstante: no obstante nevertheless

obtener to obtain

octavo eighth

ocupado busy

ocurrir to happen

oficina *f.* office

ofrecer to offer

oído *m.* ear

oír (*irr.*) to hear

ojo *m.* eye

ola *f.* wave

onza *f.* ounce

opuesto opposite; opposed

órbita *f.* orbit

orden *m.* order

ordinario ordinary, common

oreja *f.* ear

orilla *f.* shore, bank

oro *m.* gold

oscuro dark

oso *m.* bear

otro other

P

paciencia *f.* patience

paella *f.* yellow rice with saffron, meat, seafood, and vegetables

pagar (gu) to pay

página *f.* page

pago *m.* payment

país *m.* country

pájaro *m.* bird

pala *f.* shovel

palabra *f.* word

palmera *f.* palm tree

pan *m.* bread

panadero(-era) baker

pantalones *m. pl.* pants

pantera *f.* panther

pantufla *f.* slipper

pañuelo *m.* handkerchief; **pañuelo de papel** tissue

papa *f.* potato

papagayo *m.* cockatoo

papel *m.* paper; **papel higiénico** toilet paper

para for, (in order) to

parabrisas *m.* windshield

parachoques *m.* bumper

parada *f.* stop; **parada de autobús** bus stop

paraguas *m. sing. & pl.* umbrella

paraíso *m.* paradise, heaven

parar to stop

parecer to seem; **al parecer** apparently; **¿qué le parece?** what do you think?

parecido similar

pareja *f.* couple, pair

parte *f.* part; **en cualquier parte** anywhere; **en todas partes** everywhere

partida *f.* certificate; **partida de matrimonio** marriage certificate; **partida de nacimiento** birth certificate

partido *m.* game, match

pasado *m.* past; **el lunes (mes, verano, año) pasado** last Monday (month, summer, year)

pasaje *m.* ticket, pass

pasajero(-era) passenger

pasaporte *m.* passport

pasar to pass; to spend (time); to happen; **¿qué pasa?** what's going on?, what's up?; **pase por aquí** come this way

paseo *m.* stroll, walk; **dar** (*irr.*) **un paseo** to take a walk

pasillo *m.* corridor, lobby, hall

pasta *f.* paste; **pasta de dientes** toothpaste

pastel *m.* cake, pastry

pastilla *f.* tablet; **pastilla para la tos** cough drop

pata *f.* animal leg or foot

patata *f.* potato

patín *m.* skate

patinaje *m.* skating

patinar to skate

patrulla *f.* police squad car

pavo *m.* turkey

payaso(-a) clown

paz *f.* peace

peatón *m.* pedestrian

pedir (i) to order, ask for, request; **pedir prestado** to borrow

peinar to comb; **peinarse** to comb one's hair

peine *m.* comb

pelear to fight

película *f.* film

peligroso dangerous

pelo *m.* hair

pelota *f.* ball

peluquero(-era) hairdresser

pena *f.* sorrow; **¡qué pena!** what a shame!

pensar (ie) to think

pequeño small, little

perder (ie) to lose

periódico *m.* newspaper

periodista *m. & f.* reporter, journalist

perito *m.* expert

perla *f.* pearl

permiso *m.* permission; permit

permitir to permit

pero but

perro *m.* dog

perseguir (i, g) to pursue

pesa *f.* weight; **levantar pesas** to lift weights

pesadilla *f.* nightmare

pesado heavy

pesar to weigh

pescado *m.* fish

pescar (qu) to fish, go fishing

peso *m.* weight

picante hot (spicy)

pie *m.* foot; **pie cuadrado** square foot

piedra *f.* stone

piel *f.* skin; leather

pijama *m.* pajama

píldora *f.* pill

piloto *m.* pilot

pingüino *m.* penguin

piraña *f.* piranha

pirata *m.* pirate

piscina *f.* swimming pool

piso *m.* floor

pistola *f.* pistol

placa *f.* license plate

planear to plan

planeta *m.* planet

planta *f.* plant

plata *f.* silver

plato *m.* dish, plate

playa *f.* beach

plaza *f.* public square

plazo *m.* installment

poción *f.* potion

poco little

poder (ue) (*irr.*) to be able, can

poder *m.* power

poema *m.* poem

policía *m. & f.* police officer; *f.* police force

pollo *m.* chicken

ponche *m.* punch

poner (*irr.*) to put; **ponerse** to put on

por for, by, through, along; **¿por qué?** why?

porque because

poseer to possess

posible possible; **todo lo posible** everything possible

postre *m.* dessert

precio *m.* price

precioso lovely, beautiful

preferido favorite

preferir (ie) to prefer

pregunta *f.* question; **hacer** (*irr.*) **una pregunta** to ask a question

preguntar to ask

premio *m.* prize

prenda *f.* article of clothing

prendedor *m.* pin, brooch

preocupado worried

preocuparse to worry

preparar to prepare

prestado: pedir prestado to borrow

prestar to lend; **prestar atención** to pay attention

primerísimo foremost

primero first

primo(-a) cousin

principio *m.* beginning; **al principio** at the beginning

principiante *m. & f.* beginner

probar (ue) to try; **probarse** to try on

problema *m.* problem

programa *m.* program

programador(-ora) computer programmer

promesa *f.* promise

pronto quickly, soon; **por lo pronto** meanwhile

propiedad *f.* property

proprietario(-a) owner

propio own

proponer (*irr.*) to propose

propósito *m.* purpose; **a propósito** by the way

proteger (j) to protect

próximo next

psiquiatra *m. & f.* psychiatrist

publicar (qu) to publish

puerta *f.* door

pues well, then

puesto *m.* job, position

pulsera *f.* bracelet; **reloj de pulsera** *m.* wristwatch
punto *m.* point; period; **en punto** on the dot

Q

que that; **más que** more than; **¿qué?** what?
quedar to remain; to be (located); **quedarse** to stay, remain; **quedarse con** to keep
querer (ie) (*irr.*) to want, wish for; **querer decir** to mean
querido dear
¿quién? who?; **¿a quién?** whom?; **¿de quién?** whose?
quinto fifth
quiropráctica *f.* chiropractic
quitarse to take off
quizás perhaps, maybe

R

rana *f.* frog
rápido fast
raqueta *f.* racket
rascacielos *m. sing. & pl.* skyscraper
ratón *m.* mouse
raya *f.* stripe; **a rayas** striped
razón *f.* reason; **tener** (*irr.*) **razón** to be right; **no tener razón** to be wrong
reaccionar to react
realizar (c) to realize, fulfill
realmente really
receta *f.* prescription
recibir to receive; to go and meet
reciclamiento *m.* recycling
recientemente recently
recoger (j) to pick up; to gather
reconocer to recognize
recordar (ue) to remember
recostado leaning on; **estar** (*irr.*) **recostado** to be lying down
red *f.* net
refinado refined
reflejar to reflect
refresco *m.* soft drink; **refrescos** refreshments

refrigerador *m.* refrigerator
refrito refried
regalar to give (away)
regalo *m.* present, gift
regla *f.* rule; ruler
regresar to return
reír(se) (i) to laugh
relajarse to relax
reloj *m.* watch; **reloj de pulsera** wristwatch
remar to row
remitir to send
rendido exhausted
repente: de repente suddenly
repetir (i) to repeat
reservado reserved
resolver (ue) to resolve, solve
respetar to respect
respuesta *f.* answer, response
restar to subtract
restaurante *m.* restaurant
resultado *m.* result
retraso *m.* delay
revelar to reveal
revisar to check, go through
revista *f.* magazine
rey *m.* king
ridículo ridiculous
rincón *m.* corner
río *m.* river
robar to steal
robo *m.* theft
roca *f.* stone, rock
rodear to surround
rodilla *f.* knee
rojo red
romper to break
ropa *f.* clothes
rubí *m.* ruby
rubio blond
rueda *f.* wheel

S

sábado Saturday
saber (*irr.*) to know
sacar (qu) to take out, remove; to get (grade); **sacar fotos** to take pictures
saco *m.* coat, jacket; **saco de sport** sport jacket
sal *f.* salt

sala *f.* living room; **sala de conciertos** concert hall
salir to go out, leave
salsa *f.* sauce
saltamontes *m. sing. & pl.* grasshopper
saltar to jump
salud *f.* health
saludar to greet, say hello
salvaje savage, wild
salvavidas *m. & f., sing. & pl.* lifeguard
satélite *m.* satellite
secadora *f.* dryer
sección *f.* section
seda *f.* silk
seguir (i) to follow; to continue
según according to
segundo *m.* second; *adj.* second
seguro sure, certain
sello *m.* stamp
semáforo *m.* traffic light
semana *f.* week; **la semana pasada** last week; **la semana que viene** next week
señal *f.* signal, sign
sentado seated
sentar (ie) to seat; **sentarse** to sit down
sentido *m.* sense
sentimiento *m.* feeling
sentir(se) (ie) to feel; **lo siento** I'm sorry
séptimo seventh
sepultado buried
ser (*irr.*) to be; *m.* being
seriamente seriously
serie *f.* series
serio serious, reserved
serpiente *f.* snake, serpent
servir (i) to serve; to be useful; **¿en qué puedo servirle?** what can I do for you?
sexto sixth
si if
siempre always
siglo *m.* century
significar (qu) to mean
siguiente following

silla *f.* chair; **silla de playa** beach chair

sillón *m.* armchair

simpático nice, pleasant

sin without

sincero sincere

siquiera: ni siquiera not even

sirena *f.* siren

sitio *m.* place, spot

sobre on, on top of, over; about; *m.* envelope

sobrenatural supernatural

socorro *m.* help

sofa *m.* sofa, couch

sofisticado sophisticated

sol *m.* sun; **tomar el sol** to sunbathe

solamente only

soldado *m.* soldier

solo only, just; alone

soltero single

sombra *f.* shadow

sombrero *m.* hat

sombrilla *f.* umbrella, sunshade

sonar (ue) to sound, ring; **sonarse las narices** to blow one's nose

sonido *m.* sound

sonreir (í) to smile

soñar (ue) con to dream of

sopa *f.* soup

sorprender to surprise

sortija *f.* ring

su his, her, its, your, their

subir to climb, to go (come) up

subterráneo *m.* subway

sucio dirty

sudadera *f.* warm-up suit

suegra *f.* mother-in-law

sueldo *m.* salary

sueño *m.* sleep; dream; **tener (irr.) sueño** to be sleepy

suerte *f.* luck; **tener suerte** to be lucky

suéter *m.* sweater

suficiente enough

sumar to add (up)

supuesto: por supuesto of course, naturally

suspiro *m.* sigh; **echar un suspiro** to sigh

T

tabla *f.* board

tacaño stingy

talla *f.* size

también also

tampoco neither; **ni yo tampoco** neither do I

tanque *m.* tank

tanto so much; **tanto como** as much as

tarde *f.* afternoon late; **más tarde** later; **por la tarde** in the afternoon

tarea *f.* homework

tarjeta *f.* card; **tarjeta postal** postcard

tela *f.* fabric, material

telaraña *f.* spider's web, cobweb

teléfono *m.* telephone; **hablar por teléfono** to be on the phone; **llamar por teléfono** to telephone

televidente *m. & f.* TV viewer

televisor *m.* TV set

temor *m.* fear, dread

temprano early

tener (irr.) to have; **tener * años** to be * years old; **tener cuidado** to be careful; **tener miedo** to be afraid; **tener sueño** to be sleepy

teniente *m. & f.* lieutenant

tercero third

terciopelo *m.* velvet

terco stubborn

terminar to finish, end

termómetro *m.* thermometer

ternera *f.* veal

terrestre terrestrial, earthly

tesoro *m.* treasure

testigo *m. & f.* witness

tiburón *m.* shark

tiempo *m.* time; weather

tienda *f.* store

tierno tender

tierra *f.* earth; land

tímido shy

tinta *f.* ink

típico typical, traditional

tipo *m.* type

tirar to throw

títere *m.* puppet

toalla *f.* towel

tocar (qu) to touch; to knock; to play (musical instrument); **tocar a la puerta** to knock on the door; **tocar madera** to knock on wood

todavía yet

todo all, everything; **todos** everybody

tomar to take; to drink; **tomar asiento** to take a seat; **tomar el sol** to sunbathe

tontería *f.* silly thing, foolishness; **tonterías** nonsense

tonto foolish, silly

toro *m.* bull

torta *f.* cake

tortilla *f.* cornmeal pancake; omelette

tortuga *f.* turtle

tos *f.* cough

toser to cough

trabajo *m.* work

traer (irr.) to bring

traje *m.* suit; **traje de baño** bathing suit

tránsito *m.* traffic

transporte *m.* transportation

tratar to treat, to deal with; **tratar de** to try to

trato *m.* deal

través: a través through

travieso mischievous

trébol *m.* clover

triste sad

truco *m.* trick

tubo *m.* tube

U

últimamente lately

último last

único original, unique, only

universitario university (*adj.*)

usar to use; to wear
uso *m.* use; **de uso** used
utilizar (c) to use

V

vacaciones *f. pl.* vacation, holidays
vacío empty
vacunación *f.* vaccination
valer to be worth; **más vale** (it's) better
valiente brave
valor *m.* value
vara *f.* stick
variedades *f. pl.* variety show
varios several, some
vaso *m.* glass
vecino(-a) neighbor
vegetal *m.* vegetable
vela *f.* sail
veloz fast, quick
venda *f.* bandage
vendado bandaged; blindfolded
vendar to bandage
vendedor(-ora) salesperson
vender to sell
venir (*irr.*) to come; **el mes que viene** next month

venta *f.* sale
ventaja *f.* advantage; **llevar ventaja a** to have the advantage over
ventana *f.* window
ventanilla *f.* small window, car window
ver to see
verano *m.* summer
veras: de veras really, truly
verdad *f.* truth; **¿verdad?** isn't that so?
verde green
vestido *m.* dress
vestir (i) to dress; **vestirse** to get dressed
veterinario(-a) veterinarian
vez *f.* time; **en vez de** instead of; **otra vez** again; **por primera vez** for the first time; **tal vez** perhaps
viajar to travel
viaje *m.* trip; **viaje espacial** space voyage; **hacer** (*irr.*) **un viaje** to take a trip
víctima *f.* victim
vida *f.* life; **mi vida** my love (term of endearment)
viejo old

viernes Friday
visa *f.* visa
visita *f.* visitor; visit
visitar to visit
vitamina *f.* vitamin
viviente living
vivir to live
volante *m.* steering wheel
volar (ue) to fly
voleibol *m.* volleyball
volver (ue) to return, to go (come) back
vuelo *m.* flight
vuelta *f.* turn; **vuelta ciclista** long-distance cycle race

Y

ya already
yodo *m.* iodine

Z

zapatero(-era) shoemaker
zapatilla *f.* slipper
zapato *m.* shoe

English-Spanish Vocabulary

The English-Spanish Vocabulary includes only those words that occur in the English-to- Spanish exercises.

A

about sobre, acerca de
address dirección *f.*
advice consejo *m.*
afterwards después
ago hace
airplane avión *m.*
airport aeropuerto *m.*
all todo, todos
also también
always siempre
answer contestar
any cualquier; alguno; **not any** ninguno; **anymore** más
anything algo; **not anything** nada
appetizer entrada *f.*
armchair butaca *f.*, sillón *m.*
arrive llegar (gu)
ask preguntar; **ask for** pedir (i)
asleep dormido; **to fall asleep** dormirse (ue)
aspirin aspirina *f.*

B

baby bebé *m. & f.*
bad malo
baker panadero(-era)
barbecue barbacoa *f.*
baseball béisbol *m.*
bath baño *m.*; **to take a bath** bañarse
bathroom cuarto de baño *m.*
bathing suit traje de baño *m.*
be estar (*irr.*); ser (*irr.*)
beach playa *f.*
bear oso *m.*
beautiful bonito, precioso
because porque
bed cama *f.*; **to go to bed** acostarse (ue)

belt cinturón *m.*
best (el / la) mejor
bicycle bicicleta *f.*
body cuerpo *m.*
bookcase librero *m.*
bookshelf estante para libros *m.*
boot bota *f.*
brake freno *m.*
breakfast desayuno *m.*
bring traer (*irr.*)
brother hermano *m.*
brush cepillo *m.*; cepillarse
building edificio *m.*
bus autobús *m.*
but pero
butcher carnicero *m.*
buy comprar

C

cafeteria cafetería *f.*
call llamar
can poder (ue) (*irr.*)
candidate candidato(-a)
careful cuidadoso; **to be careful** tener (*irr.*) cuidado
carefully cuidadosamente
chain cadena *f.*
chair silla *f.*
champion campeón(-ona)
choose escoger (j)
city ciudad *f.*
close cerrar (ie)
clothes ropa *f.*
coat abrigo *m.*
cold frío; **to be cold** hacer (*irr.*) frío
comb peine *m.*; **to comb one's hair** peinarse
come venir (*irr.*); **come back** volver (ue), regresar
comfortable cómodo

comfortably cómodamente
concert concierto *m.*
correct corregir (i, j)
cost costar (ue)
cough tos *f.*; toser
country país *m.*
crazily locamente
criminal criminal *m. & f.*
crocodile cocodrilo *m.*
cruise crucero *m.*; **to take a cruise** hacer (*irr.*) un crucero
curtain cortina *f.*

D

dangerous peligroso
day día *m.*
deodorant desodorante *m.*
dessert postre *m.*
dining room comedor *m.*
dish plato *m.*
dog perro *m.*
door puerta *f.*
downtown centro *m.*
dress vestido; **to get dressed** vestirse (i)
dresser cómoda *f.*
dressing gown bata *f.*
driver chofer *m.*
during durante

E

early temprano
earn ganar
earth tierra *f.*
easily fácilmente
eat comer; **eat out** comer afuera
elect elegir (i, j)
embrace abrazar (c)
employee empleado(-a)
English inglés *m.*

enough suficiente
enter entrar
envelope sobre *m.*
every cada; **every day** todos los días; **every morning** todas las mañanas
example ejemplo *m.*
exhibit exhibición *f.*
explain explicar (qu)

F

face cara *f.*
family familia *f.*
fast rápido, rápidamente
father padre *m.*, papá *m.*
favorite preferido
fender guardafango *m.*
film película *f.*
fingerprint huella digital *f.*
firefighter bombero(-era)
first primero
fish pescar (qu)
follow seguir (i, g)
food comida *f.*
football fútbol *m.*
freezer congelador *m.*
friend amigo(-a)
fun diversión *f.*; **to have fun** divertirse (ie)
furniture muebles *m. pl.*

G

game partido *m.*; juego *m.*
gas gasolina *f.*
get up levantarse
giraffe jirafa *f.*
give dar (*irr.*)
go ir (*irr.*); **to go away** irse
good bueno
grandparents abuelos *m. pl.*

H

hair pelo *m.*
hairdresser peluquero(-era)
hand mano *f.*
happy contento
hat sombrero *m.*
have haber (*irr.*); tener (*irr.*); **to have to** tener que
headlight faro *m.*, luz *f.*

helmet casco *m.*
here aquí
hike dar (*irr.*) una caminata
homework tarea *f.*
hood cubierta *f.*, capó *m.*
hour hora *f.*
house casa *f.*
how? ¿cómo?; **how old are you?** ¿cuántos años tienes?
hundred cien

I

idea idea *f.*
intelligently inteligentemente
invite invitar
island isla *f.*

J

jacket chaqueta *f.*; **sports jacket** saco de sport *m.*
jail cárcel *f.*
job puesto *m.*, trabajo *m.*
judge juez *m. & f.*

K

knock (on the door) tocar (qu) a la puerta
know saber (*irr.*); **(to be acquainted with)** conocer

L

land aterrizar (c)
large grande
last último; **last summer** el verano pasado
lawyer abogado(-a)
learn aprender
leave salir, irse (*irr.*)
lend prestar
leopard leopardo *m.*
license plate placa *f.*
lie mentira *f.*
light luz *f.*
like gustar
listen escuchar
little pequeño, chico; poco
live vivir
long largo
look (at) mirar; **to look for** buscar (qu)

lot: a lot mucho
lotion loción *f.*; **suntan lotion** loción bronceadora
lunch almuerzo *m.*; **to have lunch** almorzar (ue, c)

M

magazine revista *f.*
mailbox buzón *m.*
mail carrier cartero(-era)
many muchos; **how many?** ¿cuántos?
married casado
meal comida *f.*
meat carne *f.*
menu menú *m.*
mirror espejo *m.*; **rear-view mirror** espejo retrovisor
mistake error *m.*
Monday lunes
money dinero *m.*
moon luna *f.*
morning mañana *f.*
mother madre *f.*, mamá *f.*
movies cine *m.*
much mucho; **how much?** ¿cuánto?

N

name nombre *m.*; **what's your name?** ¿cómo te llamas?
near cerca (de)
need necesitar
neighborhood barrio *m.*
neither tampoco; **neither . . . nor** ni . . . ni
never nunca, jamás
new nuevo
newspaper periódico *m.*; diario *m.*
night noche *f.*
nobody nadie
none ninguno
nothing nada
now ahora

O

obtain conseguir (i, g)
often a menudo; frecuentemente

oil aceite *m.*

old viejo; **older, oldest** mayor;
   to be . . . years old tener (*irr.*)
   . . . años; **how old are you?**
   ¿cuántos años tienes?

one un, uno

only sólo, solamente

open abrir

outing excursión *f.*

P

pail cubo *m.*

pajama pijama *m.*

palm tree palmera *f.*

pants pantalones *m. pl.*

parents padres *m. pl.*

party fiesta *f.*

people gente *f.*

perfectly perfectamente

photographer fotógrafo(-afa)

picture foto *f.*; **to take pictures**
   sacar (qu) fotos

pilot piloto *m. & f.*

place lugar; **to take place** tener
   (*irr.*) lugar

planet planeta *m.*

plate plato *m.*

play jugar (ue, gu)

player jugador(-ora)

political político

postcard tarjeta postal *f.*

prefer preferir (ie)

professional profesional

programmer programador
   (-ora)

protect proteger (j)

pursue perseguir (i, g)

put poner (*irr.*); **to put on**
   ponerse

pyramid pirámide *f.*

Q

quickly rápidamente; pronto

quietly en silencio, sin hacer
   ruido

R

rain llover (ue)

raincoat impermeable *m.*,
   gabardina *f.*

ready listo; **to be ready** estar
   (*irr.*) listo

really realmente

reporter periodista *m. & f.*

ring anillo *m.*, sortija *f.*

river río *m.*

robbery robo *m.*

room cuarto *m.*

row remar

rubber goma *f.*

rug alfombra *f.*

rule regla *f.*

ruler regla *f.*

run correr; **to run away**
   escaparse

S

sailboat barco de vela *m.*

sand arena *f.*

sandcastle castillo de arena *m.*

say decir (*irr.*)

scream gritar

sea mar *m.*

seashell concha *f.*

see ver

seriously seriamente

serve servir (i)

shark tiburón *m.*

shine brillar

shirt camisa *f.*

shoe zapato *m.*

shoemaker zapatero(-era)

shovel pala *f.*

sister hermana *f.*

sit (down) sentarse (ie)

ski esquiar

sleep dormir (ue)

slipper pantufla *f.*, zapatilla *f.*

snake culebra *f.*, serpiente *f.*

soap jabón *m.*

soccer fútbol *m.*

sock calcetín *m.*, media *f.*

somebody alguien

something algo

soon pronto

sorry perdón; **I'm sorry** lo
   siento

soup sopa *f.*

speak hablar

spider araña *f.*

squirrel ardilla *f.*

stamp estampilla *f.*, sello *m.*

star estrella *f.*

station estación *f.*; **police
   station** estación de policía

steering wheel volante *m.*

stop parar; parada *f.*

store tienda *f.*

story cuento *m.*, historia *f.*

stove estufa *f.*

strong fuerte

study estudiar

style moda; **in style** de moda

summer verano *m.*

sun sol *m.*

sunbathe tomar el sol

Sunday domingo

sunglasses gafas de sol *f. pl.*

sweater suéter *m.*

swim nadar

swimming pool piscina *f.*

syrup jarabe *m.*; **cough syrup**
   jarabe para la tos

T

table mesa *f.*; **coffee table**
   mesita de café; **night table**
   mesita de noche

take tomar; llevar; **to take
   away** llevarse; **to take off**
   quitarse

tank tanque *m.*

team equipo *m.*

tell decir (*irr.*); contar (ue)

thermometer termómetro *m.*

there ahí, allí

thief ladrón *m.*

thing cosa *f.*

tie corbata *f.*

tiger tigre *m.*

time tiempo *m.*; vez *f.*; **at what
   time?** ¿a qué hora?; **on time**
   a tiempo

tire llanta *f.*

tissue pañuelo de papel *m.*

today hoy

toilet paper papel higiénico *m.*

tomorrow mañana

too también

toothbrush cepillo de dientes *m.*

toothpaste pasta de dientes *f.*
towel toalla *f.*
train tren *m.*
travel viajar
tree árbol *m.*
trip viaje *m.*
trunk maletero *m.*
t-shirt camiseta *f.*
Tuesday martes
turkey pavo *m.*
turtle tortuga *f.*

U

umbrella paraguas *m. & f.*;
  sombrilla *f.*
underneath debajo de
understand comprender,
  entender (ie)
undress desvestirse (i)
use usar, utilizar

V

vacation vacaciones *f.* pl.
vase florero *m.*

very muy
vest chaleco *m.*
veterinarian veterinario(-a)
victim víctima *f.*
visit visitar

W

waiter mesero *m.*; camarero *m.*
wake up despertarse (ie)
wall pared *f.*
want querer (ie) (*irr.*)
wash lavar; **to wash oneself**
  lavarse
watch mirar
wear llevar, usar
weekend fin de semana *m.*
well bien
whale ballena *f.*
what? ¿qué?
wheel rueda *f.*
when cuando; **when?**
  ¿cuándo?
where? ¿dónde?; **where (to)?**
  ¿adónde?

which? ¿cuál? ¿qué?
who? ¿quién?
whole entero, todo
whom ¿a quién?
whose? ¿de quién?
why? ¿por qué?
window ventana *f.*
with con
word palabra *f.*
work funcionar; trabajar
write escribir

Y

year año *m.*
yesterday ayer
young joven; **younger,**
  youngest menor, más
  pequeño; **young man** joven
  m.; **young woman** joven *f.*

Z

zoo (parque) zoológico *m.*

Grammatical Index

Topical Index